Real-Resumes For Administrative Support, Office & Secretarial Jobs

...including real resumes used to change careers
and gain federal employment

Anne McKinney, Editor

PREP PUBLISHING

FAYETTEVILLE, NC

PREP Publishing

1110 ½ Hay Street

Fayetteville, NC 28305

(910) 483-6611

Library of Congress Cataloging-in-Publication Data

Real-resumes for administrative support, office & secretarial jobs--including real resumes used to change careers and gain federal employment / Anne McKinney, editor.
       p. cm. -- (Real-resumes series)
  ISBN 1-885288-37-9 (alk. paper)
  1. Resumes (Employment)--United States. 2. Clerical occupations--United States. 3. Career changes--United States. 4. Civil service positions--United States. I. McKinney, Anne, 1948-
II. Series.

  HF5383.R39527 2004
  650.14'2--dc22   2004041420

Printed in the United States of America

PREP Publishing

Contents

Real-Resumes For Administrative Support, Office & Secretarial Jobs

Anne McKinney, Editor

A WORD FROM THE EDITOR:
ABOUT THE REAL-RESUMES SERIES

Welcome to the Real-Resumes Series. The Real-Resumes Series is a series of books which have been developed based on the experiences of real job hunters and which target specialized fields or types of resumes. As the editor of the series, I have carefully selected resumes and cover letters (with names and other key data disguised, of course) which have been used successfully in real job hunts. That's what we mean by "Real-Resumes." What you see in this book are *real* resumes and cover letters which helped real people get ahead in their careers.

The Real-Resumes Series is based on the work of the country's oldest resume-preparation company known as PREP Resumes. If you would like a free information packet describing the company's resume preparation services, call 910-483-6611 or write to PREP at 1110½ Hay Street, Fayetteville, NC 28305. If you have a job hunting experience you would like to share with our staff at the Real-Resumes Series, please contact us at preppub@aol.com or visit our website at www.prep-pub.com.

The resumes and cover letters in this book are designed to be of most value to people already in a job hunt or contemplating a career change. If we could give you one word of advice about your career, here's what we would say: Manage your career and don't stumble from job to job in an incoherent pattern. Try to find work that interests you, and then identify prosperous industries which need work performed of the type you want to do. Learn early in your working life that a great resume and cover letter can blow doors open for you and help you maximize your salary.

We hope the superior samples will help you manage your current job campaign and your career so that you will find work aligned to your career interests.

**Introduction:
The Art of
Changing
Jobs...
and Finding
New Careers**

As the editor of this book, I would like to give you some tips on how to make the best use of the information you will find here. Because you are considering a career change, you already understand the concept of managing your career for maximum enjoyment and self-fulfillment. The purpose of this book is to provide expert tools and advice so that you *can* manage your career. Inside these pages you will find resumes and cover letters that will help you find not just a job but the type of work you want to do.

Overview of the Book

Every resume and cover letter in this book actually worked. And most of the resumes and cover letters have common features: most are one-page, most are in the chronological format, and most resumes are accompanied by a companion cover letter. In this section you will find helpful advice about job hunting. Step One begins with a discussion of why employers prefer the one-page, chronological resume. In Step Two you are introduced to the direct approach and to the proper format for a cover letter. In Step Three you learn the 14 main reasons why job hunters are not offered the jobs they want, and you learn the six key areas employers focus on when they interview you. Step Four gives nuts-and-bolts advice on how to handle the interview, send a follow-up letter after an interview, and negotiate your salary.

The cover letter plays such a critical role in a career change. You will learn from the experts how to format your cover letters and you will see suggested language to use in particular career-change situations. It has been said that "A picture is worth a thousand words" and, for that reason, you will see numerous examples of effective cover letters used by real individuals to change fields, functions, and industries.

The most important part of the book is the Real-Resumes section. Some of the individuals whose resumes and cover letters you see spent a lengthy career in an industry they loved. Then there are resumes and cover letters of people who wanted a change but who probably wanted to remain in their industry. Many of you will be especially interested by the resumes and cover letters of individuals who knew they definitely wanted a career change but had no idea what they wanted to do next. Other resumes and cover letters show individuals who knew they wanted to change fields and had a pretty good idea of what they wanted to do next.

Whatever your field, and whatever your circumstances, you'll find resumes and cover letters that will "show you the ropes" in terms of successfully changing jobs and switching careers.

Before you proceed further, think about why you picked up this book.
- Are you dissatisfied with the type of work you are now doing?
- Would you like to change careers, change companies, or change industries?
- Are you satisfied with your industry but not with your niche or function within it?
- Do you want to transfer your skills to a new product or service?
- Even if you have excelled in your field, have you "had enough"? Would you like the stimulation of a new challenge?
- Are you aware of the importance of a great cover letter but unsure of how to write one?
- Are you preparing to launch a second career after retirement?
- Have you been downsized, or do you anticipate becoming a victim of downsizing?
- Do you need expert advice on how to plan and implement a job campaign that will open the maximum number of doors?
- Do you want to make sure you handle an interview to your maximum advantage?

- Would you like to master the techniques of negotiating salary and benefits?
- Do you want to learn the secrets and shortcuts of professional resume writers?

Using the Direct Approach

As you consider the possibility of a job hunt or career change, you need to be aware that most people end up having at least three distinctly different careers in their working lifetimes, and often those careers are different from each other. Yet people usually stumble through each job campaign, unsure of what they should be doing. Whether you find yourself voluntarily or unexpectedly in a job hunt, the direct approach is the job hunting strategy most likely to yield a full-time permanent job. The direct approach is an active, take-the-initiative style of job hunting in which you choose your next employer rather than relying on responding to ads, using employment agencies, or depending on other methods of finding jobs. You will learn how to use the direct approach in this book, and you will see that an effective cover letter is a critical ingredient in using the direct approach.

Lack of Industry Experience Not a Major Barrier to Entering New Field

"Lack of experience" is often the last reason people are not offered jobs, according to the companies who do the hiring. If you are changing careers, you will be glad to learn that experienced professionals often are selling "potential" rather than experience in a job hunt. Companies look for personal qualities that they know tend to be present in their most effective professionals, such as communication skills, initiative, persistence, organizational and time management skills, and creativity. Frequently companies are trying to discover "personality type," "talent," "ability," "aptitude," and "potential" rather than seeking actual hands-on experience, so your resume should be designed to aggressively present your accomplishments. Attitude, enthusiasm, personality, and a track record of achievements in any type of work are the primary "indicators of success" which employers are seeking, and you will see numerous examples in this book of resumes written in an all-purpose fashion so that the professional can approach various industries and companies.

The Art of Using References in a Job Hunt

You probably already know that you need to provide references during a job hunt, but you may not be sure of how and when to use references for maximum advantage. You can use references very creatively during a job hunt to call attention to your strengths and make yourself "stand out." Your references will rarely get you a job, no matter how impressive the names, but the way you use references can boost the employer's confidence in you and lead to a job offer in the least time.

You should ask from three to five people, including people who have supervised you, if you can use them as a reference during your job hunt. You may not be able to ask your current boss since your job hunt is probably confidential.

A common question in resume preparation is: "Do I need to put my references on my resume?" No, you don't. Even if you create a references page at the same time you prepare your resume, you don't need to mail, e-mail, or fax your references page with the resume and cover letter. Usually the potential employer is not interested in references until he meets you, so the earliest you need to have references ready is at the first interview. Obviously there are exceptions to this standard rule of thumb; sometimes an ad will ask you to send references with your first response. Wait until the employer requests references before providing them.

The "direct approach" is the style of job hunting most likely to yield the maximum number of job interviews.

Using references in a skillful fashion in your job hunt will inspire confidence in prospective employers and help you "close the sale" after interviews.

An excellent attention-getting technique is to take to the first interview not just a page of references (giving names, addresses, and telephone numbers) but an actual letter of reference written by someone who knows you well and who preferably has supervised or employed you. A professional way to close the first interview is to thank the interviewer, shake his or her hand, and then say you'd like to give him or her a copy of a letter of reference from a previous employer. Hopefully you already made a good impression during the interview, but you'll "close the sale" in a dynamic fashion if you leave a letter praising you and your accomplishments. For that reason, it's a good idea to ask supervisors during your final weeks in a job if they will provide you with a written letter of recommendation which you can use in future job hunts. Most employers will oblige, and you will have a letter that has a useful "shelf life" of many years. Such a letter often gives the prospective employer enough confidence in his opinion of you that he may forego checking out other references and decide to offer you the job on the spot or in the next few days.

With regard to references, it's best to provide the names and addresses of people who have supervised you or observed you in a work situation.

Whom should you ask to serve as references? References should be people who have known or supervised you in a professional, academic, or work situation. References with big titles, like school superintendent or congressman, are fine, but remind busy people when you get to the interview stage that they may be contacted soon. Make sure the busy official recognizes your name and has instant positive recall of you! If you're asked to provide references on a formal company application, you can simply transcribe names from your references list. In summary, follow this rule in using references: If you've got them, flaunt them! If you've obtained well-written letters of reference, make sure you find a polite way to push those references under the nose of the interviewer so he or she can hear someone other than you describing your strengths. Your references probably won't ever get you a job, but glowing letters of reference can give you credibility and visibility that can make you stand out among candidates with similar credentials and potential!

The approach taken by this book is to (1) help you master the proven best techniques of conducting a job hunt and (2) show you how to stand out in a job hunt through your resume, cover letter, interviewing skills, as well as the way in which you present your references and follow up on interviews. Now, the best way to "get in the mood" for writing your own resume and cover letter is to select samples from the Table of Contents that interest you and then read them. A great resume is a "photograph," usually on one page, of an individual. If you wish to seek professional advice in preparing your resume, you may contact one of the professional writers at Professional Resume & Employment Publishing (PREP) for a brief free consultation by calling 1-910-483-6611.

Part One: Some Advice About Your Job Hunt

What if you don't know what you want to do?

Your job hunt will be more comfortable if you can figure out what type of work you want to do. But you are not alone if you have no idea what you want to do next! You may have knowledge and skills in certain areas but want to get into another type of work. What *The Wall Street Journal* has discovered in its research on careers is that most of us end up having at least three distinctly different careers in our working lives; it seems that, even if we really like a particular kind of activity, twenty years of doing it is enough for most of us and we want to move on to something else!

Figure out what interests you and you will hold the key to a successful job hunt and working career. (And be prepared for your interests to change over time!)

That's why we strongly believe that you need to spend some time figuring out *what interests you* rather than taking an inventory of the skills you have. You may have skills that you simply don't want to use, but if you can build your career on the things that interest you, you will be more likely to be happy and satisfied in your job. Realize, too, that interests can change over time; the activities that interest you now may not be the ones that interested you years ago. For example, some professionals may decide that they've had enough of retail sales and want a job selling another product or service, even though they have earned a reputation for being an excellent retail manager. We strongly believe that interests rather than skills should be the determining factor in deciding what types of jobs you want to apply for and what directions you explore in your job hunt. Obviously one cannot be a lawyer without a law degree or a secretary without secretarial skills; but a professional can embark on a next career as a financial consultant, property manager, plant manager, production supervisor, retail manager, or other occupation if he/she has a strong interest in that type of work and can provide a resume that clearly demonstrates past excellent performance in *any* field and *potential* to excel in another field. As you will see later in this book, "lack of exact experience" is the last reason why people are turned down for the jobs they apply for.

How can you have a resume prepared if you don't know what you want to do?

You may be wondering how you can have a resume prepared if you don't know what you want to do next. The approach to resume writing which PREP, the country's oldest resume-preparation company, has used successfully for many years is to develop an "all-purpose" resume that translates your skills, experience, and accomplishments into language employers can understand. What most people need in a job hunt is a versatile resume that will allow them to apply for numerous types of jobs. For example, you may want to apply for a job in pharmaceutical sales but you may also want to have a resume that will be versatile enough for you to apply for jobs in the construction, financial services, or automotive industries.

"Lack of exact experience" is the last reason people are turned down for the jobs for which they apply.

Based on more than 20 years of serving job hunters, we at PREP have found that your best approach to job hunting is **an all-purpose resume** and **specific cover letters tailored to specific fields** rather than using the approach of trying to create different resumes for every job. If you are remaining in your field, you may not even need more than one "all-purpose" cover letter, although the cover letter rather than the resume is the place to communicate your interest in a narrow or specific field. An all-purpose resume and cover letter that translate your experience and accomplishments into plain English are the tools that will maximize the number of doors which open for you while permitting you to "fish" in the widest range of job areas.

Your resume will provide the script for your job interview.
When you get down to it, your resume has a simple job to do: Its purpose is to blow as many doors open as possible and to make as many people as possible want to meet you. So a well-written resume that really "sells" you is a key that will create opportunities for you in a job hunt.

This statistic explains why: The typical newspaper advertisement for a job opening receives more than 245 replies. And normally only 10 or 12 will be invited to an interview.

But here's another purpose of the resume: it provides the "script" the employer uses when he interviews you. If your resume has been written in such a way that your strengths and achievements are revealed, that's what you'll end up talking about at the job interview. Since the resume will govern what you get asked about at your interviews, you can't overestimate the importance of making sure your resume makes you look and sound as good as you are.

So what is a "good" resume?
Very literally, your resume should motivate the person reading it to dial the phone number or e-mail the screen name you have put on the resume. When you are relocating, you should put a local phone number on your resume if your physical address is several states away; employers are more likely to dial a local telephone number than a long-distance number when they're looking for potential employees.

If you have a resume already, look at it objectively. Is it a limp, colorless "laundry list" of your job titles and duties? Or does it "paint a picture" of your skills, abilities, and accomplishments in a way that would make someone want to meet you? Can people understand what you're saying? If you are attempting to change fields or industries, can potential employers see that your skills and knowledge are transferable to other environments? For example, have you described accomplishments which reveal your problem-solving abilities or communication skills?

How long should your resume be?
One page, maybe two. Usually only people in the academic community have a resume (which they usually call a *curriculum vitae*) longer than one or two pages. Remember that your resume is almost always accompanied by a cover letter, and a potential employer does not want to read more than two or three pages about a total stranger in order to decide if he wants to meet that person! Besides, don't forget that the more you tell someone about yourself, the more opportunity you are providing for the employer to screen you out at the "first-cut" stage. A resume should be concise and exciting and designed to make the reader want to meet you in person!

Should resumes be functional or chronological?
Employers almost always prefer a chronological resume; in other words, an employer will find a resume easier to read if it is immediately apparent what your current or most recent job is, what you did before that, and so forth, in reverse chronological order. A resume that goes back in detail for the last ten years of employment will generally satisfy the employer's curiosity about your background. Employment more than ten years old can be shown even more briefly in an "Other Experience" section at the end of your "Experience" section. Remember that your intention is not to tell everything you've done but to "hit the high points" and especially impress the employer with what you learned, contributed, or accomplished in each job you describe.

Your resume is the "script" for your job interviews. Make sure you put on your resume what you want to talk about or be asked about at the job interview.

The one-page resume in chronological format is the format preferred by most employers.

Once you get your resume, what do you do with it?
You will be using your resume to answer ads, as a tool to use in talking with friends and relatives about your job search, and, most importantly, in using the "direct approach" described in this book.

When you mail your resume, always send a "cover letter."
A "cover letter," sometimes called a "resume letter" or "letter of interest," is a letter that accompanies and introduces your resume. Your cover letter is a way of personalizing the resume by sending it to the specific person you think you might want to work for at each company. Your cover letter should contain a few highlights from your resume—just enough to make someone want to meet you. Cover letters should always be typed or word processed on a computer—never handwritten.

Never mail or fax your resume without a cover letter.

1. Learn the art of answering ads.
There is an "art," part of which can be learned, in using your "bestselling" resume to reply to advertisements.

Sometimes an exciting job lurks behind a boring ad that someone dictated in a hurry, so reply to any ad that interests you. Don't worry that you aren't "25 years old with an MBA" like the ad asks for. Employers will always make compromises in their requirements if they think you're the "best fit" overall.

What about ads that ask for "salary requirements?"
What if the ad you're answering asks for "salary requirements?" The first rule is to avoid committing yourself in writing at that point to a specific salary. You don't want to "lock yourself in."

What if the ad asks for your "salary requirements?"

There are two ways to handle the ad that asks for "salary requirements."
First, you can ignore that part of the ad and accompany your resume with a cover letter that focuses on "selling" you, your abilities, and even some of your philosophy about work or your field. You may include a sentence in your cover letter like this: "I can provide excellent personal and professional references at your request, and I would be delighted to share the private details of my salary history with you in person."

Second, if you feel you must give some kind of number, just state a range in your cover letter that includes your medical, dental, other benefits, and expected bonuses. You might state, for example, "My current compensation, including benefits and bonuses, is in the range of $30,000-$40,000."

Analyze the ad and "tailor" yourself to it.
When you're replying to ads, a finely tailored cover letter is an important tool in getting your resume noticed and read. On the next page is a cover letter which has been "tailored to fit" a specific ad. Notice the "art" used by PREP writers of analyzing the ad's main requirements and then writing the letter so that the person's background, work habits, and interests seem "tailor-made" to the company's needs. Use this cover letter as a model when you prepare your own reply to ads.

Date

Exact Name of Person
Exact Title
Exact Name of Company
Address
City, State, Zip

Dear Exact Name of Person (or Dear Sir or Madam if answering a blind ad):

With the enclosed resume, I would like to make you aware of my interest in exploring employment opportunities with your company.

As you will see from my resume, I have excelled in every job I have held and can provide outstanding references from all employers, including my current employer. At the present time I manage accounts payable for a medical business with locations in two states, and I handle a variety of special projects for the CEO. I have used QuickBooks for accounts payable management, inventory control, and accounts receivable management.

In my first job out of high school, I began as a LAN Administrative Assistant and was promoted to Sales Agent for Delta Airlines in Ft. Lauderdale, where I was involved in technical problem solving and local area network troubleshooting as well as customer service. In a subsequent job with an international corporation, I served as Secretary to the Vice Presidents of the North American and Latin American sales regions. For several years as Finance & Accounting Manager for a construction company, I managed accounts payable and receivable, payroll and tax preparation, and the negotiation of customer contracts.

Although I am held in the highest regard by my current employer, I am selectively exploring other opportunities. I have a friendly personality and sunny disposition which enables me to quickly establish rapport with others, and I am skilled in working with the general public as well as with any type of accounting software or financial management system. Many of my positions have involved serving as the "personal assistant" to busy executives, so I have gained versatile problem-solving abilities through assisting in resolving profitability and customer issues at top levels.

With an outstanding personal and professional reputation, I am confident that I could become a valuable asset to a company which seeks intelligent hard workers who are committed to maximizing growth and profitability. If you have interest in my skills and talents, I hope you will contact me to suggest a time when we might meet to discuss your needs.

Yours sincerely,

Andrea B. Caldwell

Employers are trying to identify the individual who wants the job they are filling. Don't be afraid to express your enthusiasm in the cover letter!

2. Talk to friends and relatives.

Don't be shy about telling your friends and relatives the kind of job you're looking for. Looking for the job you want involves using your network of contacts, so tell people what you're looking for. They may be able to make introductions and help set up interviews.

About 25% of all interviews are set up through "who you know," so don't ignore this approach.

3. Finally, and most importantly, use the "direct approach."

The "direct approach" is a strategy in which you choose your next employer.

More than 50% of all job interviews are set up by the "direct approach." That means you actually mail, e-mail, or fax a resume and a cover letter to a company you think might be interesting to work for.

To whom do you write?

In general, you should write directly to the *exact name* of the person who would be hiring you: say, the vice-president of marketing or data processing. If you're in doubt about to whom to address the letter, address it to the president by name and he or she will make sure it gets forwarded to the right person within the company who has hiring authority in your area.

How do you find the names of potential employers?

You're not alone if you feel that the biggest problem in your job search is finding the right names at the companies you want to contact. But you can usually figure out the names of companies you want to approach by deciding first if your job hunt is primarily geography-driven or industry-driven.

In a **geography-driven job hunt,** you could select a list of, say, 50 companies you want to contact **by location** from the lists that the U.S. Chambers of Commerce publish yearly of their "major area employers." There are hundreds of local Chambers of Commerce across America, and most of them will have an 800 number which you can find through 1-800-555-1212. If you and your family think Atlanta, Dallas, Ft. Lauderdale, and Virginia Beach might be nice places to live, for example, you could contact the Chamber of Commerce in those cities and ask how you can obtain a copy of their list of major employers. Your nearest library will have the book which lists the addresses of all chambers.

In an **industry-driven job hunt,** and if you are willing to relocate, you will be identifying the companies which you find most attractive in the industry in which you want to work. When you select a list of companies to contact **by industry,** you can find the right person to write and the address of firms by industrial category in *Standard and Poor's, Moody's,* and other excellent books in public libraries. Many Web sites also provide contact information.

Many people feel it's a good investment to actually call the company to either find out or double-check the name of the person to whom they want to send a resume and cover letter. It's important to do as much as you feasibly can to assure that the letter gets to the right person in the company.

On-line research will be the best way for many people to locate organizations to which they wish to send their resume. It is outside the scope of this book to teach Internet research skills, but librarians are often useful in this area.

What's the correct way to follow up on a resume you send?

There is a polite way to be aggressively interested in a company during your job hunt. It is ideal to end the cover letter accompanying your resume by saying, "I hope you'll welcome my call next week when I try to arrange a brief meeting at your convenience to discuss your current and future needs and how I might serve them." Keep it low key, and just ask for a "brief meeting," not an interview. Employers want people who show a determined interest in working with them, so don't be shy about following up on the resume and cover letter you've mailed.

It pays to be aware of the 14 most common pitfalls for job hunters.

STEP THREE: Preparing for Interviews

But a resume and cover letter by themselves can't get you the job you want. You need to "prep" yourself before the interview. Step Three in your job campaign is "Preparing for Interviews." First, let's look at interviewing from the hiring organization's point of view.

What are the biggest "turnoffs" for potential employers?

One of the ways to help yourself perform well at an interview is to look at the main reasons why organizations *don't* hire the people they interview, according to those who do the interviewing.

Notice that "lack of appropriate background" (or lack of experience) is the *last* reason for not being offered the job.

The 14 Most Common Reasons Job Hunters Are Not Offered Jobs (according to the companies who do the interviewing and hiring):

1. Low level of accomplishment
2. Poor attitude, lack of self-confidence
3. Lack of goals/objectives
4. Lack of enthusiasm
5. Lack of interest in the company's business
6. Inability to sell or express yourself
7. Unrealistic salary demands
8. Poor appearance
9. Lack of maturity, no leadership potential
10. Lack of extracurricular activities
11. Lack of preparation for the interview, no knowledge about company
12. Objecting to travel
13. Excessive interest in security and benefits
14. Inappropriate background

Department of Labor studies have proven that smart, "prepared" job hunters can increase their beginning salary while getting a job in *half* the time it normally takes. (4½ months is the average national length of a job search.) Here, from PREP, are some questions that can prepare you to find a job faster.

Are you in the "right" frame of mind?

It seems unfair that we have to look for a job just when we're lowest in morale. Don't worry *too* much if you're nervous before interviews. You're supposed to be a little nervous, especially if the job means a lot to you. But the best way to kill unnecessary fears about job hunting is through 1) making sure you have a great resume and 2) preparing yourself for the interview. Here are three main areas you need to think about before each interview.

Do you know what the company does?

Don't walk into an interview giving the impression that, "If this is Tuesday, this must be General Motors."

Find out before the interview what the company's main product or service is. Where is the company heading? Is it in a "growth" or declining industry? (Answers to these questions may influence whether or not you want to work there!)

Information about what the company does is in annual reports, in newspaper and magazine articles, and on the Internet. If you're not yet skilled at Internet research, just visit your nearest library and ask the reference librarian to guide you to printed materials on the company.

Do you know what you want to do for the company?

Before the interview, try to decide how you see yourself fitting into the company. Remember, "lack of exact background" the company wants is usually the last reason people are not offered jobs.

Understand before you go to each interview that the burden will be on you to "sell" the interviewer on why you're the best person for the job and the company.

How will you answer the critical interview questions?

Put yourself in the interviewer's position and think about the questions you're most likely to be asked. Here are some of the most commonly asked interview questions:

Q: "What are your greatest strengths?"
A: Don't say you've never thought about it! Go into an interview knowing the three main impressions you want to leave about yourself, such as "I'm hard-working, loyal, and an imaginative cost-cutter."

Q: "What are your greatest weaknesses?"
A: Don't confess that you're lazy or have trouble meeting deadlines! Confessing that you tend to be a "workaholic" or "tend to be a perfectionist and sometimes get frustrated when others don't share my high standards" will make your prospective employer see a "weakness" that he likes. Name a weakness that your interviewer will perceive as a strength.

Q: "What are your long-range goals?"
A: If you're interviewing with Microsoft, don't say you want to work for IBM in five years! Say your long-range goal is to be *with* the company, contributing to its goals and success.

Q: "What motivates you to do your best work?"
A: Don't get dollar signs in your eyes here! "A challenge" is not a bad answer, but it's a little cliched. Saying something like "troubleshooting" or "solving a tough problem" is more interesting and specific. Give an example if you can.

Research the company before you go to interviews.

Anticipate the questions you will be asked at the interview, and prepare your responses in advance.

Q: "What do you know about this organization?"

A: Don't say you never heard of it until they asked you to the interview! Name an interesting, positive thing you learned about the company recently from your research. Remember, company executives can sometimes feel rather "maternal" about the company they serve. Don't get onto a negative area of the company if you can think of positive facts you can bring up. Of course, if you learned in your research that the company's sales seem to be taking a nose-dive, or that the company president is being prosecuted for taking bribes, you might politely ask your interviewer to tell you something that could help you better understand what you've been reading. Those are the kinds of company facts that can help you determine whether or not you want to work there.

Go to an interview prepared to tell the company why it should hire you.

Q: "Why should I hire you?"

A: "I'm unemployed and available" is the wrong answer here! Get back to your strengths and say that you believe the organization could benefit by a loyal, hard-working cost-cutter like yourself.

In conclusion, you should decide in advance, before you go to the interview, how you will answer each of these commonly asked questions. Have some practice interviews with a friend to role-play and build your confidence.

STEP FOUR: Handling the Interview and Negotiating Salary

Now you're ready for Step Four: actually handling the interview successfully and effectively. Remember, the purpose of an interview is to get a job offer.

A smile at an interview makes the employer perceive of you as intelligent!

Eight "do's" for the interview

According to leading U.S. companies, there are eight key areas in interviewing success. You can fail at an interview if you mishandle just one area.

1. **Do wear appropriate clothes.**

   You can never go wrong by wearing a suit to an interview.

2. **Do be well groomed.**

   Don't overlook the obvious things like having clean hair, clothes, and fingernails for the interview.

3. **Do give a firm handshake.**

   You'll have to shake hands twice in most interviews: first, before you sit down, and second, when you leave the interview. Limp handshakes turn most people off.

4. **Do smile and show a sense of humor.**

   Interviewers are looking for people who would be nice to work with, so don't be so somber that you don't smile. In fact, research shows that people who smile at interviews are perceived as more intelligent. So, smile!

5. **Do be enthusiastic.**

   Employers say they are "turned off" by lifeless, unenthusiastic job hunters who show no special interest in that company. The best way to show some enthusiasm for the employer's operation is to find out about the business beforehand.

6. Do show you are flexible and adaptable.

An employer is looking for someone who can contribute to his organization in a flexible, adaptable way. No matter what skills and training you have, employers know every new employee must go through initiation and training on the company's turf. Certainly show pride in your past accomplishments in a specific, factual way ("I saved my last employer $50.00 a week by a new cost-cutting measure I developed"). But don't come across as though there's nothing about the job you couldn't easily handle.

7. Do ask intelligent questions about the employer's business.

An employer is hiring someone because of certain business needs. Show interest in those needs. Asking questions to get a better idea of the employer's needs will help you "stand out" from other candidates interviewing for the job.

8. Do "take charge" when the interviewer "falls down" on the job.

Go into every interview knowing the three or four points about yourself you want the interviewer to remember. And be prepared to take an active part in leading the discussion if the interviewer's "canned approach" does not permit you to display your "strong suit." You can't always depend on the interviewer's asking you the "right" questions so you can stress your strengths and accomplishments.

An important "don't": Don't ask questions about salary or benefits at the first interview. Employers don't take warmly to people who look at their organization as just a place to satisfy salary and benefit needs. Don't risk making a negative impression by appearing greedy or self-serving. The place to discuss salary and benefits is normally at the second interview, and the employer will bring it up. Then you can ask questions without appearing excessively interested in what the organization can do for you.

Now...negotiating your salary

Even if an ad requests that you communicate your "salary requirement" or "salary history," you should avoid providing those numbers in your initial cover letter. You can usually say something like this: "I would be delighted to discuss the private details of my salary history with you in person."

Once you're at the interview, you must avoid even appearing *interested* in salary before you are offered the job. Make sure you've "sold" yourself before talking salary. First show you're the "best fit" for the employer and then you'll be in a stronger position from which to negotiate salary. **Never** bring up the subject of salary yourself. Employers say there's no way you can avoid looking greedy if you bring up the issue of salary and benefits before the company has identified you as its "best fit."

Interviewers sometimes throw out a salary figure at the first interview to see if you'll accept it. You may not want to commit yourself if you think you will be able to negotiate a better deal later on. Get back to finding out more about the job. This lets the interviewer know you're interested primarily in the job and not the salary.

When the organization brings up salary, it may say something like this: "Well, Mary, we think you'd make a good candidate for this job. What kind of salary are we talking about?" You may not want to name a number here, either. Give the ball back to the interviewer. Act as though you hadn't given the subject of salary much thought and respond something like this: "Ah, Mr. Jones, I wonder if you'd be kind enough to tell me what salary you had in mind when you advertised the job?" Or ... "What is the range you have in mind?"

Employers are seeking people with good attitudes whom they can train and coach to do things their way.

Don't appear excessively interested in salary and benefits at the interview.

Don't worry, if the interviewer names a figure that you think is too low, you can say so without turning down the job or locking yourself into a rigid position. The point here is to negotiate for yourself as well as you can. You might reply to a number named by the interviewer that you think is low by saying something like this: "Well, Mr. Lee, the job interests me very much, and I think I'd certainly enjoy working with you. But, frankly, I was thinking of something a little higher than that." That leaves the ball in your interviewer's court again, and you haven't turned down the job either, in case it turns out that the interviewer can't increase the offer and you still want the job.

Salary negotiation can be tricky.

Last, send a follow-up letter.

Mail, e-mail, or fax a letter right after the interview telling your interviewer you enjoyed the meeting and are certain (if you are) that you are the "best fit" for the job. The people interviewing you will probably have an attitude described as either "professionally loyal" to their companies, or "maternal and proprietary" if the interviewer also owns the company. In either case, they are looking for people who want to work for *that* company in particular. The follow-up letter you send might be just the deciding factor in your favor if the employer is trying to choose between you and someone else. You will see an example of a follow-up letter on page 16.

A follow-up letter can help the employer choose between you and another qualified candidate.

A cover letter is an essential part of a job hunt or career change.

Many people are aware of the importance of having a great resume, but most people in a job hunt don't realize just how important a cover letter can be. The purpose of the cover letter, sometimes called a **"letter of interest,"** is to introduce your resume to prospective employers. The cover letter is often the critical ingredient in a job hunt because the cover letter allows you to say a lot of things that just don't "fit" on the resume. For example, you can emphasize your commitment to a new field and stress your related talents. The cover letter also gives you a chance to stress outstanding character and personal values. On the next two pages you will see examples of very effective cover letters.

A cover letter is an essential part of a career change.

Please do not attempt to implement a career change without a cover letter. A cover letter is the first impression of you, and you can influence the way an employer views you by the language and style of your letter.

Special help for those in career change

We want to emphasize again that, especially in a career change, the cover letter is very important and can help you "build a bridge" to a new career. A creative and appealing cover letter can begin the process of encouraging the potential employer to imagine you in an industry other than the one in which you have worked.

As a special help to those in career change, there are resumes and cover letters included in this book which show valuable techniques and tips you should use when changing fields or industries. The resumes and cover letters of career changers are identified in the table of contents as "Career Change" and you will see the "Career Change" label on cover letters in Part Two where the individuals are changing careers.

Date

**Addressing the Cover
Letter:** Get the exact
name of the person to
whom you are writing. This
makes your approach
personal.

Exact Name of Person
Exact Title
Exact Name of Company
Address
City, State, Zip

Dear Exact Name of Person: (or Dear Sir or Madam if answering a blind ad):

First Paragraph: This
explains why you are
writing.

With the enclosed resume, I would like to make you aware of my background in business management and office operations as well as my versatile history of accomplishments in a fast-paced, growth-oriented environment.

Second Paragraph: You
have a chance to talk
about whatever you feel is
your most distinguishing
feature.

As you will see from my resume, I have enjoyed a track record of advancement with Bellarmine Industrial Laundries, and I have played an important role in its growth. The company was a year old, had first-year sales of $500,000, and employed approximately 20 people when I joined it as the Bookkeeper. As the company grew, I was able to hire assistants and became the Office Manager as the number of employees rose to 40. In 2000 I became the Business Manager. Bellarmine now has 60 employees, annual sales of around $3.5 million, and operates in two states. It was recently acquired by a Tennessee-based firm which has two offices in Kentucky and Illinois and an additional 20 offices in six other states.

Third Paragraph: You
bring up your next most
distinguishing qualities and
try to
sell yourself.

As the company has grown, I have continued to take on new duties and have become recognized for my problem-solving skills and ability to handle diverse tasks while keeping my staff focused on providing timely support for accounts payable, accounts receivable, general ledger, and payroll. On my own initiative, I played a significant role in automating accounting and bookkeeping functions in order to allow the company to keep up with growth and expansion.

Fourth Paragraph: Here
you have another
opportunity to reveal
qualities or achievements
which will impress your
future employer.

Although I am held in high regard in my current position, I am selectively exploring career opportunities in other organizations.

If you can use an experienced, mature, and dependable professional known for high levels of initiative and vision, I hope you will welcome my call soon when I try to arrange a brief meeting to discuss your goals and how my background might serve your needs. I can provide outstanding references at the appropriate time.

Final Paragraph: She
asks the employer to
contact her. Make sure
your reader knows what
the "next step" is.

Sincerely,

Kelly D. Inman

**Alternate Final
Paragraph:** It's more
aggressive (but not too
aggressive) to let the
employer know that you
will be calling him or her.
Don't be afraid to be
persistent. Employers are
looking for people who
know what they want to
do.

Alternate Last Paragraph:
I hope you will write or call me soon to suggest a time when we might meet to discuss your needs and goals and how my background might serve them. I can provide outstanding references at the appropriate time.

Date

Three blank spaces

Exact Name of Person
Title or Position   Address
Name of Company
Address (number and street)
Address (city, state, and zip)

Dear Exact Name of Person: (or Dear Sir or Madam if answering a blind ad.)   Salutation
                                                                                     One blank space

Can you use an articulate and knowledgeable assistant who offers a reputation as an enthusiastic and energetic individual with outstanding computer skills? Mr. Nate Lipscomb recommended that I contact you.

As you will see from my resume, I am currently excelling as an Executive Secretary with Pfizer, Inc., where I have been involved in planning appointments and travel schedules for a busy executive while also composing, proofreading, editing, and processing office correspondence. Described as "writing with remarkable clarity and consistency," I demonstrated my exceptional communication skills while playing a key role in the creation and publication of Pfizer's first Human Resources Manual.

Body

Although I am highly regarded by my present employer and can provide outstanding references at the appropriate time, I have decided to permanently relocate back to my native Canada. I am interested in exploring career options with companies that can use a highly skilled, dedicated administrative assistant.

My computer skills are top-notch and include proficiency with Word, Excel, Access, PowerPoint, and other popular software programs. A highly motivated individual known for unlimited personal initiative, I offer skills, experience, and knowledge which would make me a valuable addition to any organization searching for a versatile and adaptable professional.

I hope you welcome my call soon when I try to arrange a brief meeting to discuss your needs and how I might help you. Thank you in advance for your time.

Sincerely,

Signature

Samuel Jackson

cc: Mr. Nate Lipscomb   cc: Indicates you are sending
                                                         a copy of the letter to
                                                         someone

Date

Exact Name of Person
Title or Position
Name of Company
Address (number and street)
Address (city, state, and zip)

Follow-up Letter

A great follow-up letter
can motivate the
employer
to make the job offer,
and the salary offer may
be influenced by the
style and tone of your
follow-up
letter, too!

Dear Exact Name:

I am writing to express my appreciation for the time you spent with me on 9 December, and I want to let you know that I am sincerely interested in the position of Executive Assistant which we discussed.

I feel confident that I could skillfully interact with your 20-person executive staff, and I am confident that I possess the superior computer knowledge you require, including proficiency with QuickBooks. I offer a proven ability to rapidly master new software programs and operating systems.

As you described to me what you are looking for in the person who fills this position, I had a sense of "déjà vu" because my current employer was in a similar position when I went to work for his business. The managing partner needed someone to come in and be his "right arm" and take on an increasing amount of his management responsibilities so that he could be freed up to do other things. I have played a key role in the growth and profitability of his firm, and that business has come to depend on my strong personal initiative and interpersonal skills. Since this is one of the busiest times of the year in my employer's business, I feel that I could not leave during that time. I could certainly make myself available by mid-January.

It would be a pleasure to work for a successful individual such as yourself, and I feel I could contribute significantly to your hotel chain not only through my administrative skills but also through my strong qualities of loyalty, reliability, and trustworthiness. I am confident that I could become a trusted personal assistant to you, and I would welcome being trained to do things your way.

Yours sincerely,

Jacob Evangelisto

PART TWO:

Resumes & Cover Letters for Administrative Support, Office & Secretarial Jobs

In this section, you will find resumes and cover letters of professionals seeking employment, or already employed, in the administrative and office support field. How do these individuals differ from other job hunters? Why should there be a book dedicated to people seeking jobs such as these? Based on more than 20 years of experience in working with job hunters, this editor is convinced that resumes and cover letters which "speak the lingo" of the field you wish to enter will communicate more effectively than language which is not industry-specific. This book is designed to help people (1) who are seeking to prepare their own resumes and (2) who wish to use as models "real" resumes of individuals who have successfully launched careers in the administrative and office support field or advanced in the field. You will see a wide range of experience levels reflected in the resumes in this book. Some of the resumes and cover letters were used by individuals seeking to enter the field; others were used successfully by senior professionals to advance in the field.

Newcomers to an industry sometimes have advantages over more experienced professionals. In a job hunt, junior professionals can have an advantage over their more experienced counterparts. Prospective employers often view the less experienced workers as "more trainable" and "more coachable" than their seniors. This means that the mature professional who has already excelled in a first career can, with credibility, "change careers" and transfer skills to other industries.

Newcomers to the field may have disadvantages compared to their seniors.
Almost by definition, the inexperienced professional—the young person who has recently entered the job market, or the individual who has recently received certifications respected by the industry—is less tested and less experienced than senior managers, so the resume and cover letter of the inexperienced professional may often have to "sell" his or her potential to do something he or she has never done before. Lack of experience in the field she wants to enter can be a stumbling block to the junior employee, but remember that many employers believe that someone who has excelled in anything—academics, for example—can excel in many other fields.

Some advice to inexperienced professionals...
If senior professionals could give junior professionals a piece of advice about careers, here's what they would say: Manage your career and don't stumble from job to job in an incoherent pattern. Try to find work that interests you, and then identify prosperous industries which need work performed of the type you want to do. Learn early in your working life that a great resume and cover letter can blow doors open for you and help you maximize your salary.

Special help for career changers...
For those changing careers, you will find useful the resumes and cover letters marked "Career Change" on the following pages. Consult the Table of Contents for page numbers showing career changers.

ACCOUNTING SUPERVISOR (CAREER CHANGE)

Date

Exact Name of Person
Exact Title
Exact Name of Company
Address
City, State, Zip

ACCOUNTING SUPERVISOR
for a CPA's office

Dear Exact Name of Person: (or Dear Sir or Madam if answering a blind ad):

With the enclosed resume, I would like to make you aware of my background as a resourceful accounting supervisor who offers an extensive background in accounts payable, data analysis, account relationship management, and staff supervision.

As you will see from my resume, I have served Baldwin Financial Services in Dallas, TX with distinction as I supervise office personnel while directing accounts payable clerks involved in posting to accounts and ledgers. Responsible for general ledger accountability and financial statement preparation, I handle accounting for and deposits of state sales and use taxes.

Although I was highly regarded by everyone at Baldwin Financial and can provide outstanding personal and professional references at the appropriate time, I have decided to pursue my long-term career objectives in an environment where I can make more extensive use of my strong customer focus. I feel that there may be a good "fit" between your organization's needs and my unique combination of ability and experience.

If you can use a loyal and experienced finance professional, I would enjoy meeting with you to discuss your needs. I hope you will welcome my call soon when I try to arrange a brief meeting to discuss how my background might serve your needs.

Sincerely,

Iris H. Zylka

Alternate last paragraph:
If you can use a loyal, articulate, and experienced accounting professional, I hope you will write or call me soon to suggest a time when we might meet to discuss your needs and goals and how my background might serve them.

IRIS H. ZYLKA

1110½ Hay Street, Fayetteville, NC 28305　•　preppub@aol.com　•　(910) 483-6611

OBJECTIVE

To benefit an organization that can use a resourceful planner, organizer, and manager with expertise as an accountant along with vast experience in financial research and analysis.

EDUCATION

Associate of Science, Business and Accounting, Victoria College, Victoria, TX, 1992.
One-year accounting certificate, Temple College, 1989.
Extensive executive development courses and experience related to payroll preparation, accounts receivable and payable, management/data analysis, and full charge bookkeeping.
In 2004, completed professional seminar on sales and use taxes.

COMPUTERS

Operate mainframes and PCs with software for word processing, data base management, spreadsheet analysis, and graphics; have evaluated and selected software applications including databases, spreadsheets, and word processing.

EXPERIENCE

ACCOUNTING SUPERVISOR. Baldwin Financial Services, Dallas, TX (2004-present). Supervise office personnel while directing/advising accounts payable clerk in ensuring correct posting to accounts and ledgers. Responsible for general ledger accountability and financial statement preparation; coordinate with CPA. Handle accounting for and deposits of state sales and use taxes.
- Act as Human Resource Manager and advise on personnel/financial matters.
- Prepare accounts and ledgers for corporate merger with parent company in Louisiana.
- Directed downsizing of the office, resulting in improved efficiency and lower costs.
- Acquired hands-on expertise in all facets of human resource management including payroll, benefits, workers' compensation, and selection/retention/dismissal.

ADMINISTRATIVE ASSISTANT. Beneficial of Texas, Dallas, TX (2002-04). Prepared family financial programs for presentation to clients; contacted clients and prospective clients by mail and telephone while also scheduling appointments, preparing literature for mailing, and designing seminar materials and other marketing products.
- Developed office procedures "from scratch" for a new sales operation.
- Planned, purchased, and organized work stations to efficiently use space.

Excelled in the following track record of promotion with World-Wide Food Distributors:
2002: SUPERVISORY ACCOUNTING TECHNICIAN. Mexico. Wrote standard operating procedures used in physical inventories of the world's largest government food distribution center while coordinating accounting transactions for 80 commissaries domestic and abroad locations; supervised 8 accounting technicians maintaining accounting records/transactions for a $41 million semi-perishable grocery warehouse that had a complete turnover of inventory monthly.
- Acted as consultant to 80 warehouses in solving accounting and computer problems.
- Managed all accounts for this $41 million warehouse within 1% allowable tolerance.

2001-02: LEAD ACCOUNTING TECHNICIAN. Dallas, TX. Coordinated transactions for more than 80 retail groceries in maintaining accounts for a $35 million semi-perishable food warehouse; analyzed data and reported findings to the Regional Accounting Branch while compiling monthly reports, reconciling internal control document log to the summary audit log, and reviewing the postings to the general ledger.

Other experience:
SYSTEM ADMINISTRATOR/AUDITOR. Concord, Inc., Victoria, TX (1992-01). Began as an administrative assistant and was promoted to manage typing, printing, auditing, and distribution of financial programs to offices throughout the US after auditing financial program worksheets submitted by sales agents to the Regional Headquarters.
- On my own initiative, established automation including PC work stations, laser printers, and office design for a sales region that had no computer knowledge; developed training program, integrated software, and established security and backup systems that became the "model" of computer efficiency.

PERSONAL

Known for attention to detail. Member, National Association of Administrative Assistants.

ACCOUNTS PAYABLE SUPERVISOR

Date

Exact Name of Person
Exact Title
Exact Name of Company
Address
City, State, Zip

Dear Exact Name of Person (or Dear Sir or Madam if answering a blind ad):

With the enclosed resume, I would like to make you aware of my interest in exploring employment opportunities with your company.

As you will see from my resume, I have excelled in every job I have held and can provide outstanding references from all employers, including my current employer. At the present time I manage accounts payable for a medical business with locations in two states, and I handle a variety of special projects for the CEO. I have used QuickBooks for accounts payable management, inventory control, and accounts receivable management.

In my first job out of high school, I began as a LAN Administrative Assistant and was promoted to Sales Agent for Delta Airlines in Ft. Lauderdale, where I was involved in technical problem solving and local area network troubleshooting as well as customer service. In a subsequent job with an international corporation, I served as Secretary to the Vice Presidents of the North American and Latin American sales regions. For several years as Finance & Accounting Manager for a construction company, I managed accounts payable and receivable, payroll and tax preparation, and the negotiation of customer contracts.

Although I am held in the highest regard by my current employer, I am selectively exploring other opportunities. I have a friendly personality and sunny disposition which enables me to quickly establish rapport with others, and I am skilled in working with the general public as well as with any type of accounting software or financial management system. Many of my positions have involved serving as the "personal assistant" to busy executives, so I have gained versatile problem-solving abilities through assisting in resolving profitability and customer issues at top levels.

With an outstanding personal and professional reputation, I am confident that I could become a valuable asset to a company which seeks intelligent hard workers who are committed to maximizing growth and profitability. If you have interest in my skills and talents, I hope you will contact me to suggest a time when we might meet to discuss your needs.

Yours sincerely,

Andrea B. Caldwell

ANDREA B. CALDWELL

1110½ Hay Street, Fayetteville, NC 28305   •   preppub@aol.com   •   (910) 483-6611

OBJECTIVE   To contribute to an organization that can use a versatile professional who offers an ability to use computers and perform clerical and administrative tasks while also providing outstanding customer support and customer service in environments which require excellent interpersonal skills and problem-solving abilities.

COMPUTERS   Proven ability to rapidly master new software programs and operating systems.
Proficient with Windows and Microsoft Suite including Word, Excel, Access, PowerPoint, Publisher, Outlook.
Knowledgeable of accounting and financial software including QuickBooks 2003, Quicken, and Coins.
Experienced in using Business Works for accounting and inventory control.
Experienced in using FileMaker Pro and Tenant Pro. Experienced with Oracle and Business Objects.
Have used the Sabre airlines reservation system.
Highly skilled in performing Internet research.

EXPERIENCE   **ACCOUNTS PAYABLE MANAGER & EXECUTIVE ASSISTANT.** Cape Fear Orthotics and Prosthetics, Charlotte, NC (2001-present). For a diversified operation which has prosthetics businesses in two states (NC and VA), utilize a computer daily with QuickBooks accounting software in order to manage accounts payable while aggressively taking advantage of credits for quick payment from major vendors.
- As the company's first Accounts Payable Manager, helped the CEO establish the accounts payable system and subsequently streamlined the system we established when a second location of the business was established in Pennsylvania. Now handle accounts payables for the newly started Richmond operation.
- Maintain revenue spreadsheets for corporate executives.
- In a special project for six months during 2003, assumed the responsibility of handling accounts receivable as well as shipping and receiving for an affiliated book publishing company. Performed liaison with large accounts including Borders and Barnes & Noble. Provided oversight for warehouse operations.

OFFICE MANAGER'S ASSISTANT & PROJECT ASSISTANT. American Construction Company, Charlotte, NC (2000-01). As the assistant to three busy executives (the Office Manager, Vice President, and Assistant Vice President), prepared correspondence and input accounting data into computer spreadsheets. Demonstrated my ability to handle multiple tasks while simultaneously acting as Assistant to the Grading Department Manager and an Assistant VP. Performed support related to inventory control and accounting.

EXECUTIVE SECRETARY. Smith & Associates, Raleigh, NC (1998-99). Began with this company as a Sales Support Secretary responsible for compiling statistical data and handling customer service issues. Was promoted to serve as Secretary to the Regional Manager and ten sales associates in Raleigh and, after one year of outstanding performance, was promoted to the position as Secretary to the Vice Presidents of North American and Latin American sales regions.
- Compiled statistical reports using data compiled in seven sales regions in North and Latin America; generated reports on a weekly, monthly, and quarterly basis used to analyze trends and profitability.

FINANCE & ACCOUNTING MANAGER. Sandhills Construction, Raleigh, NC (1991-98). For a residential construction company which built approximately 10 houses a year, managed accounts payable, accounts receivable, payroll preparation, tax reporting, and the negotiation of customer contracts.

LAN ADMINISTRATIVE ASSISTANT & SALES AGENT. Delta Airlines, Ft. Lauderdale, FL (1988-91). Excelled in a track record of promotion with Delta Airlines. As a LAN Administrative Assistant, assisted with technical problem solving and local area network troubleshooting while serving as a member of a development team for installation of a new reservation information system. As a Sales Agent, booked domestic and Caribbean reservations and provided outstanding customer service and customer support.

EDUCATION   Completed Accounting courses, Charlotte Technical Community College, Charlotte, NC.
Extensive computer training sponsored by Delta Airlines. Graduated from the Associated School of Travel in Ticketing and Reservations.

PERSONAL   Licensed Notary Public. Offer a friendly personality and sunny disposition which enables me to establish rapport quickly with supervisors, co-workers, customers, and outside organizations. Outstanding communication skills.

ADMINISTRATIVE AIDE

Date

Exact Name of Person
Title or Position
Name of Company
Address (no., street)
Address (city, state, zip)

Dear Exact Name of Person: (or Dear Sir or Madam if answering a blind ad.)

I would appreciate an opportunity to talk with you soon about how I could contribute to your organization through my proven ability to "get things done" as well as through my management aptitude, communication skills, and versatile customer service/public relations ability.

You will see from my resume that I have excelled in jobs which helped me refine my ability to serve the public in a gracious manner. I completely financed my college education while simultaneously pursuing a rigorous business management curriculum and excelling as a member of the varsity tennis team and varsity track team. I hope this will demonstrate to you that I am a hard worker with a proven ability to set high goals and then organize my time in the most efficient manner for achieving those goals.

In my current job with the Malone College Athletic Sales Office, I display my ability to handle numerous simultaneous activities including sales, billing and finance, scheduling, statistical analysis, media relations, office administration, and data entry. I have been commended for my excellent problem-solving and decision-making skills.

You would find me to be an enthusiastic young professional who prides myself on adding value to any organization of which I am a part. I can provide outstanding personal and professional references at your request.

I hope you will call or write me soon to suggest a time convenient for us to meet and discuss your current and future needs and how I might serve them. Thank you in advance for your time.

Sincerely yours,

Stacia M. Walker

STACIA M. WALKER

1110½ Hay Street, Fayetteville, NC 28305 • preppub@aol.com • (910) 483-6611

OBJECTIVE

To contribute to an organization that can use a highly motivated self-starter with excellent customer service and public relations skills, along with a proven ability to solve problems and discover efficient new operational methods.

EDUCATION

Bachelor of Science degree, Sports Administration, Clark State Community College, Springfield, OH, 2004.

EXPERIENCE

ADMINISTRATIVE AIDE. Tier Stadium Sports Connection, Malone College Athletic Sales Office, Canton, OH (2003-present). Excelled in this part-time job while personally financing all my college educational expenses.

- **Sales:** Coordinated the sale of season tickets for the athletic sales office.
- **Scheduling:** Established and administered the schedule for the use of athletic facilities.
- **Statistics:** Analyzed data and prepared statistical reports which analyzed factors pertaining to athletes and facilities.
- **Mass mailings:** Prepared bulk mailings.
- **Billing & finance:** Handled accounts receivable and coordinated the billing of season ticket holders.
- **Computer operation:** Performed data entry and routinely used a computer for word processing and spreadsheet preparation.
- **Media relations:** Learned to deal effectively with television, radio, and print media through frequent telephone conversations and through information I prepared for media press kits.
- **Office administration:** Operated a wide variety of office machines and contributed to the efficient administration of this bustling office.

WAITRESS. J.D. Hunter Golf Club, Canton, OH (2003). In a summer job between my junior and senior year of college, worked at an elegant country club serving food at private parties and at special banquets.

- Was commended for my management skills after transforming a variety of tasks into an organized system for getting the job done.
- Learned how to deal with demanding customers and keep them very satisfied.

SUPERVISOR/CLERK. Citgo, Canton, OH (2002). In a summer job, excelled at cashiering, inventory control, and employee supervision in the absence of the owner.

- In my first management job, learned how to supervise others while doing my own job.

SALES ASSOCIATE. Gordon's Jewelers, Springfield, OH (2000-01). Conducted sales, cashiering, inventory control, data entry, and display design and setup; was responsible for opening and closing the store.

SALES ASSOCIATE. Dillard's Department Store, Springfield, OH (1998-00). While learning the basics of retail management, was responsible for conducting sales, operating the cash register, performing inventory, and scheduling employees.

PERSONAL

Am able to get along with people from all different backgrounds. Adapt new environments quickly and easily. Outstanding references on request.

ADMINISTRATIVE ASSISTANT

Date

Exact Name of Person
Title or Position
Name of Company
Address (number and street)
Address (city, state, and zip)

ADMINISTRATIVE ASSISTANT
for a city office in Richmond

Dear Exact Name of Person: (or Sir or Madam if answering a blind ad.)

I would appreciate an opportunity to talk with you soon about how I could contribute to your organization through my experience in administrative management and skills in computer operations.

With a keen eye for detail and an ability to quickly learn and resourcefully apply new concepts, I offer a reputation as a professional who can be depended on for personal integrity and dedication to excellence in everything I attempt.

As you will see from my enclosed resume, I have been employed for the last two years with the Public Affairs Office of Richmond in a position which was originally a six-month temporary assignment. Cited for my accomplishments in this highly visible role, I plan, coordinate, and conduct guided tours for school and church groups as well as visiting dignitaries. Proficient with a wide variety of popular software programs, I provide expert support related to data entry, the preparation of charts used in briefings and reports, and inventory control.

I can provide strong references at the appropriate time, and I am known as a hard worker with unlimited personal initiative. You will notice from my resume that I earned my Associate's degree in Finance at night while excelling in my full-time position with the city of Richmond. I consistently seek new ways in which to advance my skills and knowledge, and I have mastered numerous software programs in my spare time.

I hope you will welcome my call soon to arrange a brief meeting to discuss your current and future needs and how I might serve them. Thank you in advance for your time.

Sincerely,

Rex W. Hubbard

Alternate last paragraph:
I hope you will call or write me soon to suggest a time convenient for us to meet and discuss your current and future needs and how I might serve them. Thank you in advance for your time.

REX W. HUBBARD

1110½ Hay Street, Fayetteville, NC 28305 • preppub@aol.com • (910) 483-6611

OBJECTIVE

Through my attention to detail as well as my strong project management abilities, I seek to contribute to an organization that can use a creative administrative specialist with excellent verbal and written communication skills.

SPECIAL SKILLS

Through experience and training, am knowledgeable of computer applications, office equipment and procedures, and administrative operations including the following:
computers: proficient in using Microsoft Word, PowerPoint, and Excel software programs
other: operate fax machines, copiers, and all standard office equipment

EXPERIENCE

Earned a reputation as a well-organized and skilled administrative specialist while serving with the City of Richmond, VA:
2002-present: TOUR COORDINATOR and **ADMINISTRATIVE ASSISTANT.** For the Public Affairs Office of City Hall, plan and carry out guided tours of the installation for school and church groups as well as visiting dignitaries.
- Develop and maintain detailed records of the arrangements which result in each tour and use the data to plan informative tours for similar groups.
- Provide five individual offices with support in meeting their requests for supplies of everything from pencils and pens, to state-of-the-art camera equipment and radio components.
- Improved the documentation process and created new request information forms accepted for use in all city offices.
- Use my computer skills and job knowledge to prepare detailed and informative flow charts used in briefing executives.
- Was asked by the Mayor's Office to assist in the preparation of a resource book: researched and obtained statistical information from all city offices while also designing the cover.
- Received special recognition for my efforts in providing outstanding two and three-day tours which supported recruiting efforts and helped educate young people on the advantages of volunteering within the community.

2000-02: PERSONNEL ADMINISTRATIVE AIDE. As the "right arm" to the city's Human Resources Director, played a key role in overseeing personnel administration for more than 40 employees including transfers and reassignments, job reclassifications, applications for advanced training, and awards.
- Handled promotion processing for personnel within the city: accepted initial requests, organized promotion boards, determined eligibility, updated promotion lists, and typed the final documents authorizing the promotion. Maintained up-to-date records of requests from the Mayor's Office for reassigning people to other departments.

1998-00: PERSONNEL ADMINISTRATION CLERK. Gained a strong base of experience in maintaining and updating personnel files using an automated computer system to track and record data for more than 40 people.
- Received special recognition for completing work assignments accurately and on schedule.
- Received cross training in payroll and financial reporting.

EDUCATION

Associate of Science degree in **Finance,** J. S. Reynolds Community College, Richmond, VA, 2001.

PERSONAL

Excellent personal and professional references are available upon request.

ADMINISTRATIVE ASSISTANT

Date

Exact Name of Person
Title or Position
Name of Company
Address (number and street)
Address (city, state, and zip)

**ADMINISTRATIVE
ASSISTANT**
for a golf & country
club

Dear Exact Name of Person: (or Sir or Madam if answering a blind ad.)

With the enclosed resume, I would like to make you aware of my background and experience related to office management, computer operations, customer service, and administration.

As you will see, I offer strong computer operations skills which include Microsoft Word, Excel, and Works as well as customized financial management systems.

In my current job as Administrative Assistant for Gavilan Golf & Country Club, an elite club with 800 members, I handle payroll for the staff while coordinating employee insurance programs and managing accounting functions. I provide the highest level of customer service to club members at all times. When members have a problem with their account, it is my job to diplomatically resolve the problem, and I handle collections as necessary. The club's relationships with outside vendors are my responsibility, and I personally sign all accounts payable and payroll checks while signing vendor checks and payroll checks.

In previous jobs I have excelled as a Loan Processor, Route Manager, and Office Manager. I pride myself on the fact that I have made significant contributions to all my employers, and I offer a proven ability to rapidly master new software and operating systems.

Although I am highly regarded by my employer and can provide outstanding references at the appropriate time, I am interested in selectively exploring opportunities with other organizations.

If you can use an articulate, hardworking administrative professional, please contact me to suggest a time when we might meet in person to discuss your needs. I can assure you in advance that I could become a valuable part of your operation and would enthusiastically seek opportunities to make valuable contributions to your business. Thank you in advance for your time.

Yours sincerely,

Jeanna A. Wilbourne

JEANNA A. WILBOURNE

1110½ Hay Street, Fayetteville, NC 28305 • preppub@aol.com • (910) 483-6611

OBJECTIVE   To benefit an organization that can use an articulate professional with strong communication and organizational skills along with experience in office administration, sales, and customer service.

SKILLS   Microsoft Word   Microsoft Excel   Microsoft Works
             Micros and Novell Network   Ten Key by Touch   BK Business System

EXPERIENCE   **ADMINISTRATIVE ASSISTANT.** Gavilan Golf & Country Club, Los Angeles, CA (2001-present). For this 800-member, year-round country club with golf, tennis, pool, restaurant, catering, and fine dining, handle payroll for hourly, flex, and salaried employees. Manage petty cash, cash reconciliation, training of new employees, and other areas; sign paychecks and accounts payable checks.

- Played the key role in implementing the club's new computer system, and train other employees.
- Type minutes for committee meetings; assemble packets for board of directors meetings; prepare end-of-month member statements; and resolve problems with member accounts.
- Write checks for vendors and receive inventory; handle garnishments and tax payments.
- Act as insurance coordinator for employee insurance and workman's compensation.
- Provide leadership in setting up employee-paid dental insurance program, and set up new insurance for medical benefits; manage payroll direct deposit.
- Handle bank draft for member accounts for their bill paying; handle collections and set up new member accounts; process information related to member accounts.
- Type and proofread the club's monthly newsletter; file and answer multiline phones.
- During the club's golf tournaments, establish data in computer, manage collection of money and bets, and pay money to winners; manage the club's unique betting program.

ROUTE REPRESENTATIVE & ROUTE MANAGER. Modesto Exterminators, Los Angeles, CA (1999-01). Started as Secretary and was quickly promoted; excelled in handling route books for five routes including processing payments and charges for customers; was then promoted to manage a pest control route on Sacramento and Bakersfield extending down to Arizona; worked with residential and commercial customers.

- Complied with state regulations for safe transport and handling of chemicals.
- Scheduled work for Termite Department; handled collections for all departments as well as payroll and commissions; edited and typed all Form I's for Wood Destroying Insect Reports and Soil Guarantees for contractors; filed and operated a multiline phone.

SECRETARY/OFFICE MANAGER. Hainey Contractors, Los Angeles, CA (1998-99). For a major contracting project, typed all correspondence to go to Corp of Engineers; handled all invoices; and ordered materials and equipment. Maintained specifications and insurance certificates for all subcontractors.

LOAN PROCESSOR. Olsten Finance, Los Angeles, CA (1997-98). During the busy Christmas season, filled in temporarily helping to close loans, performing loan processing, credit checks, cash reconciliations, and collections in addition to answering phones, typing, and filing.

OPERATIONS CLERK. K-Mart, Los Angeles, CA (1995-97). After excelling as a Sales Clerk, processed invoices for payments, payroll, and inventory; set prices for products received by vendors; performed cash register reconciliations; handled mark downs, write-offs, scheduling, typing, filing, video rental, customer service, and telephones.

OFFICE MANAGER. Weimann Industrial Services, Los Angeles, CA (1994-95). In charge of all accounting procedures including inventory, job costing, taxes, customer service, invoicing, collections, and purchasing; provided leadership in automating accounting, using various software applications.

ADMINISTRATIVE SPECIALIST. U.S. Air Force, Barksdale AFB, LA (1991-94). Typed correspondence for the administrative staff, handled feeder reports, inventory, and finance problems; answered phones and provided customer service in a 130-person organization.

EDUCATION   Graduate of Adelphi High School, Los Angeles, CA, 1991; Vice-President of the Student Union.

ADMINISTRATIVE ASSISTANT

Date

Exact Name of Person
Title or Position
Name of Company
Address (number and street)
Address (city, state, and zip)

Dear Exact Name of Person: (or Sir or Madam if answering a blind ad.)

With the enclosed resume, I would like to make you aware of my interest in the position of Call Center Manager.

As you will see from my resume, I offer call center experience along with a proven ability to manage multiple activities in environments where priorities must rapidly adjust to constantly changing bottom-line needs. For two years, I worked at Netcom Communications, where I was promoted rapidly from Call Center Operator to Sales Verifier. I became skilled in listening to calls made by telemarketers in order to determine if policies and procedures were being observed. I am very knowledgeable of the quality controls which must be adhered to in a call center environment. I resigned from Netcom because I thought I wanted to be a stay-at-home mom, but I realized after a few months that I wanted to work. Although I can provide an excellent reference from the Netcom organization and am eligible for rehire there, I subsequently went to work for a Fortune 500 company—Berkshire Hathaway.

While working for Berkshire Hathaway since 1999, I have been promoted quickly from Technician, to Switchboard Operator of a 170-phone switchboard, to Administrative Assistant. I am currently being groomed to handle even more complex responsibilities. In the process of earning numerous "perfect attendance" quarterly awards, I have demonstrated my ability to handle multiple simultaneous responsibilities. Known for my ability to work well with others while "juggling" multiple tasks, I handle a variety of management responsibilities related to executive support, purchasing, human resources, and financial management.

I would enjoy the opportunity to discuss the possibility of working for your organization. I feel certain that I could contribute significantly to your company's success. I am eager to discuss your needs and I look forward to talking with you.

Yours sincerely,

Peggy G. Lipscomb

PEGGY G. LIPSCOMB

1110½ Hay Street, Fayetteville, NC 28305   •   preppub@aol.com   •   (910) 483-6611

OBJECTIVE

I want to contribute to an organization that can use a professional communicator with a background that includes call center and switchboard operations experience along with a proven ability to manage multiple projects, people, and programs in an environment of rapidly shifting priorities.

EXPERIENCE

Have recently excelled in a track record of promotion with a division of Berkshire Hathaway, a major Fortune 500 company:
2004-present: ADMINISTRATIVE ASSISTANT. Was promoted to act as Administrative Assistant to the division manager; continue to operate a 170-phone switchboard while handling multiple responsibilities. Have won quarterly awards for perfect attendance.
- **Executive support services:** Provide support to managerial staff including the controller, materials manager, IT manager, and three other executives; create PowerPoint presentations and handle word processing. Attend executive meetings and prepare minutes.
- **Purchasing:** Was recently promoted to oversee purchasing paperwork for the entire facility.
- **Employee services:** Coordinate the mailing of birthday and anniversary cards for all employees.
- **Management:** Monitor monthly reports for American Express card program; coordinate paperwork with AMEX for the 50 corporate users of the American Express card. Manage four other purchasing cards for the company which cover expenses including meetings and luncheons, supplies, telephone bills, and computer equipment repairs. Book all air travel, hotel, and car reservations.

2002-04: SWITCHBOARD OPERATOR. Received and routed all calls; received all visitors while ordering supplies for 350 employees.
1999-02: TECHNICIAN. After only six months of working as an assembly technician, was promoted to Acting Team Leader.

CALL CENTER OPERATOR & SALES VERIFIER. Netcom Communications, Miami, FL (1997-99). Excelled as Call Center Operator and was promoted to Sales Verifier after several months; delivered scripts for Nordstrom, Dillards, Sears, insurance companies, credit card companies, and other companies.
- Became skilled in listening to calls made by telemarketers and determining if sales were legitimate and if policies were being followed.

LICENSED REAL ESTATE AGENT. Century 21 Realtors, Miami, FL (1996-97). Listed and sold residential properties.

Other experience: Excelled as a Department of the Treasury employee in positions worldwide.
BUDGET ASSISTANT. (1994-96). Analyzed weekly and monthly costs and posted expense data to commitment ledgers. Validated accounting classifications and assisted in establishing an audit trail. Reviewed cost reports. Assisted in the preparation of financial reports. Received a prestigious medal and was praised for my contributions to accurate fund control, reconciliation, and budget forecasting.

ACCOUNTING TECHNICIAN. (1990-94). Was promoted from Accounting Clerk to Accounting Technician; managed accounting for multiple programs and developed cost estimates and funds certification; prepared monthly reports monthly. Reviewed invoices and travel documents. Checked for fraud, waste, abuse, and compliance with fiscal control guidelines. Received a prestigious medal and was praised for "untiring commitment to excellence, and caring attitude, and unselfish devotion."

SUPPLY CLERK & CUSTOMER SERVICE SUPERVISOR. (1988-89). Inspected items being turned into a warehouse and prepared reports. Supervised employees providing customer service.

EDUCATION

Completed more than two years of college-level training at institutions including the Miami-Dade Community College and Barry University related to quality assurance, management, interpersonal skills, manufacturing, and other areas.
Extensive training in automated data systems and computer operations sponsored by Berkshire Hathaway; gained proficiency with Microsoft Word, Excel, and PowerPoint.

HONORS

Received numerous awards for "outstanding achievements" and "sustained superior performance."

PERSONAL

Hard worker with high energy. Experienced in dealing with a broad range of people. Honest. Loyal.

ADMINISTRATIVE ASSISTANT

Date

Exact Name of Person
Title or Position
Name of Company
Address (number and street)
Address (city, state, and zip)

ADMINISTRATIVE ASSISTANT
for a social services organization

Dear Exact Name of Person: (or Sir or Madam if answering a blind ad.)

I would appreciate an opportunity to talk with you soon about how I could contribute to your organization through my education in accounting, my experience in financial operations, and my technical skills in data entry and word processing.

With a keen eye for detail and a proven ability to learn new tasks quickly, I offer a background in accounting and bookkeeping along with strong analytical skills. I am very self-reliant and work well independently and as part of a dedicated team. In my current position I am involved in posting daily transactions into journals, auditing financial records, and balancing receipts which average $12,000 weekly. Known for my strong personal initiative, I created a new system for registering Child Development Center applicants which greatly improved efficiency while generating goodwill with prospective applicants.

You will see from my enclosed resume that I am attending University of Nevada pursuing a degree in Accounting. Earlier I excelled academically while completing a one-year diploma program in Accounting and Bookkeeping with the Community College of Southern Nevada.

I hope you will welcome my call soon to arrange a brief meeting to discuss your current and future needs and how I might serve them. Thank you in advance for your time.

Sincerely,

Dorothy Tillison

Alternate last paragraph:
I hope you will call or write me soon to suggest a time convenient for us to meet and discuss your current and future needs and how I might serve them. Thank you in advance for your time.

DOROTHY TILLISON

1110½ Hay Street, Fayetteville, NC 28305 • preppub@aol.com • (910) 483-6611

OBJECTIVE

To benefit an organization that can use my education in accounting along with my experience in positions which required strong computer skills, the ability to deal with the public, and a keen eye for detail.

EDUCATION

Attend the University of Nevada, Las Vegas, NV: have completed 62 credit hours toward a bachelor's degree in Accounting. Presently hold a cumulative 3.76 GPA.

Earned a diploma in Accounting and Bookkeeping, Community College of Southern Nevada, North Las Vegas, NV, 2003; excelled in studies emphasizing bookkeeping, posting to journals and ledgers, and completing income statements, balance sheets, and trial balances.

SPECIAL SKILLS

Through training and experience, have gained knowledge of office equipment operations and standard office procedures:

Computers: am familiar with Microsoft Word, Excel and Access, as well as software specific to the child development field (CD-SAMS).

Other: 12-key business calculators, multiline phones, fax machines, copiers, and typewriters.

EXPERIENCE

ADMINISTRATIVE ASSISTANT. Department of Social Services, Las Vegas, NV (2003-present). After originally being hired as an Educational Technician, was selected for advanced training and then promoted into an administrative position for the Human Resources Division.

- Was selected for my ability to work independently while meeting tight deadlines.
- On my own initiative, created a new system for registering Child Development Center applicants which has increased efficiency and promoted goodwill.
- Post daily transactions in journals and into computer files while also processing bank deposits, balancing receipts which averaged $12,000 a week, and depositing payments.
- Receive telephone calls and schedule appointments.
- Audit financial records and handle administrative technician's duties including typing exceptions to policy and performing quality assurance checks.
- Provide customers with information on areas of eligibility, privileges, and application procedures.
- Excelled as an **Educational Technician** developing and overseeing age-appropriate developmental activities for three and four-year-olds.

DATA ENTRY CLERK. Systel, Las Vegas, NV (2002-03). Applied my attention to detail and data entry skills while performing technical and administrative actions including data entry and word processing.

- Reviewed and proofread all material and made determinations on additions, deletions, and changes to documents or lists.

SALES ASSOCIATE and **CASHIER.** Sears, Las Vegas, NV (2001-02). Advised customers and helped them make decisions on which merchandise to choose while also operating scannable cash registers; accounted for $70,000 worth of merchandise.

- Assisted in the customer service office by accepting credit card payments and layaway sales.
- Processed and posted cash and check transaction vouchers.

RESERVATIONS CLERK. Winngate Inn, Las Vegas, NV (1999-01). Became known for my ability to deal with people in a busy international reservations office while working with customers in person and by phone.

- Gained experience in using the corporation's specific software program to accept, change, or eliminate reservations and built my typing speed up to 65 wpm.

DEPARTMENT SECRETARY and **RECEPTIONIST.** University of Nevada, Finance Office, Las Vegas, NV (1997-98). Handled departmental correspondence and maintained student files.

- Attended meetings and conferences in order to take minutes and then record them.
- Answered incoming calls and scheduled student-faculty conferences.

PERSONAL

Offer knowledge of medical terminology. Studied engineering at the University of Nevada before changing my area of concentration to accounting. Outstanding references on request.

ADMINISTRATIVE ASSISTANT

Date

Exact Name of Person
Exact Title
Exact Name of Company
Address
City, State, Zip

ADMINISTRATIVE ASSISTANT
for a nationwide lease trucking service

Dear Exact Name of Person (or Dear Sir or Madam if answering a blind ad):

I would appreciate an opportunity to talk with you soon about how I could contribute to your organization through my versatile skills in office operations, computer applications, and quality control.

As you will see from my enclosed resume, I am a self-motivated professional who is totally committed to delivering the highest level of customer satisfaction through quality products and services. I enjoy the challenge of developing methods of improving productivity and effectiveness while reducing costs. Through my excellent verbal and written communication skills, I have become known as one who can be counted on to prepare accurate and timely reports and correspondence and to work well with others in leadership roles while contributing to team efforts.

In my current job as an Administrative Assistant at Global Transports, Inc., I handle a wide range of office and production activities. I prioritize work, provide quality assurance support, control inventory, and word process a variety of reports, documents, and spreadsheets. I also file and answer multiline phones. I have become known for my outstanding problem-solving skills in the process of troubleshooting a variety of customer issues by phone.

I am confident that my commitment to increasing efficiency and reducing costs would make me a valuable asset to any organization seeking a dedicated hard worker. I hope you will contact me to suggest a time when we might meet to discuss your needs. I can assure you in advance that I could rapidly become an asset to your organization.

Sincerely,

Davida G. Valdez

DAVIDA G. VALDEZ

1110½ Hay Street, Fayetteville, NC 28305   •   preppub@aol.com   •   (910) 483-6611

OBJECTIVE   To offer experience in developing and maintaining efficient office operations and effective customer service.

EXPERIENCE   **ADMINISTRATIVE ASSISTANT.** Global Transports, Inc., Boston, MA (2000-present). In the regional office of this firm which provides leased labor services of nationwide truck drivers, spend a great deal of my time on the phone coordinating arrangements between the customers and drivers.
- Schedule D.O.T. physicals, drug screenings, and road tests as well as processing drivers' files to ensure they complete all required tests before being assigned.
- Create and maintain an efficient work station and process large volumes of computer records.
- Deal on a regular basis with my peers in other regional offices as well as with personnel in the Trenton corporate office.

OFFICE MANAGER. Orkin Pest Control, Boston, MA (1997-00). Handled administrative functions ranging from processing payroll for five people, to scheduling appointments, to bookkeeping, to filing, to word processing and typing records.
- Increased profits through improvements such as reorganizing office procedures in the areas of scheduling appointments and automating payroll and bookkeeping functions.
- Learned to prepare payroll for employees who included hourly, salaried, and commissioned workers.

ADMINISTRATIVE ASSISTANT. Tiny Tots Day Care Center, Boston, MA (1995-97). Learned the value of being patient while dealing with both children and their parents in a church-operated day care center.
- Spent half of each day taking care of infants as well as children needing after-school care.
- Handled a wide range of responsibilities during the afternoons spent in the center's office answering phones, collecting fees, filing, and typing correspondence and forms.

ASSISTANT TO THE GENERAL MANAGER. Vanderpool Mobile Homes, Boston, MA (1987-95). Played a key role in transforming a poorly run mobile home park into a clean and popular residential area while handling the day-to-day operation of this family-owned business.
- Was instrumental in taking a 14-unit park/duplex apartment complex which had nine vacancies and, after making minor repairs, we rented all units.
- Maintained no lower than a 85% occupancy rate through solid management and a determination to keep the park clean, safe, and attractive.
- Handled activities including preparing advertising, doing the company bookkeeping, arranging for minor repairs to be completed, and contracting for major repairs.
- Greeted and screened prospective tenants, checked their references, and processed applications.
- Inspected units as they became vacant and saw that they were cleaned and quickly ready for occupancy.
- Oversaw and performed lawn maintenance and grounds keeping activities.

Highlights of earlier experience:
Gained valuable work experience as a Title Clerk and Receptionist for an automobile dealership and as a File Clerk in the Bookkeeping Department of an insurance company.

EDUCATION &   Studied Medical and Business Administration, Simmons College, Boston, MA, 1997-99.
TRAINING   Was chosen to complete Global Transports, Inc. computer training at the Trenton office, 2003.

OFFICE SKILLS   Offer knowledge and experience with the following operations and equipment:
Software: various programs such as Microsoft Word, Excel, Access and PageMaker
Typing: approximately 80 wpm
Other: computerized fax programs, copiers, and multiline phones

PERSONAL   Offer a talent for dealing with the public. Enjoy meeting and getting to know people. Am very well organized and effective at finding ways to increase profitability and efficiency.

ADMINISTRATIVE ASSISTANT

Date

Exact Name of Person
Title or Position
Name of Company
Address (number and street)
Address (city, state, and zip)

Dear Exact Name of Person: (or Sir or Madam if answering a blind ad.)

I would appreciate an opportunity to talk with you soon about how I could contribute to your organization through my skills in data entry along with my knowledge of office operations, dedication to quality customer service, and ability to work well with others.

With a keen eye for detail and ability to learn quickly, I offer a reputation as a professional who can be depended on for personal integrity, resourcefulness, and dedication to excellence in everything I attempt. In my present job as an Administrative Assistant, I handle a variety of day-to-day activities while controlling supply levels, processing all fax traffic, answering phones, providing excellent customer service, and processing payroll for 200 employees.

In my previous job, I excelled as a Data Entry Operator and Dispatcher for four years and was recognized for speed and accuracy in entering data into an automated system. On my own initiative, I created a new labeling system for use by warehouse personnel which improved order-filling accuracy by nearly 50%. That boost in accuracy had the immediate effect of improving customer satisfaction and increasing repeat orders.

I have become proficient in using Microsoft Word and company-specific software programs and offer a working knowledge of Excel and Access.

If you can use a mature young professional who can competently handle pressure and deadlines while providing expertise in data entry and office operations, I hope you will welcome my call soon to arrange a brief meeting to discuss your current and future needs and how I might serve them. Thank you in advance for your time.

Sincerely,

Amy Williams

Alternate last paragraph:
I hope you will call or write me soon to suggest a time convenient for us to meet and discuss your current and future needs and how I might serve them. Thank you in advance for your time.

AMY WILLIAMS

1110½ Hay Street, Fayetteville, NC 28305 • preppub@aol.com • (910) 483-6611

OBJECTIVE

To utilize my skills in data entry for the benefit of an organization that can use a detail-oriented professional with excellent computer operations skills as well as knowledge of office procedures and the ability to develop productive working relationships with my peers, superiors, and customers.

SPECIAL SKILLS

Through training and experience, am familiar with equipment and functions including:
Computers: proficient with Microsoft Word and company-specific software programs; working knowledge of Excel and Access.
Office equipment: operate computers, copiers, multiline phones, 10-key calculators, and fax machines.
Office procedures: experienced in customer service, routing and scheduling activities, processing time cards and preparing payroll, and filing.

EXPERIENCE

ADMINISTRATIVE ASSISTANT. Albany Daily News, Albany, GA (2004-present). Have quickly earned the respect of my superiors and peers for my versatility and ability to take charge of a wide range of office operations with an emphasis on controlling supply levels as well as other support activities.
- Process all fax traffic: receive incoming faxes, route them to the correct department and person within the company, and send outgoing faxes.
- Collect and process time cards for approximately 200 employees.
- Answer phones and sort incoming mail.
- Oversee fax and copy machine operations to include maintaining adequate levels of supplies and scheduling maintenance and repairs.
- Coordinate with vending machine companies to ensure machines are kept full and maintenance performed as soon as possible in the event of any breakdown.
- Learned the importance of maintaining cordial relationships and keeping communication lines open with people whose work ethic and performance standards did not match my own.
- Recognized for my control and ability to remain calm in an emergency, was selected to chaperone any employee who was injured on the job and needed to be taken to the hospital.

FULL-TIME STUDENT and **HOMEMAKER.** Darton College, Albany, GA (2002-04). Refined my time management skills and organizational abilities attending school full time while simultaneously taking care of a home and family.

DATA ENTRY OPERATOR and **DISPATCHER.** Alliant Food Services, Albany, GA (1998-02). Developed new procedures for scheduling deliveries while taking care of day-to-day activities including keying data into computer records, answering phones, providing helpful customer service, and performing light filing for this large food service industry supplier.
- Was cited for my accuracy and speed while entering numeric values into the computer so that incoming orders could be processed and the correct items delivered.
- Completed check-in procedures as approximately 15 drivers finished their assigned delivery routes: sorted invoices and ensured that checks and cash collected matched invoice amounts.
- Supported large commercial accounts such as the Bullard, Clark, and other nearby county school systems as well as numerous restaurants.
- Gained recognition for my positive attitude, cheerful personality, and willingness to take on increasing amounts of responsibility.
- Created a new labeling system for use by warehouse personnel which helped ensure that the correct items were pulled and loaded for delivery: established the logical step of placing the first orders to be delivered on the truck last for ease in handling. Guaranteed that the system became a smooth routine so that all phases of ordering, processing, pulling, loading, and delivery fell into place properly.

EDUCATION

Completed approximately two years of college course work with an emphasis on Administrative Operations, Darton College, Albany, GA, 2002-04.

PERSONAL

Am very self-motivated with a talent for motivating those around me to work to the best of their abilities. Enjoy expanding my knowledge of computer applications. Outstanding references.

ADMINISTRATIVE ASSISTANT (CAREER CHANGE)

Date

Exact Name of Person
Title or Position
Name of Company
Address (no., street)
Address (city, state, zip)

ADMINISTRATIVE ASSISTANT
for a health & life insurance company. Sometimes the best time to change careers is immediately after earning a new academic credential or degree.

Dear Exact Name of Person: (or Dear Sir or Madam if answering a blind ad.)

I would appreciate an opportunity to talk with you soon about how I could contribute to your organization through my excellent office skills as well as through my proven ability to apply my creativity and initiative in solving problems in the work place.

As you will see from my resume, I recently received my B.S. degree in Management and Human Resources. I excelled academically while also excelling in the full-time and part-time jobs I held in order to finance my college education. Based on my grades and character, I was inducted into a prestigious service organization, and I played a key role in producing a video that taught customer service skills. In my most recent job, when the company learned that I would be relocating to Wichita, I was asked to interview and train my successor because of the confidence the employer had in me. In that position as an Administrative Assistant, I developed a new marketing plan for group health insurance that the company is still using today.

A computer-knowledgeable young professional, I offer the ability to rapidly master new software and hardware, and I am knowledgeable of Microsoft Word, Access, Excel spreadsheets, PowerPoint, and dBase III.

You will also see from my resume that I am not exactly "new" to Wichita. I lived and worked in Wichita from 1996-02. During that period, I excelled in jobs with First Federal Bank as well as with other companies on assignments through Olsten Staffing Services. I can provide outstanding personal and professional references at your request.

You would find me to be an outgoing young professional who understands the importance of first-class customer service and public relations.

I hope you will write or call me to suggest a time when we might meet to discuss your needs and goals and how I might serve them. Thank you in advance for your time.

Sincerely yours,

Meredith J. Pugh

MEREDITH J. PUGH

1110½ Hay Street, Fayetteville, NC 28305   •   preppub@aol.com   •   (910) 483-6611

OBJECTIVE

To contribute to the success of an organization that can use a hardworking and creative young professional who offers excellent analytical and problem-solving skills, a highly motivated and resourceful nature, as well as a gracious style of dealing with the public.

EDUCATION

Earned **Bachelor of Science (B.S.) degree in Management and Human Resources,** Ft. Hays State University, Hays, AZ, 2004.
- Excelled academically while working to finance my education; was named to the Dean's List and Honor Roll.
- Based on my character, leadership, and academic standing, was selected for induction into the prestigious REACH ("Research, Education, Advise, Counsel, and Help") service organization; co-wrote, co-directed, and co-starred in a video produced by REACH that taught customer service skills.

COMPUTER KNOWLEDGE

Knowledgeable of Microsoft Word, Access, and PowerPoint software programs.
Have studied dBase III and Excel spreadsheets in computer science course work.

EXPERIENCE

ADMINISTRATIVE ASSISTANT. Provincial Insurance, Hays, AZ (2002-04). For a fast-growing company selling health and life insurance products and services, rapidly became a highly valued employee because of my outstanding office skills as well as the personal initiative and creativity I displayed in finding ways to improve my employer's methods of marketing its services to customers.

- Developed a presentation for marketing group health insurance plans; in order to do this, I had to teach myself to use Microsoft Word while simultaneously learning how to research individual health plans and where to find answers to health care questions.
- Was asked to interview, select, and train my replacement; derived much satisfaction from leaving my employer with a well-trained employee who could "follow in my footsteps."
- On my own initiative, completed a self-study program on life and health insurance and received my Life, Health, and Disability license in Kansas.
- Excelled in preparing documents for insurance processing; prepared correspondence; directed all office functions; performed services for clients such as changing items on policies; prepared payroll and payroll taxes; and supervised temporary file clerks.

RECEPTIONIST. O'Neill & Quillen Realtors, Hays, AZ (2002). In this part-time job on the weekend, received and directed all incoming calls on an eleven-line telephone switchboard system while warmly greeting customers in the lobby of the building and directing traffic to numerous offices.

- Became known for my outgoing personality and positive attitude as well as for my ability to handle numerous activities simultaneously.
- Learned how to soothe angry and dissatisfied customers through my listening skills and patient disposition.

SECRETARY. Olsten Staffing Services, Wichita, KS (2000-02). Excelled in jobs as a receptionist, data entry clerk, and engineering department secretary.
- On a long-term assignment for an engineering company, handled purchase orders, typed correspondence, typed reports, and distributed mail.

SECRETARY. First Federal Bank, Wichita, KS (1996-99). Excelled as a commercial loan secretary; prepared documentation and presentations, researched customer accounts, and mastered the inhouse word processing system. Promoted to commercial loan secretary based on top-notch work as a file clerk.

PERSONAL

Am a self-motivated and well organized person who is skilled in prioritizing tasks and organizing my time for maximum efficiency. Enjoy working with customers and coworkers.

ADMINISTRATIVE ASSISTANT

Date

Exact Name of Person
Exact Title
Exact Name of Company
Address
City, State, Zip

**ADMINISTRATIVE
ASSISTANT**
for a manufacturing
company

Dear Exact Name of Person (or Dear Sir or Madam if answering a blind ad):

With the enclosed resume, I would like to acquaint you with my exceptional organizational, communication, and computer skills as well as my background in purchasing and inventory control, customer service, and office supervision.

As you will see, I have excelled in a variety of positions at Black & Decker. In my most recent position, I oversaw control and disbursement of the company's travel reimbursement fund as well as the purchasing of office supplies and company shirts. In that capacity, I reduced supply expenditures by 50% without compromising the effectiveness of the department. I also read and analyzed engineering diagrams and entered data into an Excel database, and I updated information using Black & Decker's proprietary computer software.

In positions as Coordinator of Administrative Services and Computer Terminal Operator, I mastered Microsoft Word, Excel, PowerPoint, Outlook, and the FoxBase engineering program while also operating a mainframe computer. I provided customer service for seven Black & Decker facilities and was involved in purchasing, processing invoices and receipts, and reconciling discrepant orders and invoices.

Although I was highly regarded by my employer and can provide excellent references at the appropriate time, a downturn in business forced Black & Decker to reduce its work force, displacing me and many of my coworkers. Nevertheless, I am certain that my extensive knowledge of computer hardware and software, as well as my background in office management and customer service, are valuable assets which will be transferable to any organization.

If you can use a highly motivated, articulate professional with strong administrative skills, I hope you will contact me. I can assure you that I have an excellent reputation and could quickly become a valuable asset to your organization.

Sincerely,

Donielle E. Richardson

DONIELLE E. RICHARDSON

1110½ Hay Street, Fayetteville, NC 28305 • preppub@aol.com • (910) 483-6611

OBJECTIVE

To benefit an organization that can use an experienced office manager, administrative assistant, and data entry professional with exceptional computer skills along with a background in purchasing and inventory control, customer service, manufacturing, and the supervision and training of personnel.

EDUCATION

Division System Specialist Program, Black & Decker training program, 2003.
Continuous Flow Workshop, Black & Decker training program, 2002.
Completed courses in Customer Service (1992) and Basic First Aid (1998), Calhoun Community College, Decatur, AL.

COMPUTERS

Proficient in the following software programs:
- *Office:* Microsoft Word, Excel, PowerPoint, and Outlook
- *Mainframe:* Skilled in the operation of FoxBase engineering software and EDI ordering system

EXPERIENCE

With Black & Decker, was promoted to positions of increasing responsibility in this busy manufacturing facility, Charlotte, NC.

2002-04: **ADMINISTRATIVE ASSISTANT.** Performed a variety of clerical and administrative duties for this busy manufacturing facility.
- Answered multiline phones and operated the switchboard, routing calls and taking messages.
- Assisted and instructed employees on the operation of the various components of the Microsoft Office Suite, including Word, Excel, PowerPoint, and Outlook.
- Read engineering drawings and entered data into an Excel database.
- Released customer orders for manufacture and shipment.
- Oversaw the maintenance and distribution of the travel reimbursement fund; booked all travel and entertainment arrangements for employees and their guests.
- Purchased office supplies and company shirts; reduced office supply expenditures by 50%.
- Performed routine maintenance on copiers and fax machines.
- Was responsible for troubleshooting and correction of order processing problems.
- Updated information on Black & Decker's proprietary software platform.

1997-02: **COORDINATOR OF ADMINISTRATIVE SERVICES.** Was promoted to this position from computer terminal operator; utilized my organizational and problem-solving skills to ensure that administration support was provided to the facility in an efficient and effective manner.
- Processed engineered customer orders and released them for manufacture.
- Supervised and trained all temporary employees assigned to the department.
- Assisted the scheduler with the purchase of production materials.
- Read engineered drawings and entered pertinent data into an Excel database.
- Learned the FoxBase engineering program, as well as Microsoft Word, Excel, and PowerPoint.
- Maintained charts and graphs for the department.
- Filled in for customer service representatives and engineers as needed.

1991-1996: **COMPUTER TERMINAL OPERATOR.** In addition to administrative and clerical tasks, I was responsible for purchasing and served as the customer service representative for seven service centers.
- Entered purchase orders and receipts into an Excel database.
- Expedited and purchased production materials hardware under the direction of the senior buyer.
- Reconciled discrepancies concerning disputed purchase orders and invoices.
- Provided customer service to other Black & Decker locations and learned the purchasing system.

Other experience: SALES ASSOCIATE/SWITCHBOARD OPERATOR. McDonald Lumber & Construction Company, Decatur, AL (1988-1990). Operated the telephone switchboard and worked the sales floor, providing customer service, processing government contracts, filing invoices and compiling billing statements for this busy building supply dealer.

PERSONAL

Outstanding personal and professional references are available upon request.

ADMINISTRATIVE ASSISTANT

Date

Exact Name of Person
Exact Title
Exact Name of Company
Address
City, State, Zip

ADMINISTRATIVE
ASSISTANT
for a distribution
company

Dear Exact Name of Person (or Dear Sir or Madam if answering a blind ad):

I would appreciate an opportunity to talk with you soon about how I could contribute to your organization through my versatile experience and skills in office operations, computer applications, and quality control.

In my current job as an Administrative Assistant at Mitchell's Distribution Company, I handle a wide range of office and production activities. Because of my reputation for "attention to detail" in all things, I have been selected to handle numerous special projects. For example, I was placed in charge of a special project which achieved a perfect first-time no-defects record on units going through testing. I offer a proven ability to multi-task and my written and oral communication skills are excellent.

I hope you will contact me to suggest a time when we might meet to discuss your needs. I can assure you in advance that I could rapidly become an asset to your organization.

Sincerely,

Joyce E. Maynard

JOYCE E. MAYNARD

1110½ Hay Street, Fayetteville, NC 28305 • preppub@aol.com • (910) 483-6611

OBJECTIVE

To benefit an organization that can use my knowledge and experience in office operations, computer applications, and quality control along with my reputation as a self-motivated leader who excels in finding ways to increase productivity while reducing costs.

EDUCATION & TRAINING

Associate of Arts degree in General Studies, Hofstra University, Hempstead, NY, 2001.
Previously studied two years in the Dental Hygiene program at Kingsborough Community College of CUNY, New York, NY.
Have completed numerous training programs and seminars on subjects such as:

Team leading concepts	Continuous flow technology	Communication
Small business operations	Advertising	Small business taxes
Testing/wiring motor units	Workplace safety	Chemical hazard safety

SPECIAL SKILLS

Offer specialized knowledge and experience which includes:
Computer software: Microsoft Word, Access, and Excel
Office operations and procedures: preparing special reports, providing quality control, processing work orders, prioritizing jobs, ordering equipment and parts, answering phones, filing, typing, word processing, and preparing spreadsheets

EXPERIENCE

ADMINISTRATIVE ASSISTANT. Mitchell's Distribution Company, Brooklyn, NY (2002-present). Handle a wide range of operational activities related to production planning and quality control as well as supporting a 20-person team of specialists.
- Make decisions about which procedures and jobs are of greatest priority and organize work flow so that high-dollar jobs are properly completed in a timely manner.
- Review spreadsheets and determine whether needed parts are in stock or to be ordered from outside vendors.
- Apply my computer skills while processing memos, letters, and reports.
- Provide quality assurance and ensure schematics are followed.
- Answer incoming calls on a multiline system and route them to the correct person.
- Achieved a perfect first-time no-defects record on units going through testing.
- Established standardized locations for schematic drawings and labels.

TREASURER'S ASSISTANT. Kingsboro Community College of CUNY, Student Affairs Department, New York, NY (2001-02). Gained leadership experience and was able to play a role in finding economical ways to improve student quality of life while maintaining budget records and obtaining approval for spending for school activities.
- Compiled and presented reports to the school dean and the association.
- Served as assistant to the chairperson of the five-member budget committee.

FULL-TIME STUDENT. Hofstra University, Hempstead, NY (1999-01). Refined my time management and organizational skills while completing numerous general studies courses.

ADMINISTRATIVE ASSISTANT. Bedoin & Associates Architects, Brooklyn, NY (1995-99). Held multiple responsibilities related to approving bids and processing the contracts for architectural drawings and building blueprints for both the state and county planning divisions.
- Prepared letters, memos, and reports.
- Filed billing and sales records.
- Answered incoming multiline phones and directed calls to the appropriate person.
- Learned how to sell and how to prepare bids which resulted in profits for the company.
- Became known for my service orientation and ability to ensure customer satisfaction.

PERSONAL

Work well with others in team settings or while filling leadership roles. Excellent references.

ADMINISTRATIVE ASSISTANT (CAREER CHANGE)

Date

Exact Name of Person
Title or Position
Name of Company
Address (no., street)
Address (city, state, zip)

ADMINISTRATIVE ASSISTANT
for a financial services firm.

Dear Exact Name of Person: (or Dear Sir or Madam if answering a blind ad.)

I would appreciate an opportunity to talk with you soon about how I could benefit your organization through my experience in sales, customer service, marketing, and management. I have just relocated to the Palm Beach area, and I feel my experience and skills could be of considerable value to your organization.

Most recently I have excelled as an Administrative Assistant for a financial services firm, and I handled a variety of tasks in areas which included pre-sale, underwriting, customer service, computer operation, accounts payable/receivable, and health insurance processing. In prior jobs, I gained excellent time-management and organizational skills in the process of working at a variety of jobs while attending school full-time. I am experienced in handling a wide range of financial procedures and possess excellent communication, planning, and time-management abilities.

I have earned a reputation for my ability to rapidly master new tasks and solve thorny problems. I am accustomed to operating on the "front line," making decisions and maximizing resources while handling a wide range of financial transactions in a fast-paced environment. You would find me to be a congenial person who prides myself on my ability to rapidly become a valuable part of a team.

The address and phone number on my resume are those of my parents, because my husband and I are in the process of househunting in the Palm Beach area and do not yet have a telephone connected. My parents will be able to get messages to me reliably and quickly, so please call them and leave a message and I will get in touch with you right away. I hope I will have an opportunity to meet with you to discuss your needs and how I might serve them. I can guarantee that you would be getting a very valuable employee, and I can provide outstanding personal and professional references which will attest to that fact.

Sincerely yours,

Dede King

DEDE R. KING

1110½ Hay Street, Palm Beach, FL 28305 • preppub@aol.com • (910) 483-6611

OBJECTIVE

To benefit an organization seeking a hardworking, results-oriented business and financial professional with top-notch skills in accounting, marketing, and sales as well as excellent organizational and time-management skills.

EDUCATION

Bachelor of Science degree in **Business Administration** with a minor in **Marketing**, the University of North Carolina at Charlotte, Charlotte, NC, May 2002; consistently made both Dean's List and Chancellor's List.

COMPUTERS

Proficient in Microsoft Word, Excel, PowerPoint, and software specific to insurance industry or The Principal including Quicken.

EXPERIENCE

ADMINISTRATIVE ASSISTANT. Prudential Financial Group, Raleigh, NC (2003-04). Excelled in several functional areas while working with this financial services firm. Recently resigned when I relocated to the Palm Beach area.
- *Pre-sale:* Handled correspondence including mass mailings to prospects and letters to individual prospects.
- *Underwriting:* Processed new business applications; reviewed applications for completion, completed daily, weekly, and monthly office reports and submitted applications to Home Office.
- *Customer service:* Performed extensive customer service.
- *Quicken/AR/AP:* Handled accounts receivable, accounts payable, and/or Quicken entries for bookkeeping.
- *Health insurance:* Assembled quotes from different health carriers or prepare quotes using carriers' rate book, processed applications, and prepared policies for delivery.

CHILD SUPPORT INTERN. Superior Clerk of Court, Wake County, Raleigh, NC (2002). Served a three month internship providing financial, clerical, and administrative support to the Child Support Division; performed general clerical and data entry functions.
- Handled a wide range of financial transactions, including processing bad checks.
- Prepared docket sheets for use by the Wake County District Attorney.

Paid for my college education and refined my time-management skills in the process of working in various part-time and full-time jobs while attending school full-time.
CASHIER/WAITRESS/HOSTESS. Peaden's Seafood, Charlotte, NC (2002). Wore several hats in this popular and fast-paced restaurant, including seating customers, waiting on customers, and serving as cashier.

CASHIER/SALES ASSOCIATE. Sam's Club, Charlotte, NC (1998-02). Performed a wide range of cash-handling procedures in addition to promoting and selling both individual and commercial discount club memberships.
- Provided accurate cash-flow, register reconciliation, and refunds, as well as answering and resolving customer questions and complaints.
- Assisted new members in choosing appropriate membership, completing necessary forms, and inputting data to generate membership cards and accounts.
- Provided product information and recommendations while assisting in purchases.

ADMINISTRATIVE ASSISTANT. Myers Park Junior High School, Charlotte, NC (1993-98). Acted as school's "frontline," providing a wide range of administrative and clerical procedures working in this busy office.
- Registered new students, processed and updated student files, sorted and distributed incoming mail, scheduled parent-teacher conferences, and performed clerical tasks.
- Processed purchase orders, managed inventory, made deposits, maintained petty cash.
- Prepared five-year school review report for school officials and community leaders.
- Assisted in coordinating school events and activities.

PERSONAL

Excellent references on request. Am a flexible, versatile professional who enjoys challenges, problem-solving, and maximizing resources. Have received numerous outstanding work performance evaluations.

ADMINISTRATIVE MANAGER

Date

Exact Name of Person
Title or Position
Name of Company
Address (no., street)
Address (city, state, zip)

Dear Exact Name of Person (or Dear Sir or Madam if answering a blind ad):

I would appreciate an opportunity to talk with you soon about how I could contribute to your company as an administrative manager through my background of outstanding performance in positions emphasizing computer operations, general office operations, and records management.

In my current position with the Department of Homeland Security, I have made significant contributions to internal efficiency. On my own initiative, I conducted an analysis which discovered and corrected 200 discrepancies in an inventory of security badges. I also implemented procedural changes which greatly reduced security incidents, and those changes are being reviewed for possible implementation at other locations of Homeland Security. I recently persuaded my boss to implement an employee suggestions program which has produced some outstanding ideas related to improving organizational morale and efficiency.

With a reputation as a highly motivated professional, I excel at finding ways to increase productivity and achieve outstanding results in all areas of performance. I offer a high degree of administrative know-how along with a proven ability to optimize the use of scarce resources.

I hope you will call or write me soon to suggest a time convenient for us to meet and discuss your current and future needs and how I might serve them. Thank you in advance for your time.

Sincerely yours,

Katherine B. O'Donnell

KATHERINE B. O'DONNELL

1110½ Hay Street, Fayetteville, NC 28305　　•　　preppub@aol.com　　•　　(910) 483-6611

OBJECTIVE

To offer extensive experience in office administration to an organization in need of a mature self starter with a talent for finding methods of increasing productivity and efficiency while maximizing individual employees' strengths for the benefit of the organization as a whole.

SPECIAL SKILLS & TRAINING

Familiar with Microsoft Word, Access and Excel as well as answering multiline phones.
Experienced in information security, have held a Top Secret security clearance.
Was selected for training in leadership, postal operations, and security management.

EXPERIENCE

ADMINISTRATIVE MANAGER. Department of Homeland Security, Philadelphia, PA (2002-present). In an affiliate office of the Department of Homeland Security, have improved the efficiency of daily operations while overseeing the training of administrative support staff and managing records in a 200-person department; supervise three administrative specialists.

- Have applied my knowledge and expertise to successfully train five administrative technicians from other affiliate operations. Was specially selected to train these individuals because of my reputation for productivity and efficiency.
- On my own initiative, conducted an analysis which discovered and corrected 200 discrepancies in an inventory of security badges. Implemented procedural changes which greatly reduced security incidents. The changes are now being reviewed for possible implementation at all Homeland Security locations.
- Persuaded my boss to implement an employee suggestions program which has produced some outstanding ideas related to improving organizational morale and efficiency.
- Prepare and present weekly information security reports for the senior executive. Utilize PowerPoint to create effective visual presentations.

ADMINISTRATIVE ASSISTANT. J.H. Wright Appraisal Company, Philadelphia, PA (2000-02). Praised for my attention to detail, knowledge, and abilities, received excellent ratings during company inspections in a job which included document security, records management, and typing.

- Ensured documents were filed, distributed, logged, and destroyed in accordance with all applicable regulations while coordinating document management with other departments. Received a certificate of achievement for contributions while rewriting a procedure that improved operations.

Consistently excelled in positions of trust and responsibility while broadening my base of knowledge and experience of office automation and administration, U.S. Army:
1999-00: PUBLICATIONS, FORMS, AND ADMINISTRATION MANAGER. Fort Meade, MD. Operated an information transfer center which processed official mail; provided advice and guidance to smaller departments and sections throughout the community.

- Implemented the Record Information Management System (RIMS) ahead of schedule.
- Displayed strong managerial skills providing 24-hour support services during wartime efforts.
- Developed a strong team of employees despite an early 50% personnel turnover.
- Totally reorganized the filing system which eliminated the likelihood of lost records.

1998-99: ADMINISTRATIVE BRANCH MANAGER. Fort Hood, TX. Promoted to this position on the basis of my ability to work under pressure and offer outstanding managerial abilities as a Control Center Manager, proceeded to find ways to eliminate wasted time and efforts in this operations center.

- Streamlined recordkeeping and reporting procedures and completed a major reorganization project ahead of schedule. Managed a $250,000 account for sensitive and secure communications equipment.

1995-97: ADMINISTRATIVE ASSISTANT, OPERATIONS AND PLANS BRANCH. Italy. Contributed to the smooth operation of a regional headquarters by providing control, records maintenance, and distribution for both classified and unclassified materials and by administering personnel actions including performance reports.

- Earned praise for my performance which included achieving a 40% reduction in the backlog of one type of report while meeting high performance standards for my typing, filing, and handling of classified correspondence. Refined computer skills and streamlined procedures.

PERSONAL

Earned four commendation medals for outstanding performance, loyalty, and dedication. Offer proven abilities as a planner and organizer. Challenge employees to high standards.

ADMINISTRATIVE SPECIALIST

Date

Exact Name of Person
Exact Title or Position
Company Name
Company Address (street and number)
Company Address (city, state, and ZIP)

ADMINISTRATIVE SPECIALIST

for a 1000-bed medical center in Massachusetts

Dear Exact Name (or Dear Sir or Madam if answering a blind ad):

With the enclosed resume, I would like to express my interest in receiving consideration for employment with your medical facility.

In my current position, I excel in an administrative role at the Worcester County Memorial Hospital, a 1,000-bed medical center. While supervising three full-time and two part-time employees, I have made numerous contributions to efficiency and customer satisfaction through my strong personal initiative and excellent organizational abilities. For example, I created a user-friendly centralized appointment system for 125 physicians which vastly improved efficiency while putting patients and their doctors in a better mood!

Previously employed as an Assistant Manager at the Hamden Medical Center, I was known as an articulate and enthusiastic performer with an eye for detail. I have excelled in assignments where the goal was to find ways to improve customer satisfaction and maintain confidentiality of medical records. Proficient with all editions of the Microsoft Office Suite, I am knowledgeable of specialized software programs used for maintaining records and scheduling activities in medical environments.

With a strong grasp of office administration, customer service, and the applications of automated systems, I am adept at finding ways to streamline procedures and bring about even better customer service. Known for my ability to adeptly handle numerous multiple tasks, I earned an Associate of Science degree in Computer Technology in 2000 while excelling in a full-time job within an environment of frequent change and deadline pressures.

If you can use an experienced young professional with expertise in customer service, automated systems applications, and office administration, I hope you will call soon to suggest a time when we might meet to discuss your needs. I can provide excellent personal and professional references.

Sincerely,

Carolyn S. Nunley

CAROLYN S. NUNLEY

1110½ Hay Street, Fayetteville, NC 28305   •   preppub@aol.com   •   (910) 483-6611

OBJECTIVE   To contribute a strong base of experience in medical/administrative office operations with an emphasis on customer service and computer systems activities while offering a reputation as an articulate and detail-oriented professional.

EDUCATION   **Associate of Science degree in Computer Technology**, Hamden State College, Westfield, MA, 2000; 3.4 GPA.
Certification in **Medical Transcription,** Springfield Technical Community College, Springfield, MA, 1997. Completed courses in management, marketing and computer technology.

SPECIAL SKILLS   **Computers:** Proficient with Microsoft Word, Excel, PowerPoint, and many other programs.
Coding: Offer expertise related to insurance coding.
Scheduling: Adept at setting up templates for scheduling.
Payroll administration: Skilled at using a computer for payroll processing.

EXPERIENCE   **ADMINISTRATIVE SPECIALIST.** Worcester County Memorial Hospital, Worcester, MA (2000-present). In a 1,000-bed hospital, have been cited for my focus on streamlining procedures, increasing customer satisfaction, and improving employee morale. Utilize automated systems to maintain records, make appointments, and prepare a variety of reports.

- **Supervision:** Supervise and evaluate three full-time and two part-time personnel.
- **Customer service:** Became skilled at all aspects of customer service; enrolled individuals in smoking cessation classes while scheduling 16 facilitators and setting up classes.
- **Personal initiative:** Converted paper files to a compact disc storage format while maintaining the library of preventive medicine publications; trained users on the new system. On my own initiative, also created a user-friendly centralized appointment system for 125 physicians which improved efficiency.
- **Attention to detail:** Coded medical procedures with the correct insurance designation.
- **Scheduling and multi-tasking:** Scheduled, planned, and kept minutes for a multidisciplinary health care trainee forum which focused on improving health and fitness.

ASSISTANT MANAGER FOR ADMINISTRATIVE SERVICES. Hamden Medical Center, Westfield, MA (1998-00). Earned a reputation for having a "unique ability" to see the broad picture as well as the details. Resolved patient problems while greeting and checking in 1,500 patients a month in consecutive assignments in HMO and Primary Care Administrative Services departments.

- Researched patient eligibility, referred calls to the proper care provider, received and maintained an average of 150 scheduled medical records per day, distributed lab reports, and prepared and distributed daily rosters.
- Displayed resourcefulness in handling customer concerns with delicacy and respect.
- Provided cross training which increased departmental morale and productivity.
- Decreased the number of unbooked Primary Care appointments by half: as a result, complaints were significantly reduced and productivity increased 50%.

PATIENT SUPPORT SERVICES SPECIALIST. Emergicare, Southbridge, MA (1995-98). Processed paperwork for 250 people monthly under tight deadlines and emergency conditions; excelled in a time-sensitive environment supporting patients eligible for medical evacuation; coded and input data.
- Earned praise for as one who "goes out of her way" to satisfy customer needs.

Highlights of earlier experience: Managed medical records, typed reports/forms, trained personnel, and scheduled appointments as a Medical Administrative Clerk.

PERSONAL   Excellent references upon request. In my spare time, enjoy cooking, cross stitching, and physical fitness activities. Run marathons twice a year. Am an active volunteer in my community in organizations that include Habitat for Humanity, Boys & Girls Homes, and the Rape Crisis Center.

ASSISTANT PERSONNEL MANAGER

Date

Exact Name of Person
Title or Position
Name of Company
Address (number and street)
Address (city, state, and zip)

Dear Exact Name of Person: (or Dear Sir or Madam if answering a blind ad)

Can you use a hardworking and energetic young professional who offers outstanding office operations and management skills with an especially strong background in customer service?

As you will see by my enclosed resume, I am applying my abilities in an administrative role with Target Stores. As the Assistant Personnel Manager for a new store, I have played a role in organizing the personnel department. I oversee the management of personnel records, time cards, and scheduling for 150 employees and directly supervise six people. Although the Target organization has offered me an opportunity to join its management training program and make a career with Target Stores, I am selectively exploring career opportunities in other companies.

In earlier jobs, I was cited for my customer service and managerial abilities and placed in positions of responsibility usually reserved for older, more experienced managers. For instance, at a hotel in downtown Atlanta, I directed a staff of 18 people at one of the hotel's popular restaurants. While serving my country in the U.S. Army I used state-of-the-art automated equipment to maintain personnel records for over 15,000 people at Ft. Bragg, NC, the world's second largest U.S. military base.

I offer exceptional organizational, motivational, and communication skills. With a reputation as a fast learner, I am proficient in using multiple computer programs, and I enjoy the challenge of rapidly mastering new software.

I hope you will welcome my call soon to arrange a brief meeting at your convenience to discuss your current and future needs and how I might serve them. Thank you in advance for your time.

Sincerely yours,

Martha McFadyen

Alternate last paragraph:
I hope you will call or write me soon to suggest a time convenient for us to meet and discuss your current and future needs and how I might serve them. Thank you in advance for your time.

MARTHA McFADYEN

1110½ Hay Street, Fayetteville, NC 28305 • preppub@aol.com • (910) 483-6611

OBJECTIVE

To contribute through my reputation as a hardworking, enthusiastic, and energetic young professional with a broad base of experience related to data entry, computer operations, personnel management, and customer service.

SPECIAL SKILLS

Offer outstanding office skills such as the following:
Computer skills: am familiar with Microsoft Word, Access and PowerPoint software programs.
General office skills: type approximately 55 wpm and am experienced in filing and using standard office equipment including multiline phones, faxes, and copiers

EXPERIENCE

ASSISTANT PERSONNEL MANAGER. Target Stores, Charlotte, NC (2003-present). Was cited for my planning and organizational skills while contributing to the smooth operation of internal personnel activities while emphasizing outstanding customer service.

- Directly supervise six people; maintain personnel records for over 150 employees. Handle scheduling, timekeeping, and payroll preparation.
- Contribute to the store's reputation for customer service by seeing that "rain checks" are issued promptly when advertised merchandise is unavailable.
- Since this was a "start-up" of a new Target location, worked in an essentially entrepreneurial role as I played an important role in the establishment of the personnel department.
- Learned ISIS and HOST computer systems which are specialized systems for pricing, e-mail, and merchandising for the retail industry.

ADMINISTRATIVE ASSISTANT. U.S. Army, Ft. Bragg, NC (2002-03). As a member of the U.S. Army Reserves, was called into active duty during the War on Terrorism. At the second largest U.S. military base, fine tuned my general office, administrative, and customer service skills while handling dual roles as an Administrative Assistant and Personnel Information Systems Management Specialist in a department maintaining personnel records for more than 15,000 people.

- Received, analyzed, and entered data into an army-wide data base at a personnel headquarters located at the nation's largest military base.
- Was singled out for my exceptional public relations skills demonstrated while assisting customers with various needs.
- Applied a range of writing, proofreading, and typing/word processing abilities while preparing correspondence, documentation to explain awards, and narratives for written personnel evaluations.

ASSISTANT MANAGER. The Cafe, Westin Hotels, Atlanta, GA (2000-02). Was hired at the age of 20 to manage a staff of 18 people and a wide range of daily activities in the restaurant of this major downtown hotel.

- Learned what to look for and how to investigate any overages or shortages in cash drawers or in stock and supply levels.
- Trained, scheduled, and supervised employees.

ASSISTANT MANAGER. Burger King, Decatur, GA (1996-99). Originally hired as a Cashier, was soon promoted on the basis of my maturity and ability to lead others. Contributed to highly productive team work in this fast-paced environment.

- Supervised nine people while overseeing day-to-day activities including an emphasis on quick, friendly customer service.
- Was entrusted with the security of cash deposits as well as with handling cash drops and balancing cash drawers.

EDUCATION & TRAINING

Completed three years of college course work in Biology.
Excelled in approximately 724 hours of professional development training in the areas of computer systems information analysis and personnel information systems management.

PERSONAL

Am a quick learner who strongly believes in always giving 100%. Have an outgoing personality and well-developed motivational abilities. Excellent references on request.

BUSINESS MANAGER

Date

Exact Name of Person
Exact Title
Exact Name of Company
Address
City, State, Zip

Dear Exact Name of Person: (or Dear Sir or Madam if answering a blind ad):

With the enclosed resume, I would like to make you aware of my background in business management and office operations as well as my versatile history of accomplishments.

As you will see from my resume, I have enjoyed a track record of advancement with Bellarmine Industrial Laundries, and I have played an important role in its growth. The company was a year old, had first-year sales of $500,000, and employed approximately 20 people when I joined it as the Bookkeeper. As the company grew, I became the Office Manager as the number of employees rose to 40. In 2000 I became the Business Manager. Bellarmine now has 60 employees, annual sales of $3.5 million, and operates in two states. It was recently acquired by a Tennessee-based firm which has two offices in Kentucky and Illinois and an additional 20 offices in six other states. Although the new owners have strongly encouraged me to remain with the company, I am selectively and confidentially exploring other opportunities.

As the company grew, I continued to take on new duties and became recognized for my problem-solving skills and ability to expertly manage accounts payable, accounts receivable, general ledger, and payroll support. On my own initiative, I played a significant role in automating accounting and bookkeeping functions to allow the company to keep up with growth and expansion.

If you can use an experienced, mature, and dependable professional known for initiative and vision, I hope you will welcome my call soon when I try to arrange a brief meeting to discuss how my background might serve your needs. I can provide outstanding references at the appropriate time.

Sincerely,

Kelly D. Inman

Alternate last paragraph:
I hope you will write or call me soon to suggest a time when we might meet to discuss your needs and goals and how my background might serve them. I can provide outstanding references at the appropriate time.

KELLY D. INMAN

1110½ Hay Street, Fayetteville, NC 28305 • preppub@aol.com • (910) 483-6611

OBJECTIVE

To offer a strong background in business management and office operations to an organization that can benefit from my experience in a fast-paced environment where my skills in bookkeeping and computer operations contributed to growth and profitability.

EDUCATION

Completed college-level coursework in management skills and accounting.

SPECIAL SKILLS

Computers: utilize Microsoft Word and QuickBooks software for accounting.
Accounting functions: accounts payable, accounts receivable, general ledger, and payroll processing.

EXPERIENCE

Have advanced in the following "track record" with Bellarmine Industrial Laundries, of Louisville, KY, an industrial laundry service specializing in rentals and dust control:
2000-present: BUSINESS MANAGER. Manage an office staff to include supervising, training, and counseling employees. Handle payroll processing for 60 employees, and produce income statements and balance sheets for the central office of a company which operates in the two-state area of Kentucky and Illinois.

- Am providing a stabilizing presence for employees following a recent acquisition by Martinizing, Inc., a Tennessee company with two offices in Kentucky and 20 others in six mid-eastern states.
- Provide support for a business with annual sales of approximately $3.5 million.
- Was instrumental in selecting and implementing an upgraded computer system and new software required to allow the company to meet its changing needs and level of growth.
- Have been singled out for organizational and planning skills; played a vital role in establishing efficient operations during expansion into another state.
- Handle the process of seeking out and reviewing bids for business and health insurance and the annual decision process on possible changes to those programs.
- Cited on numerous occasions for my problem-solving and decision-making skills, play a leadership role by handling workmen's compensation and health insurance issues.
- Was appointed to serve on the advisory committee for the corporate profit-sharing plan; administer various aspects of the retirement plan.
- Have been honored with three "Service with Excellence" awards for outstanding service, leadership, and dedication.
- Supervise the receptionist and a data entry specialist.
- In my spare time, keep the books and handle accounting for a "family-owned" trucking industry firm.

1997-00: OFFICE MANAGER and **BOOKKEEPER.** Originally was hired as the company's Bookkeeper and then was promoted to Office Manager. Handled payroll accounting for 20 employees of a new company which had an annual revenue of $500,000 in two primary lines of business: uniform rental and the bleaching and "stone washing" of denim jeans.

- Hired two assistants as the business grew; trained and supervised them in the daily cash flow balancing and accounts receivable processes.
- Was instrumental in changing to an automated accounting system from a manual system.
- Updated and balanced the general ledger prior to sending it to the company's CPA.
- Prepared quarterly payroll reports and annual W-2 forms as the company grew to 40 employees.
- Determined gross and net income; calculated and paid federal and state withholding tax.
- As Bookkeeper, typed invoices for distribution by route deliverymen; balanced daily cash flow; processed accounts payable and receivable using a manual system.
- Calculated sales tax for Kentucky, Illinois, and Missouri.

PERSONAL

Am a past member of the National Business Association and permanent resident of Louisville. Outstanding personal and professional references available.

CALL CENTER REPRESENTATIVE

Date

Exact Name of Person
Exact Title
Exact Name of Company
Address
City, State, Zip

Dear Exact Name of Person (or Dear Sir or Madam if answering a blind ad):

With the enclosed resume, I would like to make you aware of my background as an experienced customer service professional and office manager with exceptional communication, organizational, and computer skills.

In my present position with Triton Telemarketing Services (TTS), I provide customer service and telephone direct marketing at a large call center of one of the country's largest telemarketing companies. I contact businesses and individuals to introduce them to the client's products and services, which include several long distance plans and other telephone services such as caller I.D., additional lines, voice mail, and call waiting. Because of my ability to quickly build a rapport with and tactfully deflect the objections of customers, I have frequently been the top producer on numerous campaigns.

In a previous position as Office Manager for Hunter Construction Company, I held final accountability for a number of operational areas. I processed accounts payable and accounts receivable, prepared the company's weekly payroll and monthly billing statements, and oversaw the purchasing of building materials, office supplies, and equipment. I am proficient in the use of Microsoft Word, Excel and QuickBooks accounting software.

In an earlier position with AT&T, I called on residential telephone customers to explain the benefits, features, and incentives offered by switching their long distance service to AT&T. I learned the differences between AT&T's products and services and those of its chief competitors, and I was trained in the specific workings of the long distance billing system so that I could present information on rate structures for international, domestic, and local services. I further honed my customer service skills while dealing tactfully with customers who were frequently agitated due to the number of similar offers they were receiving.

I completed three years of college course work in Business Management at Southern Methodist University, and I feel that my strong combination of education and experience would make me a great asset to your company.

If you can use an experienced professional with a strong background in customer service, office administration, telemarketing, and accounting, I hope you will contact me soon to suggest a time when we might meet to discuss your needs. I can assure you in advance that I have an excellent reputation and could quickly become a valuable addition to your organization.

Sincerely,

Jeannie C. Hunt

JEANNIE C. HUNT

1110½ Hay Street, Fayetteville, NC 28305   •   preppub@aol.com   •   (910) 483-6611

OBJECTIVE

To benefit an organization that can use an experienced customer service professional with exceptional communication and organizational skills who offers a background in telemarketing, direct sales, accounting, and office management.

EDUCATION

Completed three years of college course work towards a Bachelor of Science degree in Business Management, Southern Methodist University, Dallas, TX, 2000.

COMPUTERS

Am proficient in the operation of the most common software packages and operating systems, including Microsoft Word, Excel and QuickBooks accounting software.

EXPERIENCE

CALL CENTER REPRESENTATIVE. Triton Telemarketing Services (TTS), Dallas, TX (2003-present). Provide customer service and telephone direct marketing at a local call center for one of the largest telemarketing companies in the country.
- Contact businesses and individuals and introduce them to the products and services offered by our clients. Sell long distance services; phone services such as caller I.D., additional lines, voice mail, and call waiting; and web pages for advertising.
- Quickly develop rapport with customers, maintaining a conversational tone and ensuring strict compliance to the marketing script provided by the client.
- Frequently recognized as the top producer on numerous campaigns.
- Able to tactfully deflect customer objections through actively listening, analyzing the reason for their misgivings, and emphasizing the positive points of the product or service offered in order to overcome their reluctance.

OFFICE MANAGER and **SECRETARY.** Hunter Construction Company, Dallas, TX (2001-03). Performed a variety of administrative, office management, purchasing, accounting, and clerical duties for this busy home improvement company.
- Processed accounts payable and accounts receivable; took orders from contractors and billed them for work completed.
- Prepared weekly payroll, calculating employee hours and phoning them in to the accounting office.
- Solely responsible for all material orders for building materials, office supplies, and equipment.
- Typed letters and other correspondence; filed invoices, customer billing statements, and other paperwork; and operated various types of office equipment.
- Answered multiline phones, directing calls and taking messages.

TELEMARKETER. AT&T, Dallas, TX (2000-01). Contributed significantly to the direct marketing and sales of AT&T long distance services, working out of a large call center which utilized an autodialer system.
- Contacted residential phone customers and explained the benefits, features, and incentives offered for switching their long-distance service to AT&T.
- Became knowledgeable of the differences between the products and services offered by AT&T and those of its main competitors.
- Trained in the specific workings of the long distance billing system, with relation to different types of long distance service, rates for domestic and international long distance, and calling areas.
- Honed my customer skills while dealing tactfully and effectively with long distance consumers who were often agitated.

TELEMARKETER. DataCom Networks, Dallas, TX (1999-00). Duties included direct telephone market of various products and services, such as credit cards and long distance telephone service, as well as soliciting donations to charitable organizations.

Other experience:
Previously excelled in positions as a Medical Records Clerk for Phildrom Memorial, as well as earlier jobs as an alarm monitor and a tour bus driver the Dallas Civic Center.

PERSONAL

Excellent personal and professional references are available upon request.

CLERICAL SPECIALIST

Date

Exact Name of Person
Exact Title
Exact Name of Company
Address
City, State, Zip

Dear Exact Name of Person (or Dear Sir or Madam if answering a blind ad):

With the enclosed resume, I would like to make you aware of my interest in exploring employment opportunities with your organization.

In my current position as a Clerical Specialist for Cauldwell Printing, I have learned operations unique to the printing industry as a secretary in charge of answering phone inquiries while controlling the supply inventory. I maintain logs of long-distance phone calls, overseas shipments, and air shipments, and I type bills of lading while applying my knowledge of printing industry standards. On my own initiative, I reorganized the stockroom and filing system with the result that overall office efficiency is at an all-time high. This has led to an improvement in turnaround times for all jobs, and that has favorably impacted on customer satisfaction while also strengthening the ability of the business to compete for time-sensitive jobs.

In previous positions as a Receptionist and Customer Service Representative, I became efficient in reorganizing filing systems as I learned different types of computer software programs. I have refined my written and oral communication skills through extensive experience in preparing correspondence and presentations.

If you can use a motivated, hardworking professional who is dedicated to delivering quality results in customer-focused environments requiring attention to detail, I hope you will contact me soon. I assure you in advance that I have an excellent reputation and would quickly become an asset to your organization.

Sincerely,

Stephanie J. Hamlane

STEPHANIE J. HAMLANE

1110½ Hay Street, Fayetteville, NC 28305   •   preppub@aol.com   •   (910) 483-6611

OBJECTIVE

To benefit an organization that can use a conscientious, dedicated hard worker with an ability to rapidly master new systems along with versatile expertise related to office operations, customer service, and computer applications.

OFFICE SKILLS

- Offer experience in working with Microsoft Word, Access and PowerPoint.
- Type 65 wpm.
- Operate office equipment including 10-key adding machines, fax machines, and printers.
- Very experienced in operating Rohm 10-line and PBX switchboards.

EXPERIENCE

CLERICAL SPECIALIST. Cauldwell Printing, Alameda, CA (2002-present). Have learned operations unique to the printing industry as a secretary in charge of answering phone inquiries and directing calls to the proper person. Handle other office activities including filing and controlling the supply inventory. On my own initiative, made contributions to office efficiency which led to improved customer satisfaction.

- Maintain logs of long-distance phone calls, overseas shipments, and air shipments.
- Type bills of lading according to the strict specifications of the printing industry.
- Improved office efficiency by reorganizing the filing system and stock room procedures.
- Applied my communication skills preparing correspondence for the owners.
- Improved my computer skills by learning a new type of software.

SWITCHBOARD OPERATOR/RECEPTIONIST. Rocklin Hospital, Rocklin, CA (2000-02). Increased my computer skills while also monitoring emergency calls and ensuring the proper personnel were paged to respond to the situation.

- Gained experience in stress management and handling pressure while working in an environment with frequent emergencies.
- Used my organizational skills to update the patient information electronic filing system.

Earned advancement in recognition of my hard work and abilities, Office Depot, Alameda, CA:
1998-99: CUSTOMER SERVICE REPRESENTATIVE. Recognized as an extremely hardworking professional who handled a workload normally shared by two people, retrieved orders from computer records sent by other locations, entered data on a local network, checked to see if the items were in stock, and printed the order for the shipping department.

- Earned praise for my attention to quality customer service while following through to see that orders were filled and delivered quickly.

1990-98: SHIPPING CLERK. Beginning as a clerk/typist preparing bills of lading and logging amounts of paper products sold, earned advancement based on my increasing skills in using automated systems and finding ways to improve productivity and efficiency.

- Took the initiative to track down answers when questions came up on orders.
- Prepared special supporting documents needed to ship hazardous waste.
- Scheduled shipments for exportation and prepared all needed documentation.
- Prepared regular daily, weekly, and monthly reports and entered data in a computer network.
- Played a major role in transferring paper work to an automated data system.
- Worked with programmers to identify company's needs and then tested program to ensure it filled requirements.

Highlights of other experience: Gained experience in dealing with customers in a helpful and courteous manner as a long-distance telephone operator, corporate PBX operator, and as the switchboard operator/receptionist for a law firm.

PERSONAL

Am a fast learner who can be counted on for my loyalty and honesty. Work well with others and with the public. Received training in customer service, typing, and computer skills.

CUSTOMER SERVICE REPRESENTATIVE

Date

Exact Name of Person
Title or Position
Name of Company
Address (number and street)
Address (city, state, and zip)

**CUSTOMER
SERVICE
REPRESENTATIVE**
for a financial position
with the state of
Tennessee

Dear Exact Name of Person: (or Sir or Madam if answering a blind ad.)

I am interested in employment with your organization and believe my exceptional communication and organizational skills would be a real asset to you. I recently resigned from my position with the City of Memphis in order to relocate to the Arkansas area. I can provide outstanding references from all previous employers.

As you will see, I recently excelled in a position as Customer Service Representative for the public utility service operated by the City of Memphis, where I handled both residential and corporate accounts. I was promoted to that position because of my excellent work history in a previous position with the city. I offer strong customer service skills as well as a background in office administration and collections.

During my years of dealing with the public, I have handled a variety of responsibilities, including customer service, revenue collection, and accounts receivable. For the past decade, I have rapidly mastered new software applications and programs. I am an outgoing, energetic individual who genuinely enjoys working with the public and helping to solve the problems of others.

I am known for my ability to establish strong working relationships with fellow employees as well as with outside organizations. I am confident that I could become a valuable resource to your organization, and I can provide outstanding professional references.

If my versatile skills and talents interest you, I hope you will contact me to suggest a time when we might meet to discuss your needs. I am very flexible and open to working any hours or shifts.

Sincerely yours,

Melissa J. Escalante

MELISSA J. ESCALANTE

1110½ Hay Street, Fayetteville, NC 28305   •   preppub@aol.com   •   (910) 483-6611

OBJECTIVE

To benefit an organization that can use my strong customer service skills as well as my versatile background which includes accounting, billing, collections, as well as inside and outside sales.

COMPUTERS & OFFICE EQUIPMENT

Proficient with Microsoft Word, Excel, QuickBooks and PageMaker skilled in using Extractor Pro CIS 2.20 and CIS 2.21.
Skilled in ten-key calculator, multiline phone system, fax, copier, and postage machine usage.

EDUCATION

Completed one year of coursework in Accounting, State Technical Institute of Technology of Memphis.
Completed formal and on-the-job training related to customer service and sales; certified Notary Public.

EXPERIENCE 2002-04:

Excelled in the following track record of promotion with the City of Memphis, TN:
CUSTOMER SERVICE REPRESENTATIVE. Set up utility accounts for new service; transferred accounts; worked face-to-face with corporate and residential customers. Recently resigned my position in order to relocate to Arkansas.
- Received service requests and complaints; prepared and maintained files and records.
- Examined credit reference for acceptability and determined deposit amount required; collected deposits and fees as well as issued receipts.
- Responded to customer questions regarding opening new accounts, deposits, credit references, return checks, final bills, and other collection-related items or city services.
- Maintained accurate records of returned checks, debited accounts for checks and fees; assisted in preparing bank drafts authorized by customers, and assisted in annual reviews of deposits eligible for refund.
- Was commended for my professional style and friendly, outgoing manner.
- Worked daily on a computer in order to input data; set up payment arrangements and was cross trained to handle tasks performed by the other three customer service reps.

2000-02:

UTILITY REVENUE COLLECTIONS CLERK. Was promoted to the job above based on my excellent performance as Collector/Cashier; credited accounts and entered data into a computer using the QuickBooks and Extractor Pro software program; issued receipts.
- Handled inquiries or complaints from general public and responded to questions pertaining to utility bills; referred customers to appropriate sources.
- Opened mail; matched checks against stubs; balanced and posted receipts to accounts.
- Provided customer service by telephone and handled customer inquiries professionally.
- Balanced cash drawer against receipts and maintained records of money received.

With a private company, Trent Landscaping, which handled lawn maintenance for Martin, TN, was promoted in the following track record:

1998-00:

ACCOUNTS RECEIVABLE CLERK. Worked extensively with Excel while processing monthly billing using Microsoft Word and Excel spreadsheets; handled collections—both incoming calls and outgoing calls—on all delinquent accounts 90 days or older; answered billing questions by telephone and in person.

1997-98:

INSIDE SALES REPRESENTATIVE. Conducted telemarketing of the company's new Mastergreen Commercial Equipment; completed an average of 35 calls daily exceeding a $2,500 monthly sales quota.

1997:

CUSTOMER SERVICE REPRESENTATIVE. Answered phones and entered customer information into the company's database; conducted follow-up calls on all accounts sold.

Excelled in an insurance company and a nonprofit environment:

1996:

UNDERWRITING CLERK. Phillips Insurance, Martin, TN. Set up new insurance groups, changed status of old groups, handled filing, and provided customer service.

1994-96:

SALES REPRESENTATIVE. National Health Association of Tennessee, Martin, TN. For a company which sold pamphlets about sexually transmitted diseases for consumer education to hospitals and corporations, maintained records of invoices, handled filing, input data, and managed a 50-line switchboard averaging 500 calls daily.

PERSONAL

Outstanding references upon request.

CUSTOMER SERVICE REPRESENTATIVE

Date

Exact Name of Person
Title or Position
Name of Company
Address (number and street)
Address (city, state, and zip)

Dear Exact Name of Person: (or Sir or Madam if answering a blind ad.)

With the enclosed resume, I would like to make you aware of my interest in exploring employment opportunities with your organization. I offer a background as an experienced clerical professional who offers experience in data entry, customer service, accounts receivable, and inventory control.

In my present position with The Vista News, I have been entrusted with increasing levels of responsibility. I perform data entry, keying a large volume of distribution data into the company's proprietary software system. As a Customer Service Representative, I interact with representatives from various retail customers, providing information, resolving customer complaints, and answering questions regarding distribution of specific titles. I assist the Accounts Receivable Department, taking payment on COD accounts from the drivers and entering those figures in the appropriate logs. I am cross-trained to receive magazines and enter invoices into the system when the computer operator is not available.

Previously as a Clerk/Typist with the Department of Agriculture in Sierra Vista, I honed my administrative skills while providing clerical support in a busy office environment. I prepared administrative documents, performed all subject filing, answered multiline phones, and distributed all office mail. In earlier temporary positions as an Office Assistant, I prepared correspondence, typed and filed, acted as receptionist, and performed general office duties. I have completed 20 semester hours of college-level course work at Cochise College. I feel that my education and versatile office experience would make me a valuable addition to your company.

If you can use a hardworking administrative, clerical or data entry professional whose skills have been tested in challenging environments, I hope you will contact me to suggest a time when we might meet. I can assure in advance that I have an excellent reputation, and would quickly become an asset to your organization.

Sincerely,

Tonya A. Felder

TONYA A. FELDER

1110½ Hay Street, Fayetteville, NC 28305   •   preppub@aol.com   •   (910) 483-6611

OBJECTIVE   To contribute to an organization that can use an articulate administrative and customer service professional with strong organizational skills who offers a background in office management, accounts receivable, and inventory control.

EDUCATION   Completed 20 hours of college-level course work at Cochise College, Sierra Vista, AZ.
Have completed extensive training sponsored by my employers related to computer operations, customer service, accounts receivable management, and inventory control.

EXPERIENCE   *With The Vista News, began as a Receptionist and Distribution Clerk, and have been entrusted with increasing levels of responsibility.*
CUSTOMER SERVICE REPRESENTATIVE and **DISTRIBUTION CLERK.** Sierra Vista, AZ (2003-present). Perform data entry, customer service, and inventory control tasks while providing assistance to the Accounts Receivable Department. Duties include:

Data Entry:
- Key a large volume of distribution data into the proprietary inventory control software employed by The Vista News; enter information concerning specific titles and quantities order by retail customers, including Barnes & Noble, Kroger, and Target.

Customer Service:
- Interact with store managers and customer representatives from various retail outlets regarding overages and shortages in their orders, requests to order extra copies of special issues, and other distribution and title availability information.
- Perform liaison with publisher representatives and field agents, both on the telephone and in the office.

Accounts Receivable:
- Accept payments for cash on delivery customers from route drivers and record amount received on appropriate tracking logs in order provide accountability.
- Key in deposits report on a daily basis.

Inventory Control:
- Update and maintain data related to quantities ordered and shipped to customers which is used to determine appropriate inventory levels.
- Cross-trained to receive magazines and enter invoices into the system when the computer operator is not available.

CLERK/TYPIST. Department of Agriculture, Sierra Vista, AZ (1999-03). Performed a variety of administrative, clerical, and receptionist duties in this busy office environment.
- Prepared and assisted in the preparation of various administrative forms such as travel vouchers, accident reports, and mail surveys.
- Performed all subject filing; maintained and updated the filing system.
- Answered multiline phones, providing information, directing calls, and taking messages.

Other experience:
SUPERVISOR. Service Merchandise, Sierra Vista, AZ (1997-99). Started with Service Merchandise as a retail salesperson in the Jewelry and Electronics department; advanced to Checkout Supervisor, where I oversaw the performance of up to 20 cashiers, ensuring all customers received prompt, courteous service.

OFFICE ASSISTANT. Olsten Staffing, Sierra Vista, AZ (1996-97). Honed my administrative and clerical skills, providing general office skills to various local businesses while employed by this temporary agency.
- Performed typing and filing, prepared correspondence, handled mail, and answered multiline phones.

PERSONAL   Excellent personal and professional references are available upon request.

CUSTOMER SERVICE SECRETARY

Date

Exact Name of Person
Title or Position
Name of Company
Address (no., street)
Address (city, state, zip)

**CUSTOMER
SERVICE
SECRETARY**
for a credit union

Dear Exact Name of Person: (or Dear Sir or Madam if answering a blind ad.)

I would appreciate an opportunity to talk with you soon about how I could contribute to your organization through my secretarial skills as well as my sales and customer service experience.

As you will see from my enclosed resume, I am a Customer Service Secretary for the First Federal Credit Union of Little Rock. I began as a receptionist and was selected to handle responsibilities not normally assigned to new employees. I handle responsibilities for updating accounts and personnel files for the Credit Union and have been praised for my initiative and willingness to take charge of disorganized areas.

In a previous position as a Word Processor for Cabrillo Insurance Group, I rapidly became the "right arm" of one of the senior managers after proving my ability to handle confidential information with discretion. I became skilled at taking dictation and, after gaining familiarity with insurance paper work, I took on responsibilities for organizing and formatting information related to claims reviews. I was also entrusted with key corporate documents and learned to expertly file claims and negotiate solutions with all parties involved.

With a reputation as a fast learner with an energetic and enthusiastic manner, I feel that my greatest strengths are my resourcefulness and adaptability. Known as a good listener, I am effective at developing a sense of team work among employees and motivating them to provide high quality services. In every company for which I have worked, I have found ways to contribute to increased productivity.

I hope you will welcome my call soon to arrange a brief meeting at your convenience to discuss your current and future needs and how I might serve them. Thank you in advance for your time.

Sincerely yours,

Lillie C. Thomas

Alternate last paragraph:
I hope you will call or write me soon to suggest a time convenient for us to meet and discuss your current and future needs and how I might serve them. Thank you in advance for your time.

LILLIE C. THOMAS

1110½ Hay Street, Fayetteville, NC 28305   •   preppub@aol.com   •   (910) 483-6611

OBJECTIVE

I want to contribute to an organization that can use a polished young professional who offers excellent written and oral communication skills, strong research and analytical abilities, proven leadership strengths, as well as the capacity for hard work and long hours.

EDUCATION

Bachelor of Science (B.S.) degree in **Political Science** and **Biology**, Southern Arkansas University, Magnolia, AR, 2002.
- Was named to Dean's List several semesters.

COMPUTERS

Offer experience with software including Microsoft Word, Excel, FrontPage, and PowerPoint.

EXPERIENCE

Worked in these full-time positions in Little Rock, AR, and was commended in each one for my exceptional planning and organizational abilities as well as my knack for dealing with the public in a tactful and gracious manner.

CUSTOMER SERVICE SECRETARY. First Federal Credit Union, Little Rock, AR (2004-present). Began as a receptionist and was selected to handle responsibilities not normally assigned to new employees; handle responsibilities for updating accounts and personnel files for the Credit Union.
- Was praised for my initiative and willingness to take charge of disorganized areas.

WORD PROCESSOR. Cabrillo Insurance Group, Little Rock, AR (2002-04). Rapidly became the "right arm" of one of the senior managers after proving my ability to handle confidential information with discretion.
- Became skilled in taking dictation. After gaining familiarity with insurance paper work, assumed responsibility for organizing and formatting information related to claims reviews.
- Was entrusted with key corporate documents and learned to expertly file claims and negotiate with all parties involved in the claim.

ACTING LEGAL SECRETARY. Smith, Hines & Taylor Law Firm, Magnolia, AR (2000-02). Was a secretary for one of the nine lawyers in this legal department, and handled a wide range of responsibilities as a personal assistant and legal secretary.
- Took dictation; for all nine lawyers, logged pertinent information regarding court dates and pending litigation.
- Booked flights, reserved hotel rooms, and arranged automobile travel.
- Handled responsibilities related to case management including updating files with all information pertinent to litigation.
- Routinely handled privileged information. Participated in the development of a new database program. Prepared a wide range of written communication including letters.

SECRETARY. Department of State, Magnolia, AR (1999-00). Performed receptionist/secretarial duties and assisted in the recruitment of managerial employees; prepared and sent letters to recruit personnel; collected and organized data for presentation to top management.

WORD PROCESSOR. Liberty Mutual, Magnolia, AR (1998-99). Interviewed beneficiaries regarding benefits, answered stockholder questions; ordered office supplies and maintenance services.

PERSONAL

Enjoy tennis and piano. Also thoroughly enjoy applying my talent for planning and organizing activities. Have acquired excellent personal time management skills.

DATA ENTRY CLERK

Date

Exact Name of Person
Exact Title
Exact Name of Company
Address
City, State, Zip

DATA ENTRY CLERK
for a bank

Dear Exact Name of Person: (or Dear Sir or Madam if answering a blind ad):

With the enclosed resume, I would like to make you aware of my background in customer service and sales, as well as the outstanding communication, organizational, and data entry skills which I could offer your company.

As you will see from my resume, I am excelling in a Data Entry Clerk position with Wachovia. I key a large volume of checks into the computer daily, accurately entering check number, account number, and amount. Other duties include answering multiline telephones and providing gracious assistance to bank customers. I have been recognized by my supervisor for exemplary efficiency and attention to detail, and I have been praised for my ability to correctly enter data into the computer under extremely tight deadlines.

In a previous job with Saks Fifth Avenue in Cambridge, I assisted customers in the selection and purchase of merchandise in a fast-paced retail environment as I performed customer service, cash handling, and clerical duties. I answered multiline phones and processed a large volume of incoming customer service requests for Sak's customers.

If you can use a dedicated young professional with outstanding data entry and customer service skills, I hope you will welcome my call soon when I try to arrange a brief meeting to discuss your goals and how my background might serve your needs. I can provide outstanding references at the appropriate time.

Sincerely,

Erica L. Finley

Alternate Last Paragraph:
I hope you will write or call me soon to suggest a time when we might meet to discuss your needs and goals and how my background might serve them. I can provide outstanding references at the appropriate time.

ERICA L. FINLEY

1110½ Hay Street, Fayetteville, NC 28305 • preppub@aol.com • (910) 483-6611

OBJECTIVE

To benefit an organization that can use an experienced professional with strong time management skills who offers a background in customer service, cash handling, and data entry in fast-paced banking and retail environments.

EDUCATION

Completed nearly two years of college-level course work towards a degree in Human Services, Leslie College, Cambridge, MA.

EXPERIENCE

DATA ENTRY CLERK. Wachovia Bank, Boston, MA (2003-present). Perform data entry and telephone customer service while assigned by the Randstaff Temporary Employment Agency to this high-volume data entry position with Wachovia.
- Key a large volume of checks into the computer daily, entering check number, account number, and amount into a computer database.
- Answer multiline telephones, providing assistance to bank customers.
- Was cited by my supervisor for my efficiency and attention to detail; correctly enter all data into the computer, meeting production and accuracy objectives.

SALES ASSOCIATE. Saks Fifth Avenue, Cambridge, MA (2002-03). Assisted customers in the selection and purchase of merchandise in a fast-paced retail environment; performed customer service, cash handling, and clerical duties.
- Answered multiline phones, processing a large volume of incoming customer service requests for Sak's customers.
- Rang customer purchases, operating cash registers and the credit card verification system.
- Provided clerical support, including but not limited to light typing, operating a facsimile machine and performing other office duties.

ADMINISTRATIVE ASSISTANT. Leslie College, Cambridge, MA (2001-02). While pursuing my college education, provided a wide range of clerical and administrative support and acted as a receptionist for this busy office.
- Processed a high volume of incoming calls, answering requests for information, routing calls to the appropriate staff member, and taking messages if the party was unavailable.
- Operated various office equipment, including photocopiers, facsimile machines, 10-key calculators, personal computers, and multiline phones.
- Assisted students in scheduling appointments with faculty members.
- Typed a variety of letters, memos, and other correspondence for the office.

CUSTOMER SERVICE REPRESENTATIVE. Uniway, Cambridge, MA (2000-01). Started with the company as a Sales Associate, and was quickly given additional responsibility as the Customer Service Representative for my shift.
- Provided exceptional customer service, both on the phone and in person; answered questions and assisted in the selection and purchase of merchandise.
- Performed some stock duties, merchandising new product and straightening displays in my assigned area of the store.
- Operated a cash register, ringing up customer sales.

PERSONAL

Known as a dependable, reliable self-starter who possesses the ability to quickly learn and adapt. Excellent personal and professional references are available upon request.

DATA ENTRY SUPERVISOR

Date

Exact Name of Person
Exact Title
Exact Name of Company
Address
City, State, Zip

Dear Exact Name of Person: (or Dear Sir or Madam if answering a blind ad):

With the enclosed resume, I would like to make you aware of the customer service and sales skills which I could offer your company.

As you will see from my resume, for most of my career I worked for an online mail company in Albuquerque where I provided exceptional customer service and support via the Internet to the Data Services department and other areas of the operation. I processed a large volume of incoming customer complaints daily, working with personnel in other departments, with manufacturer's representatives, and with internal subject matter experts to quickly provide solutions to customers' problems. In an earlier position, I was entrusted with the responsibility of issuing credits and refunds in response to customer complaints.

After receiving an Associate of Arts degree in Corporate Communications from the University of New Mexico, I accepted my current position as a Data Entry Supervisor with the Department of Social Services. My supervisor has praised my efficiency and communication skills, and I have played a key role in transferring a variety of course materials, publications, and support resources into a digital format where they can be more easily accessed.

If you can use a dedicated young professional with outstanding customer service skills, I hope you will contact me to suggest a time when we might meet to discuss your goals and how my background might serve your needs. I can provide outstanding references at the appropriate time.

Sincerely,

Carmen P. Gonzalez

Alternate Last Paragraph:
I hope you will write or call me soon to suggest a time when we might meet to discuss your needs and goals and how my background might serve them. I can provide outstanding references at the appropriate time.

CARMEN P. GONZALEZ

1110½ Hay Street, Fayetteville, NC 28305 • preppub@aol.com • (910) 483-6611

OBJECTIVE

To contribute to an organization that can use a hardworking young professional with extensive customer service and public relations experience as well as knowledge of purchasing, finance and accounting, operations management, and computer operations.

EDUCATION & TRAINING

Associate of Arts in **Corporate Communications,** University of New Mexico, Albuquerque, NM, 2003. Became skilled in typing and data processing as well as in composing business correspondence. Completed numerous training courses related to Telephone Customer Service, Warranty Administration, and other areas.

COMPUTERS

Highly proficient in utilizing computers to improve office efficiency; skilled in using Microsoft Word, Excel, and PowerPoint, and proprietary office management programs for account management and tracking; quickly master new systems and software.
Perform data entry at 7000-9000 keystrokes per minute; type 45-50 wpm.

EXPERIENCE

DATA ENTRY SUPERVISOR. Department of Social Services, Albuquerque, NM (2003-present). Oversee the provision of clerical support in data entry and filing.
- Utilize Microsoft Word, Excel and PowerPoint while keying in course materials, data sheets, lists of community resources, and other materials used by the center's staff.

Completed an internship as a business assistant and was hired on a permanent basis by a major online mail company, Eudora, Inc., Albuquerque, NM:
2000-03: DATA SERVICES DEPARTMENT CUSTOMER SERVICE REPRESENTATIVE. Cited for my initiative and conscientious manner, earned promotion to a position where the emphasis was on quickly and skillfully responding to customer questions and handling complaints about online products.
- Handled a large volume of incoming e-mail complaints using Internet Explorer, Eudora Mail, and a proprietary internal customer information system.
- Worked closely with personnel in other departments including the purchasing department, manufacturers' representatives, and internal subject matter experts to resolve complaints.
- Processed complex complaints and requests for information concerning billing, accounting, and product quality; researched and solved minor technical support issues for customers.
- Completed data updates in the internal customer information system and provided assistance to customers by telephone and e-mail.
- Earned the respect of my superiors for my helpful manner and ability to work in harmony with my peers, superiors, and customers.
- Sold warranties to phone customers. Suggested products related to the merchandise they called to order.

1998-00: CUSTOMER SERVICE REPRESENTATIVE. Responded to a large volume of customer complaints and questions, ensuring customer satisfaction while providing extensive data entry support.
- Consistently exceeded production quotas for number of complaints handled and amount of time spent on each complaint while still providing exceptional customer service.
- Answered mail queries, selecting the appropriate form letters to respond quickly to customers' concerns.
- Maintained and updated a database of customer addresses and information.
- Performed data entry, keying large mailing lists of customers receiving the same form letter; issued refunds and credits for defective merchandise.

Other experience:
INTERN. (1996-98). Completed an internship in the Human Resources Department and successfully passed an oral examination given by the City of Albuquerque Government Office, leading to certification as a Business Assistant.
- Was officially evaluated as a committed and detail-oriented team player who gained a strong base of knowledge in areas including accounting, customer service, administration, personnel development, and correspondence.

PERSONAL

A native of Mexico, I am fully bilingual in English and in Spanish.

DATA ENTRY SUPERVISOR & TAX CLERK

Date

Exact Name of Person
Exact Title
Exact Name of Company
Address
City, State, Zip

DATA ENTRY
SUPERVISOR
&
TAX CLERK
for a
real estate
organization

Dear Exact Name of Person: (or Dear Sir or Madam if answering a blind ad):

With the enclosed resume, I would like to make you aware of my interest in exploring employment opportunities with your organization. I offer a background in direct customer service and sales along with outstanding communication, organizational, and clerical skills.

Currently as a Data Entry Supervisor and Tax Clerk for Berkeley County, I have contributed numerous ideas which improved office efficiency and customer service while supervising eight data entry clerks and maintaining accurate records on 102,000 real estate parcels filed by 10-digit codes. I completed a three-year property reevaluation project nine months ahead of schedule by scheduling and editing detailed records for 98,000 parcels of land. Known for my strong written communication skills, I have prepared verbal and written reports for the county tax assessor and project coordinator. Because of my vast knowledge of numerous software programs, I was specially selected to provide computer training to other employees who included data entry clerks, appraisers, and real estate professionals.

In previous experience as an Office Manager, Receptionist, and Income Tax Preparer with Jackson Hewitt Tax Services, I earned a promotion to Office Manager on the basis of my success in ensuring customer satisfaction. I became respected for my ability to maintain outstanding relations with clients and for calming upset clients in a busy tax preparation office.

If you can use a dedicated young professional with outstanding data entry, supervisory and customer service skills, I hope you will welcome my call soon when I try to arrange a brief meeting to discuss your goals and how my background might serve your needs. I can provide outstanding references at the appropriate time.

Sincerely,

Colleen M. McCampbell

Alternate Last Paragraph:
I hope you will write or call me soon to suggest a time when we might meet to discuss your needs and goals and how my background might serve them. I can provide outstanding references at the appropriate time.

COLLEEN M. McCAMPBELL

1110½ Hay Street, Fayetteville, NC 28305   •   preppub@aol.com   •   (910) 483-6611

OBJECTIVE

To benefit an organization that can use a personable and mature individual offering outstanding customer service, clerical, and computer operations skills along with the proven ability to communicate with others and provide information in a professional manner.

SPECIAL KNOWLEDGE

Am highly skilled in operating various computers using the following software programs.
Microsoft Word   Excel   Access   PowerPoint
Type 65 wpm and use other office equipment such as ten-key adding machines, calculators, multiline phone systems, and copiers.

EXPERIENCE

DATA ENTRY SUPERVISOR and **TAX CLERK**. Berkeley County, Summerville, SC (2002-present). Have contributed numerous ideas which improved office efficiency and provided better customer service while supervising eight data entry clerks and maintaining accurate records on approximately 102,000 real estate parcels filed by 10-digit codes.

- Prepare verbal and written reports for the county tax assessor and project coordinator.
- Completed a three-year property reevaluation project ahead of schedule by nine months: scheduled and edited detailed records for 98,000 parcels of land.
- Decreased downtime caused by computer problems by implementing a swing shift schedule which resulted in greater productivity than a traditional "8 to 5" schedule.
- Developed map grids and a specialized system of 500 separate neighborhood codes used in developing the 2004 Schedule of Values used in reevaluations.
- Gathered information and wrote the Users Manual for software systems used in the tax office where none previously existed: the manual is still used in Berkeley County and has been adopted for use in other counties in the area.
- Was selected on the basis of my thorough knowledge of various software programs to train other employees ranging from data entry clerks, to appraisers, to real estate professionals.

OFFICE MANAGER, RECEPTIONIST and **INCOME TAX PREPARER**. Jackson Hewitt Tax Services, Summerville, SC (1998-02). Earned promotion to office management on the basis of my success in ensuring customer satisfaction. Maintained outstanding phone and personal relations with clients and displayed a talent for calming angry clients in a busy tax preparation office.

- Answered questions from phone and walk-in customers.
- Typed and maintained files on each client.
- Purchased office supplies and furnishings within budget guidelines.
- Made copies of completed federal and state tax returns as well as organized paperwork according to all applicable regulations and requirements.
- Scheduled appointments and maintained records of hours worked weekly by each seven employees.
- Applied my communication skills while making up to 100 phone calls a day in tax season and consistently reached a 70% appointment scheduling rate during tax season.
- Scored 98% on the Jackson Hewitt Tax Services certification course final test.

Highlights of other experience: Learned the importance of remaining professional and polite in jobs that included working with elderly and disabled patients in a mental health center.

TRAINING

Excelled in courses and seminars in stress management and supervision; completed rigorous graduate-level programs on Tax Laws and Fundamentals of Tax Listing and Assessing of South Carolina at Charleston Southern University.

AFFILIATIONS

Held membership in the Berkeley County Computer Association, 2001-03.

PERSONAL

Have been commended for my tact and diplomacy in dealing with the public. Offer outstanding communication skills. Am known for my determination to see the job done right.

EXECUTIVE MARKETING ASSISTANT

Date

Exact Name of Person
Title or Position
Name of Company
Address (no., street)
Address (city, state, zip)

EXECUTIVE
MARKETING
ASSISTANT
for an
office
automation
company

Dear Exact Name of Person: (or Dear Sir or Madam if answering a blind ad.)

I would appreciate an opportunity to talk with you soon about how I could contribute to your organization through my exceptionally strong office administration, sales, and secretarial skills.

As you will see from my resume, I am currently working as an Executive Marketing Assistant for Coeco Office Systems. I have become known for efficiency while working as the secretary for a six-person sales staff involved in the sale of office automation equipment and business machines worldwide. I draft and type proposals, write letters, and input customer data into the computer system. A very fast worker, I am known for excellent typing (65 wpm) skills. I specialize in complex statistical typing of budgetary data, often under very tight deadlines, and am continuously involved in inputting large volumes of data related to sales, accounts receivable, finance, and purchasing.

While relying on my excellent technical skills in performing complex statistical typing accurately and quickly, the sales staff also depends upon me to graciously handle customers and vendors. In my current and previous secretarial jobs, I have prepared a variety of forms and documents including stock market analyses, invoices and payroll paperwork, and business letters. I have often been commended for my excellent English grammar and spelling skills, and I am known for my punctual work habits, positive attitude, reliability, and honesty.

I feel certain I could rapidly become a valuable part of your organization. I can provide outstanding references from all employers, including from my current organization, which I would appreciate your not contacting until we meet.

I hope you will welcome my call soon to arrange a brief meeting at your convenience to discuss your current and future needs and how I might serve them. Thank you in advance for your time.

Sincerely yours,

Lynnette L. Aaron

Alternate last paragraph:
I hope you will call or write me soon to suggest a time convenient for us to meet and discuss your current and future needs and how I might serve them. Thank you in advance for your time.

LYNNETTE L. AARON

1110½ Hay Street, Fayetteville, NC 28305 • preppub@aol.com • (910) 483-6611

OBJECTIVE

To contribute to the success of an organization that can use a skilled office professional who offers proven planning and organizational skills along with experience in preparing reports, analyzing data, and maintaining excellent working relationships with people at all levels.

EDUCATION

Associate of Science in Office Technology, Butler County Community College, Butler, PA, 1999.
- Studied secretarial sciences, business math, English grammar, shorthand, property management, and other subjects at BCCC.

EXPERIENCE

EXECUTIVE/MARKETING ASSISTANT. Coeco Office Systems, Philadelphia, PA (2002-present). Became known for my efficiency while working as the secretary for a six-person sales staff involved in the sale of office automation equipment and business machines worldwide; draft and type proposals, write letters, and input customer data into the computer system.
- A very fast worker known for excellent typing (65 wpm) skills, specialize in complex statistical typing including the typing of budgetary data; often under very tight deadlines, input large volumes of data related to sales, accounts receivable, finance, and purchasing; type legal documents.
- Prepare invoices; requisition supplies as needed.
- Am respected for my gracious ability to serve the public while acting as receptionist to incoming guests and customers; operate a telephone switchboard.
- Control postal meter machine; affix postage on daily mail and prepare FedEx packages.

LOAN PROCESSING CLERK. First Federal Mortgage Corporation, Philadelphia, PA (2001-02). Demonstrated proficiency in mortgage financing while taking loan applications and setting up files for processing VA, FHA, and Conventional loans; was commended for my strong communication skills in coordinating with other professionals including attorneys, appraisers, lenders, surveyors, contractors, and real estate agents.
- Maintained up-to-date log on interest rates available at all area financial institutions; drafted and typed letters for the general manager. Prepared blueprints and builder plans for VA approval.
- Learned the vocabulary of mortgage financing and the construction industry.

SALES ASSOCIATE. Aaron Realty, Butler, PA (1998-01). Arranged financing terms and explained financial options to sellers and buyers while marketing real estate for sale; prospected for listings and advertised my own listings.
- Wrote sales contracts; interpreted and explained these to buyers and sellers.
- Performed market analysis of both commercial and residential properties in order to determine fair market value and probable selling price.
- Became known for my ability to articulate effectively while explaining highly technical terms to buyers and sellers in language laymen could understand.

PROPERTY MANAGER/SALES ASSOCIATE. All Pro Property Management, Butler, PA (1995-98). Marketed and sold properties; managed 68 properties including collecting rent monies and ensuring that the money was distributed to the appropriate property owners; handled repairs, advertising, and financial reporting; kept books and reconciled bank statements.
- Completed office support functions including inputting all MLS data into computer.
- While typing, filing, and answering phones, was involved in a wide variety of data collection and analysis.
- Gathered and compiled data and prepared reports concerning company operations and stock market operations affecting the grain industry. Established and maintained a variety of records and files including personnel, payroll, safety, and attendance.

COMPUTER SKILLS & LICENSURES

Proficient with Microsoft Word, Excel, PowerPoint and QuarkXpress
Fax, Copiers, Calculators, Projectors and Dictaphone
PA Notary Public; PA Real Estate License; PA driver's license

PERSONAL

Can provide exceptionally strong personal and professional references from all my employers. Pride myself on my positive attitude, punctual work habits, reliability, and honesty.

EXECUTIVE SECRETARY

Date

Exact Name of Person
Title or Position
Name of Company
Address (no., street)
Address (city, state, zip)

EXECUTIVE
SECRETARY
for a
military
intelligence
organization

Dear Exact Name of Person: (or Dear Sir or Madam if answering a blind ad.)

    I would appreciate an opportunity to talk with you soon about how I could contribute to your organization through my experience as an Executive Secretary/Administrative Assistant accustomed to providing support to busy executives in fast-paced environments.

    As you will see from my resume, I offer a track record of outstanding accomplishments based on my expertise in computer operations. With strong analytical and research skills as well as the ability to prioritize and coordinate complex activities, I am known for sound judgment and strong interpersonal skills.

    During my years as Executive Secretary in the US Army, I have consistently been described as extremely articulate and capable of controlling activities in dynamic, multi-task organizations. I offer the ability to work under pressure and anticipate the needs of busy executives. I have become skilled in interacting with congressional liaisons, city and state officials, and the public. I was entrusted with a Secret security clearance.

    Throughout my career, I have earned rapid advancement to higher levels of responsibility based on my accomplishments and professionalism. I hope you will welcome my call soon to arrange a brief meeting at your convenience to discuss your current and future needs and how I might serve them. Thank you in advance for your time.

Sincerely yours,

Karen C. Brockett

Alternate last paragraph:
    I hope you will call or write me soon to suggest a time convenient for us to meet and discuss your current and future needs and how I might serve them. Thank you in advance for your time.

KAREN C. BROCKETT

1110½ Hay Street, Fayetteville, NC 28305 • preppub@aol.com • (910) 483-6611

OBJECTIVE

To offer my strong background of outstanding performance as an executive secretary and administrative assistant to an organization that can use an experienced and articulate professional with superior written and verbal communication skills.

EXPERIENCE

Earned a reputation as an exceptionally talented and skilled professional in positions requiring the ability to remain tactful and composed in fast-paced, high-level executive environments while providing full-range support for executives, United States Army (1995-present):

2004-present: EXECUTIVE SECRETARY. Ft. Campbell, KY. Participated in managing staff activities and prioritized personnel and budget actions while providing secretarial and administrative support for a senior executive of a military intelligence organization with 42 locations throughout the United States and South Korea.

- Initiated a project to publish a quarterly newsletter: edited and typed articles contributed from each of the 42 subordinate offices.

2003-04: ADMINISTRATIVE ASSISTANT. Ft. Gordon, GA. As personal secretary to the director of Special Operations, controlled activities ranging from screening visitors and calls, scheduling meetings, making travel arrangements, and supervising preparation of official correspondence including editing and proofreading. Earned rapid promotion from Secretary/Stenographer.

1999-03: EXECUTIVE SECRETARY. Ft. Drum, NY. Dealt daily with high-ranking military and civilian officials in a department overseeing resource management and integration of special operations actions for a senior executive, members of Congress, as well as city and state officials.

- Attended to the complex details of maintaining appointment calendars and schedules for an executive traveling extensively for a large, geographically scattered organization.
- Selected on the basis of my expertise displayed in the Resource Management Division for a military training center, played a key role in setting up new offices.

1995-99: SENIOR SECRETARY, LOGISTICS OFFICE. US Army Reserves Office, Charleston, SC. Provided my expertise in a wide range of day-to-day functions including screening and directing visitors, mail, and phone calls; maintained yearly travel budgets; created suspense files and systems for logging information; collected data and prepared reports; sent/received e-mail worldwide.

- Rapidly advanced from Typist/Stenographer to Senior Secretary; displayed the ability to remain calm while producing quality work under tight deadlines; was selected for promotion.
- Screened, prioritized, and referred inquiries. Maintained appointment and travel schedules while gathering information and preparing detailed and accurate reports.

Highlights of earlier experience: Gained a broad base of experience in jobs as a Medical Secretary, Stenographer, and Dictating Machine Transcriber.
Volunteer experience: Enhanced my interpersonal and planning skills while organizing and leading family support groups with up to 80 members; as a choir director and accompanist, used my musical talents to lead children and adult choirs.

SPECIAL SKILLS

Am experienced with computer applications and software including:

Excel	MS Word	Internet Explorer	PowerPoint

Type 90 wpm and take shorthand at 100 wpm.

TRAINING

Excelled in extensive training programs and workshops in areas including managerial techniques for administrative assistants/secretaries, presentations and briefing techniques, customer relations, leadership skills for women, and computer operations.

- Was handpicked to create and implement training for division-level secretaries.

PERSONAL

Was entrusted with a Secret security clearance. Have consistently been described as extremely articulate, tactful, poised, and diplomatic. Excellent references upon request.

EXECUTIVE SECRETARY

Date

Exact Name of Person
Title or Position
Name of Company
Address (no., street)
Address (city, state, zip)

EXECUTIVE SECRETARY
for a
cookware
manufacturing
company

Dear Exact Name of Person: (or Dear Sir or Madam if answering a blind ad.)

I would appreciate an opportunity to talk with you soon about how I could contribute to your organization through my experience in office operations, inventory control, and project management.

In my current position as Executive Secretary with Tappan Cookware Manufacturing, I provide administrative functions and act as the company community liaison. While working for Tappan, I have coordinated and implemented logistics for worldwide product transportation, including scheduling vehicles and drivers and overseeing packing.

Because of my reputation as a "go-getter" with unlimited personal initiative, I was specially selected for my current position as Executive Secretary for a department of seven engineers. In this fast-paced job, I apply my knowledge of software including Word, Excel, and PowerPoint.

You would find me to be a hardworking and reliable professional who prides myself on always giving "110%" to every job I undertake. I can provide excellent personal and professional references upon request.

I hope you will call or write me soon to suggest a time convenient for us to meet and discuss your current and future needs and how I might serve them. Thank you in advance for your time.

Sincerely,

Wendy Allenbough

WENDY ALLENBOUGH

1110½ Hay Street, Fayetteville, NC 28305   •   preppub@aol.com   •   (910) 483-6611

OBJECTIVE

To benefit an organization seeking an enthusiastic young professional experienced in office management, inventory control, and project management who possesses excellent communication, time-management, and planning abilities.

EDUCATION

Currently enrolled in the Paralegal degree program, Lansing Community College, Lansing, MI; related subjects include legal procedures, accounting, algebra, and ethics.
Graduated from Braxton-Mitchell High School, Lansing, MI, 1997.

EXPERIENCE

Have an excellent track record of being promoted to increasing responsibilities while employed at Tappan, a well-known cookware manufacturer in Detroit, MI:
2004-present: EXECUTIVE SECRETARY. Utilize outstanding planning and organizational skills while providing administrative and technical support for a department of seven engineers.
- Utilize software applications including Excel, Cadcam, and Access. Apply computer expertise to compile and create weekly production charts, graphs, and reports while handling a wide range of office responsibilities.
- Schedule and give plant tours to schools, churches, and other community groups.
- Process a high volume of incoming calls, answering requests for information, routing calls to the appropriate staff member, and taking messages if the party was unavailable.
- Operate various office equipment, including photocopiers, facsimile machines, 10-key calculators, personal computers, and multiline phones.
- Assist supervisors in scheduling appointments with clients.
- Type a variety of letters, memos, and other correspondence for the office.

2001-04: OFFICE ASSISTANT & SHIPPING ASSISTANT. Rapidly promoted from Order Entry Clerk to receiving, tracking, and shipping orders to retailers worldwide. Manage inventory control.
- Liaised with truck companies to coordinate shipping logistics.
- Processed all bills of lading, return invoices, and other documents.
- Answered and resolved all customer questions and complaints.
- Maintained necessary stock levels of all products and accounted for returned merchandise, issuing credits where appropriate.
- Ensured all products were shipped in a timely, accurate manner.
- Assisted marketing personnel with special projects and focus groups.
- Compiled and wrote weekly and monthly reports for forwarding to top-level management.
- Learned to pick and print shipment orders.
- Assisted in coordinating and implementing the annual fiscal inventory, including counting, key punching, and verifying stock.
- Earned a reputation for easily establishing rapport with people from diverse cultural and socioeconomic backgrounds.

SKILLS

Proficient with computer operating systems, hardware, and software including Microsoft Word, Excel spreadsheets, and dBase; skilled with 10-key calculators and adding machines.

PERSONAL

Am a dedicated, hardworking professional who enjoys challenges, problem-solving, and decision-making. Have consistently received excellent work evaluations.

EXECUTIVE SECRETARY

Date

Exact Name of Person
Exact Title
Exact Name of Company
Address
City, State, Zip

Dear Exact Name of Person: (or Dear Sir or Madam if answering a blind ad):

With the enclosed resume, I would like to make you aware of my background as a skilled administrative professional with exceptional leadership and administrative skills. I offer a track record of accomplishments in office management.

As you will see from my resume, I am currently working as an Executive Secretary to a Vice President and a Chief Executive Officer of a busy insurance company. I prepare and process provider contracts and maintain listings for distribution to the home office, field agents, and third-party administrators. I am responsible for producing expense reports, prescription benefits brochures, employee evaluation forms, employer applications, and enrollment forms. I have trained approximately 30 employees in Microsoft Word.

Throughout my career, I have been lauded for my outstanding initiative, administrative expertise, and intense devotion to my work. Whether implementing plans to automate administrative functions or redesigning commonly used forms to increase their utility and reduce processing time, my efforts have consistently been credited with improving efficiency, reducing costs, and increasing profitability.

If you can use a talented and experienced administrative professional whose skills have been proven in a variety of fast-paced, challenging environments, I hope you will welcome my call soon when I try to arrange a brief meeting to discuss your goals and how my background might serve your needs. I can provide outstanding references at the appropriate time.

Sincerely,

Carolina H. York

Alternate last paragraph:
I hope you will write or call me soon to suggest a time when we might meet to discuss your needs and goals and how my background might serve them. I can provide outstanding references at the appropriate time.

CAROLINA H. YORK

1110½ Hay Street, Fayetteville, NC 28305   •   preppub@aol.com   •   (910) 483-6611

OBJECTIVE   To benefit an organization that can use a self-motivated, experienced administrative assistant and executive secretary with excellent communication and organizational skills along with an extensive background in computer operation, desktop publishing, and word processing.

EDUCATION   **Associate of Applied Science degree in General Office Technology,** St. Louis Community College at Florissant Valley, St. Louis, MO, 2003.
Completed a number of courses directly related to office administration, including:

Business English	Business Correspondence for Word Processors
Records Management	Machine Transcription

COMPUTERS   Am skilled in the operation of the following computer software:

Microsoft Word	PageMaker	dBase IV	Excel

EXPERIENCE   **EXECUTIVE SECRETARY.** Allstate Insurance Company, St. Louis, MO (2003-present). Perform a variety of office administration and clerical duties for the Vice President and Chief Executive Officer of this busy insurance provider.
- Utilize a wide variety of computer software to design forms, business cards, and letterheads as well as brochures.
- Operate computers, printers, facsimile machines, photocopiers, typewriters, and transcribers on a day-to-day basis.
- Type letters, memos, and correspondence; type 60 wpm.
- Prepare and process provider contracts and maintain listings for distribution to the home office, field agents, and third-party administrators.
- Create forms such as expense reports, prescription benefits brochures, employee evaluation forms, employer applications, and enrollment forms for group insurance.
- Trained approximately 30 employees from the word processing department in the operation of Microsoft Word.
- Enhanced routine correspondence through addition of charts, graphs, shadowboxes, and other desktop publishing elements.

OFFICE ASSISTANT. Registrar's Office, St. Louis Community College, St. Louis, MO (2002-03). While completing my college education, worked in the registrar's office, providing assistance to students and office workers.

CHURCH SECRETARY. True Vine Ministries, St. Louis, MO (1998-02). Performed clerical and secretarial duties at this local church while pursuing my Associate of Applied Science degree program at St. Louis Community College.
- Typed all letters, memos, church bulletins, and other correspondence.
- Sorted and distributed all incoming mail and processed outbound mail.
- Answered multiline phones, taking messages and directing calls.
- Conducted periodic inventories of materials and supplies used by the church.
- Purchased supplies for the office as well as for the church; ran errands.

Other experience:
ENGLISH TUTOR. While stationed in Puerto Rico with the US Air Force, demonstrated my exceptional communication skills teaching English to employees of several Hispanic companies as well as private individuals.

PERSONAL   Excellent personal and professional references are available upon request.

FACILITIES DIRECTOR

Date

Exact Name of Person
Title or Position
Name of Company
Address (number and street)
Address (city, state, and zip)

Dear Exact Name of Person: (or Sir or Madam if answering a blind ad.)

I would appreciate an opportunity to talk with you soon about how I could contribute to your organization through my extensive experience in financial management, operations management, events management, and personnel management.

As you will see from my resume, I am currently working as Officer Manager and Facilities Director for Wetherford Farms, Ltd., a resort community owned for decades by the Locklear family. The land was recently sold to the government for use by the military, and I am assisting in the orderly transition of this property to government ownership. I have shouldered a wide range of management responsibilities including managing a 10-person household staff catering to the Locklear family and guests while also overseeing a 25-person staff involved in farming, maintenance, and in the upkeep of facilities which include skeet ranges, tennis courts, swimming pools, riding stables, an 18-hole golf course, and nature trails. I have become an expert in nearly every aspect of hospitality management since we routinely host private parties and corporate events. I have been the property's only on-site person handling accounting procedures as well, and I have excelled in cost control while utilizing accounting software programs to maintain data.

In my previous job with Phillip Hughes Oil Company, a diversified business which included car washes, convenience stores, and a large trailer park, I was the "right arm" to the owner and worked faithfully for him from 1990 to 2003, when I joined the Wetherford Group.

I can provide outstanding references, and I can assure you that I have multiple talents and abilities which would permit me to become a valuable member of any organization.

I hope you will welcome my call soon to arrange a brief meeting to discuss your current and future needs and how I might serve them. Thank you in advance for your time.

Sincerely,

Carol G. Parker

Alternate last paragraph:
I hope you will call or write me soon to suggest a time convenient for us to meet and discuss your current and future needs and how I might serve them. Thank you in advance for your time.

CAROL G. PARKER

1110½ Hay Street, Fayetteville, NC 28305 • preppub@aol.com • (910) 483-6611

OBJECTIVE

To contribute to an organization that can use a highly motivated self-starter with expert knowledge of financial accounting and bookkeeping operations along with proven management skills in organizing private parties and corporate events, managing large-scale property assets and associated personnel, and coordinating the use and upkeep of leisure amenities/facilities.

EXPERIENCE

FACILITIES DIRECTOR & OFFICE MANAGER. Wetherford Farms, Ltd., Bozeman, MT (2003-present). After being introduced and recommended to the Locklear family by the accounting firm of Reid, Roberts, and Boyd, became employed to oversee a 25-person staff of laborers, farmers, mechanics, and grounds personnel as well as a 10-person household staff comprised of cooks, housekeepers, servers, and domestic personnel serving the Locklear family and guests.

- Act as a financial agent for all the business and leisure activities, and manage financial relationships between several partnerships and corporations in the Wetherford Group.
- As the estate's only person handling on-site accounting, utilize Microsoft Word software for accounting and Excel to maintain accounting information; perform P & L analysis and prepare all documentation for the accounting firm which prepared the taxes while continuously optimizing cash management and handling day-to-day transactions.
- Coordinate menu planning for private parties and corporate events held at the estate.
- Assure maintenance of facilities including a skeet shooting range, nature trails, an 18-hole golf course, hunting areas, riding stables, indoor and outdoor swimming pools, as well as tennis courts. Assure impeccable upkeep of five elegant family homes.
- Manage the estate's annual budget, which ranged considerably yearly depending on whether the family allocated funds for capital expenditures and which crops were to be farmed.
- Report to the General Manager and am frequently in charge of the property in his absence.
- Upon assuming my position, immediately identified areas in which we could cut costs while maintaining or improving quality; cut operating costs dramatically.
- Became skilled in dealing with all sorts of people: day laborers; skilled, white collar professionals; high-income guests; vendors and suppliers; supervisors; and coworkers.
- Since this estate was recently purchased by the government, am currently assisting in the orderly transition of the assets to government ownership.

OFFICE MANAGER. Phillip Hughes Oil, Inc., Bozeman, MT (1990-03). Worked continuously for this company and was the owner's "right arm" except for a brief period in 1995-96 when I resigned after the death of a family member; was rehired by Mr. Hughes and played a key role in managing and accounting for his diversified business which included the oil company as well as five convenience stores, two car washes, and a trailer park with more than 50 rental units.

- Was responsible for all accounting activities, general ledger, accounts payable and receivable, payroll, and all taxes including sales tax, payroll tax, excise taxes, and state and federal taxes.
- Performed manual and computerized bookkeeping for this company and two other subcompanies; maintained and reconciled six bank accounts.
- Maintained owner's personal checkbook and records and attended to his personal business.

EDUCATION

Graduated from Piedmont High School, Bozeman, MT, where I graduated with honors, was selected a class President in my junior year, and was member of the National Honor Society.

PERSONAL

Am a loyal and dedicated employee with outstanding references. Enjoy new challenges.

FINANCE MANAGER (CAREER CHANGE)

Date

Exact Name of Person
Title or Position
Name of Company
Address (no., street)
Address (city, state, zip)

**FINANCE
MANAGER**
for an
automobile
dealership
in Reno

Dear Exact Name of Person: (or Dear Sir or Madam if answering a blind ad.)

With the enclosed resume, I would like to make you aware of my background as an articulate young professional who offers a strong customer service focus as well as exceptional communication and negotiation skills that have been proven in challenging positions in the automobile industry.

Although I have applied my exceptional communication skills in automotive dealership environments for the last eight years, I think you will see that the abilities that I honed in these positions would make me a valuable addition in any customer service environment. As Finance Manager for Hinton Automotives, I oversee funding of all customer loans, conducting negotiations with representatives from various lending institutions in order to acquire loan approval at the best possible annual percentage rate. Additionally, I hold final responsibility for closing the sale and have excelled at tactfully overcoming last-minute objections and convincing the customer to sign the purchase agreement.

Earlier as a Customer Service Representative and Automotive Salesperson for Reno Nissan Dealers, I provided direct customer service for this busy dealership. In addition to tracking individual and dealership compliance with customer service goals, I recorded, investigated, and resolved customer complaints. Prior to that position, I served as a Service Advisor for Storey Used Cars. There I learned to deal with agitated customers in a tactful fashion. By showing empathy and suggesting resourceful solutions to customer service issues, I was able to restore their confidence in the service department and the dealership.

As you will see, I have earned an Associate of Science degree in Business Management from Meadows Community College. I feel that my education and experience, as well as my strong customer service orientation and natural sales ability, would make me a valuable addition to your team.

If you are in need of an articulate and experienced customer service professional whose communication skills have been proven in stressful situations requiring tact and diplomacy, I look forward to hearing from you soon to arrange a time when we might meet. I assure you in advance that I have an excellent reputation, and would quickly become an asset to your organization.

Sincerely,

Shana T. Voigt

SHANA T. VOIGT

1110½ Hay Street, Fayetteville, NC 28305   •   preppub@aol.com   •   (910) 483-6611

OBJECTIVE
To benefit an organization that can use an articulate young professional with exceptional communication and organizational skills whose customer service ability, finance knowledge, and salesmanship have been tested in high-volume new and used automotive dealerships.

EDUCATION
Completed two years of college-level course work towards a Bachelor of Arts degree in Business Communications, University of Nevada, Reno, NV, 2003.
Earned an **Associate of Science degree in Business Management** from Meadows Community College, Reno, NV, 2000.

EXPERIENCE
FINANCE MANAGER. Hinton Automotives, Reno, NV (2002-present). Solely responsible for all finance department operations of this busy used car dealership; work closely with the general manager and supervise up to 20 automotive sales representatives in his absence.
- An articulate communicator, I tactfully overcome last-minute customer objections to close the sale; adept at handling customers during this delicate phase in the sale process.
- Conduct negotiations with various banks, credit unions, and other lending institutions on a daily basis to obtain loan approval for customers.
- Successfully deal with customers in a tense and sometimes hostile environment on a daily basis; am instrumental in effecting increases in sales and incentives.
- Present various warranty products to customer at closing; responsible for more than 75% of the warranty sales in the dealership.
- By maintaining a high volume of aftermarket sales and obtaining favorable terms from lending institutes, achieve an average finance income of $500 per car.
- Type and process contracts and loan applications; mail completed paperwork to the lending institution that funded the deal.

CUSTOMER SERVICE REPRESENTATIVE and **AUTOMOTIVE SALESPERSON.** Reno Nissan Dealers, Reno, NV (1999-02). Performed customer service and receptionist duties; served as an automotive sales representative for this busy local new and used car dealership.
- Monitored the dealership's performance on monthly, quarterly, and annual customer service index (CSI) reports; made suggestions for improvement based on customer input.
- Processed follow-up surveys with new and repeat sales, service, and body shop customers to ensure they were satisfied with the service they received.
- Operated a computer to retrieve credit reports on sales customers from the Equifax system.
- Provided direct customer service in response to customer complaints; answered multiline phones and operated the switchboard and voice mail system.
- As an automotive sales representative, I assisted customers in the selection and purchase of new and used vehicles.

SERVICE ADVISOR. Storey Used Cars, Reno, NV (1996-99). Performed troubleshooting and diagnosis of customer's vehicle and provided price estimates for vehicle repairs and service.
- Dealt with customers in a tactful and diplomatic manner; developed and presented possible solutions to the customer's service issues.
- Wrote service orders for computer diagnostics, maintenance, or mechanical repairs; provided customer with a cost estimate on proposed repairs.
- Processed customer claims against manufacturer or aftermarket warranties; entered the customer's Vehicle Identification Number (VIN) into a computer to determine if any recall service had been ordered by the manufacturer.
- Interacted with representatives from local car rental agencies; coordinated scheduling of a rental vehicle, if repairs on the customer's vehicle were not complete.
- Assigned scheduled customer maintenance and repairs to service technicians and ordered out-of-stock parts to facilitate repairs.
- Answered multiline telephones, scheduling service appointments and assisting customers.

PERSONAL
Excellent personal and professional references are available upon request.

FINANCE SPECIALIST

Date

Exact Name of Person
Exact Title
Exact Name of Company
Address
City, State, Zip

**FINANCE
SPECIALIST**
for a
local
community
college

Dear Exact Name of Person (or Dear Sir or Madam if answering a blind ad):

With the enclosed resume, I would like to express my interest in exploring employment opportunities with your organization.

As you will see from my resume, I offer four years of experience in finance, administrative, and training support roles with Central Oregon Community College. The recipient of two "Employee of the Month" Awards for outstanding work performance, I was widely recognized for my high level of initiative and my ability to achieve quality results.

I am skilled in utilizing a variety of office automation systems which include electronic mail, database, spreadsheet, word processing, and graphics applications. My knowledge includes proficiency with Microsoft Word, Excel, Access, and PowerPoint as well as with customized database and accounting systems. I offer a proven ability to rapidly master new programs and applications, and my oral and written communication skills are excellent.

Handpicked for both of my two most recent assignments, I took over a pay section in disarray and transformed it into a model of efficiency after earlier creating an internal administrative section "from scratch" following a functional reorganization. I achieved 99% accuracy while processing accounts and receiving purchase order contracts valued as high as $25,000.

I began working while I was in high school and learned at an early age how to serve customers with a professional attitude. In my earliest jobs in retail management and food service, I was commended for my attention to detail in handling cash and was entrusted with opening and closing a retail location.

If you can use a hardworking young professional with experience in all aspects of office operations, I hope you will contact me to suggest a time when we might meet to discuss your needs. I can provide excellent personal and professional references.

Sincerely,

Jonna L. Vainwright

JONNA L. VAINWRIGHT

1110½ Hay Street, Fayetteville, NC 28305 • preppub@aol.com • (910) 483-6611

OBJECTIVE

To contribute to an organization that can use a results-oriented young professional with extensive computer operations, financial/accounting support, and customer service skills along with excellent organizational abilities and an eye for detail.

EDUCATION & TRAINING

Completed college-level courses in finance, office operations, written communication, and automated systems usage at the Central Oregon Community College, Bend, OR.
Graduated from Fairley High School, Bend, OR, 1998.

COMPUTERS

Utilize **office automation systems;** proficient with electronic mail, database, spreadsheet, word processing, and graphics applications. Am skilled in utilizing Microsoft Word, Excel, Access, and PowerPoint along with customized databases and coding systems.

EXPERIENCE

Built a reputation as a fast learner with a high level of initiative, Central Oregon Community College, Bend, OR:

2004-present: FINANCE SPECIALIST. Employed by a well respected institution, was praised by my supervisors for accomplishments made while training and supervising one subordinate in a payroll section which processes in excess of 125 customers each month. Was handpicked for this job because of outstanding results as an Administrative Clerk.

- Compose a variety of letters and reports, and have been noted for excellent grammar and written communication skills.
- Took over a section which was in disarray and where many transactions were duplicated or input inaccurately. After extensive research, transformed an unacceptable area into one recognized as a model of efficiency.
- On my own initiative, brought reject rates on all coded transactions from 78% to only 3.5%.
- Performed as Department Manager for six months in a job usually reserved for someone more experience.

2002-04: ADMINISTRATIVE CLERK and **TRAINING MANAGER.** Was specially selected to create an internal administrative section for a company with 70 employees following a functional reorganization.

- Created a filing system for matters related to finance, personnel administration, training calendars, awards and promotions, and disciplinary issues.
- Developed training schedules using SATS 4.1 and Excel software.
- Became highly skilled with the Microsoft Office Suite while word processing memoranda and letterheads as well as forms forwarded to the central office.

2000-02: COMMERCIAL ACCOUNTS MANAGER and **ACCOUNTS RECEIVABLE PROCESSOR.** Received purchase order contracts for services which included construction projects and supply support as well as for tangible goods such as office equipment, computers, and perishable items with individual contracts ranging as high as $25,000.

- Implemented a system which automated the previous manual accounting methods to a new electronic funds transfer (EFT) method; used QuickBooks for database records.
- Achieved 99% accuracy while processing more than 3,000 accounts.

Highlights of other experience: Became self-supporting while in high school; was promoted to **Assistant Manager** with Bath & Body Works, Salem, OR, after beginning as a Database Operator for Telecom, Inc.; was commended for excellent customer service and management skills.

- Gained experience in handling funds, conducting inventories, and providing customer service in retail settings.
- In an earlier job with Denny's, advanced rapidly from Waitress to Hostess; learned to deal effectively with the public.

PERSONAL

Received two "Employee of the Year" Awards for outstanding work performance. Excellent personal and professional references available upon request.

LOAN PROCESSING CLERK

Date

Exact Name of Person
Title or Position
Name of Company
Address (no., street)
Address (city, state, zip)

Dear Exact Name of Person: (or Dear Sir or Madam if answering a blind ad.)

I would appreciate an opportunity to talk with you soon about how I could contribute to your organization through my exceptionally strong office administration, sales, and secretarial skills.

In my current position with a leading bank, I have distinguished myself as a Loan Processing Clerk. I am skilled in loan closing procedures and experienced in working with attorneys, appraisers, lenders, surveyors, contractors, and the general public.

In a previous job in an organization which was named one of Georgia's fastest-growing companies, I was the sole secretary for a six-person sales staff involved in sales negotiations and transactions worldwide. While relying on my excellent technical skills in performing complex statistical typing accurately and quickly, the sales staff also depended upon me to graciously handle customers and vendors. In all my jobs, I have prepared a variety of forms and documents including stock market analyses, invoices, payroll paperwork, and business letters. I have often been commended for my excellent English grammar and spelling skills, and I am known for my punctual work habits, positive attitude, reliability, and honesty.

I feel certain I could rapidly become a valuable part of your organization as I have to all my previous employers. I can provide outstanding references from all those employers, including from my current organization, which I would appreciate your not contacting until we meet.

I hope you will welcome my call soon to arrange a brief meeting at your convenience to discuss your current and future needs and how I might serve them. Thank you in advance for your time.

Sincerely yours,

Willette Barnhill

Alternate last paragraph:
I hope you will call or write me soon to suggest a time convenient for us to meet and discuss your current and future needs and how I might serve them. Thank you in advance for your time.

WILLETTE BARNHILL

1110½ Hay Street, Fayetteville, NC 28305 • preppub@aol.com • (910) 483-6611

OBJECTIVE

To contribute to the success of an organization that can use a skilled office professional who offers proven planning and organizational skills along with experience in preparing reports, analyzing data, and maintaining excellent working relationships with people at all levels.

EDUCATION

Completed Medical Terminology Course, Macon State College, Macon, GA. Courses included Medical Office Procedures, CPT/ICD-9CM Coding Systems, Medical Office Assisting, and Pharmacology.
Completed Secretarial Science Course, DeKalb Technical College, DeKalb, GA. Courses included Business Math, English Grammar, Composition, and Shorthand.

OFFICE SKILLS & LICENSURES

Proficient with software including Microsoft Word, Excel and PageMaker
Operate copiers, fax, calculators, and dictaphone
GA Notary Public; GA Real Estate License; GA Driver's License
Specialize in complex statistical typing.

EXPERIENCE

LOAN PROCESSING CLERK. Wachovia, Macon, GA (2003-present). Demonstrate proficiency in mortgage financing while taking loan applications and setting up files for processing VA, FHA, and conventional loans; coordinate with professionals including attorneys, appraisers, lenders, surveyors, contractors, and real estate agents.
- Maintain up-to-date log on interest rates available at all area financial institutions.
- Prepare blueprints and builder plans for VA approval; draft and type letters for the general manager.

OFFICE MANAGER. Coldwell Realtors, Macon, GA (2003). Filled in as office manager while the secretary was away for eight months. Established and maintained a variety of records and files including personnel, payroll, safety, and attendance.

SECRETARY/OFFICE ASSISTANT. Reynolds Office Solutions, Macon, GA (2000-03). Became known for my efficiency while working as the secretary for a six-person sales staff involved in the sale of office automation equipment and business machines worldwide; drafted and typed proposals, wrote letters, and input customer data into the computer system.
- Earned reputation as a very fast worker known for excellent typing (65 wpm) skills.
- Input data related to payroll and typed legal documents.

SALES ASSOCIATE. Hinton Real Estate, Inc., DeKalb, GA (1997-00). Arranged financing terms and explained financial options to sellers and buyers while marketing Real Estate for sale; prospected for listings and advertised my own listings.

SECRETARY/ACCOUNTING CLERK. RELO Service, DeKalb, GA (1995-97). While typing, filing, and answering phones, was involved in a wide variety of data collection and analysis activities.
- Gathered and compiled data and prepared reports concerning company operations and stock market operations affecting the grain industry. Established and maintained a variety of records and files including personnel, payroll, safety, and attendance.

Other Experience
- Gained proficiency typing depositions while working as a *Legal Secretary*.
- After taking minutes at large corporate meetings as an *Executive Assistant*, transformed handwritten notes and dictation into concise and easily readable reports.

PERSONAL

Can provide exceptionally strong personal and professional references from all my employers. Pride myself on my positive attitude, punctual work habits, reliability, and honesty.

MARKETING ASSISTANT & MEDICAL RECEPTIONIST

Date

Exact Name of Person
Title or Position
Name of Company
Address (no., street)
Address (city, state, zip)

MARKETING ASSISTANT & MEDICAL RECEPTIONIST
for a chiropractic center

Dear Exact Name of Person: (or Dear Sir or Madam if answering a blind ad)

I would appreciate an opportunity to talk with you soon about how I could benefit your organization through my experience as a secretary and marketing assistant with outstanding skills in organization, communication, public relations, and marketing.

In my most recent position as a marketing assistant and medical secretary for a chiropractic clinic, I have developed a great interest in the medical field. Though the marketing and receptionist duties vary greatly, I have excelled in all activities.

- As a marketing assistant, I have visited locations and spoken with the public, knowledgeably informing them of available services and helping to perform free blood pressure screenings and bilateral weighings.

- As a medical receptionist, I have cultivated a natural empathy for patients and prepared them for visits. I have checked on the progress of patients between visits, keeping detailed and up-to-date records. In addition, I have ensured the readiness of examination and treatment rooms.

Through my earlier positions, I laid the foundation for the development of "top-notch" office operations skills. You would find me to be a dependable and enthusiastic professional who thrives on learning new things.

I hope you will welcome my call soon to arrange a brief meeting at your convenience to discuss your current and future needs and how I might serve them. Thank you in advance for your time.

Sincerely yours,

Cheryl Quiles

Alternate last paragraph:
I hope you will call or write soon to suggest a time convenient for us to meet and discuss your current and future needs and how I might serve them. Thank you in advance for your time.

CHERYL QUILES

1110½ Hay Street, Fayetteville, NC 28305 • preppub@aol.com • (910) 483-6611

OBJECTIVE

To apply my customer service and office management skills as well as my organizational and sales abilities to a company that can use an adaptable and motivated professional with experience in the medical and legal fields.

EXPERIENCE

MARKETING ASSISTANT & MEDICAL RECEPTIONIST. Chiro-Care Center, Hartford, CT (2003-present). Visit outside locations to meet with potential clients and inform them of services available at the clinic while also preparing patients and materials for examinations and treatments.
- Schedule examinations and treatments; confirm daily appointments.
- Keep detailed records on patient progress.
- Arrange examination rooms between client visits.
- Screen client insurance information.

RECEPTIONIST. Fields & Manning, LLP, Hartford, CT (2001-03). Excelled in both the administrative and the secretarial aspects of this position with a busy law firm, handling phone lines and correspondence in addition to confirming appointments and court dates.
- Opened and closed client files.
- Worked with a large volume of personal injury cases, gaining a basic knowledge of medical terminology.

SECRETARY/RECEPTIONIST. Tempo Temporary Services, New Haven, CT (2001-02). Polished a wide variety of secretarial skills and proved my adaptability in working for this temporary agency serving banking institutions, insurance and real estate companies, automobile dealerships, and other outlets.

SECRETARY/RECEPTIONIST. Strickland & Strickland Family Law Practice, New Haven, CT (1999-01). Aided attorneys in the preparation of legal documents while honing office operations skills to ensure efficient office functioning among partners with different styles.
- Prepared loan packages and learned many legal concepts dealing with home interest rates and mortgages.

Other experience: Gained practical work experience as a **Customer Service Representative**, **Retail Sales Clerk**, and **Cashier** in various locations (1994-99).
- Learned to effectively communicate with the public in person, by letter, and by telephone under a variety of circumstances while demonstrating poise and tact.
- Enhanced my organizational skills through stock distribution and inventory work.

EDUCATION

Excelled in course work for medical record administration and other courses such as physiology, economics and history at the Southern Connecticut State University, New Haven, CT (1999-2002).

COMPUTER & OFFICE SKILLS

Through a number of positions demanding productivity and flexibility, developed a proficiency with a broad range of clerical skills and office equipment.
- Acquired expertise with Microsoft Word for creating outgoing correspondence.
- Expertly handled office operations such as taking dictation, filing, answering a multiline switchboard, and processing paperwork and correspondence.

PERSONAL

Pride myself on highly developed communication skills. Am a flexible, cheerful professional who learns quickly. Have a sincere desire to benefit my employer through productivity and efficiency.

MEDICAL CLINIC RECEPTIONIST & CLERK TYPIST

Date

Exact Name of Person
Exact Title
Exact Name of Company
Address
City, State, Zip

**MEDICAL
CLINIC
RECEPTIONIST
&
CLERK TYPIST**
for an inner city
medical hospital

Dear Exact Name of Person (or Dear Sir or Madam if answering a blind ad):

I would appreciate an opportunity to talk with you soon about how I could contribute to your organization through my experience in administrative operations as well as my skills related to computer operations, research, and communicating with people from varied backgrounds. My husband and I have recently relocated to Texas, and I am seeking an employer who can use my administrative skills and medical knowledge.

As you will see from my enclosed resume, I refined my office management and clerical skills at the Baltimore County Hospital as a Medical Clinic Receptionist and Clerk/Typist. I was often singled out with praise for my friendly and helpful attitude while inprocessing 300 patients a day and answering phones/routing calls in support of health care providers in four clinics: optometry, ophthalmology, otolaryngology, and audiology. I was described as having "personally reduced patient complaints by 85%." These simultaneous activities allowed me an opportunity to further refine my time management and organizational skills while processing time-sensitive and confidential materials on tight schedules.

You will see that I studied Business Administration and Management at the University of Baltimore, and I am experienced in the operation of a wide variety of office equipment including Microsoft Word, Excel, Access, and PowerPoint.

If you can use an articulate, personable, and mature professional, I hope you will call or write me soon to suggest a time when we might have a brief discussion of how I could contribute to your school and to its ability to provide a safe and caring environment where students may learn and grow. I will provide excellent professional and personal references at the appropriate time.

Sincerely,

Kristina F. Oxner

KRISTINA F. OXNER

1110½ Hay Street, Fayetteville, NC 28305   •   preppub@aol.com   •   (910) 483-6611

OBJECTIVE

To apply my experience in the area of office administration as well as my abilities in medical office management, to an organization that can use an enthusiastic, friendly, and caring professional with strong computer knowledge and interpersonal communications skills.

EXPERIENCE

Refined my office management and clerical skills, Baltimore County Hospital, Baltimore, MD:
2000-present: MEDICAL CLINIC RECEPTIONIST AND CLERK/TYPIST. Was often singled out with praise for my friendly and helpful attitude while inprocessing approximately 300 patients a day as well as answering phones and routing calls in support of health care providers in four clinics: optometry, ophthalmology, otolaryngology, and audiology.
- Was described as having "personally reduced patient complaints an impressive 85%."
- Maintained patient records by entering information into the ACCESS computer system.
- Displayed thorough knowledge of clinic operations and was selected to train others.
- Contributed my clerical skills during a period of personnel shortages: prepared and typed correspondence, scheduled patient appointments, and assisted new patients.
- Reduced problems in work areas by setting up procedures including a system for tracking patients needing follow-up care.

1999-00: EMERGENCY ROOM MEDICAL CLERK AND RECEPTIONIST. Handled a variety of functions while processing approximately 200 patients a day: registered patients, coordinated referrals to clinics for less severely ill patients, answered phones, paged doctors, signed out crutches, and assisted patients to their clinics within the hospital.
- Described as a "truly concerned and caring professional," was involved in helping the families of critically injured or dying patients while they waited for chaplains or friends.
- Ordered forms and controlled inventories of important documents including lab slips.
- Maintained daily records of the status, condition, and disposition of each patient; prepared records for personnel injured on duty.
- Processed two daily and four monthly reports using Microsoft Word and Excel.
- Trained and supervised volunteers as well as "backup" secretarial personnel.
- Earned special recognition for organizing admission procedures when over 160 heat stroke/exhaustion victims were admitted within one four-hour period.
- Established a support program for employees suffering from stress and fatigue.

1998: MEDICAL CLAIMS TRANSCRIBER. Loyola Legal Services, Baltimore, MD. Used various Microsoft Office Suite programs while transcribing voice recordings and producing typed drafts of social security medical claims hearings.
- Gained a broad base of knowledge of medical terminology including proper spellings while editing and producing final drafts for signature by administrative law judges.
- Refined time management skills supporting seven judges and five attorney advisors.

Highlights of experience in other jobs:
- As Clerk/Typist for Chicora Military Magnet Academy, contributed many hours of overtime to ensure student evaluations and documentation of special accomplishments for 3,600 cadets were completed on time.
- Assisted customers, including many foreign students, locate materials in a special-interest library; ordered books and removed out-of-date materials from the catalog department.

EDUCATION & SPECIAL SKILLS

Studied Business Administration and Management, University of Baltimore, Baltimore, MD.
Am experienced in the operation of a wide variety of office equipment including:

computerized and manual typewriters	copiers	printers
microfiche/microfilm printers and readers	collating machines	dictaphones
Microsoft Word	Excel	PowerPoint

PERSONAL

Received numerous certificates and letters of appreciation/commendation for "exemplary service" and "outstanding performance." Am highly effective in reducing complaints.

MEDICAL RECORDS TRANSCRIPTION SUPERVISOR

Date

Exact Name of Person
Exact Title
Exact Name of Company
Address
City, State, Zip

**MEDICAL
RECORDS
TRANSCRIPTION
SUPERVISOR**
for a
medical
center
in
Mississippi

Dear Exact Name of Person (or Dear Sir or Madam if answering a blind ad):

I would appreciate an opportunity to talk with you soon about how I could contribute to your organization through my experience in medical administration and computer operations.

As you will see from my enclosed resume, I am currently employed as a Medical Records Supervisor with Delta Memorial Hospital. While supervising up to eight transcriptionists daily depending on our workload, I prioritize and assign transcription duties to produce accurate work on time under tight deadlines. In previous experience as a Customer Service Representative for the Department of Transportation, I gained customer service experience while providing motor vehicle information to clients and answering multiline phones.

You will see that I completed a Medical Terminology Course at Senatobia Medical Center and also completed two years of college course work in Business Management and Marketing with the Mississippi Valley State University. I feel that both my education and experience have refined my ability to excel in any environment.

If you can use an articulate, personable, and mature professional, I hope you will call or write me soon to suggest a time when we might have a brief discussion of how I could contribute to your organization. I will provide excellent professional and personal references at the appropriate time.

Sincerely,

Barbara J. Naumann

BARBARA J. NAUMANN

1110½ Hay Street, Fayetteville, NC 28305   •   preppub@aol.com   •   (910) 483-6611

OBJECTIVE   To contribute to an organization that can use a skilled young professional with excellent communication, organizational, and clerical skills who offers a proven ability to interact effectively with others.

EDUCATION   Completed Medical Terminology Course at Senatobia Medical Center, Senatobia, MS, 2003. Completed two years of college course work, Mississippi Valley State University, Itta Bena, MS, 1995-97.
- Majored in Business with a minor in Accounting; courses included Business Management, Accounting, Business Law, Psychology, Biology, Economics, Business Marketing, Spanish I & II and Writing Seminar.

COMPUTERS   Proficient with Microsoft Word, Excel and Access.
- Experienced with various patient-registration software programs used by hospitals.
- Skilled in using software of the Department of Transportation (DOT).
- Offer the ability to rapidly master new software applications.

EXPERIENCE   **MEDICAL RECORDS TRANSCRIPTION SUPERVISOR.** Delta Memorial Hospital, Jackson, MS (2003-present). While working with up to eight transcriptionists daily depending on our workload, prioritize and assign transcription to produce accurate work on time and under tight deadlines; make corrections in Microsoft Word.
- Print and chart transcription; correct transcription deficiencies on charts; file and pull medical record charts.

EMERGENCY ROOM REGISTRATION CLERK. Banner Medical Center, Senatobia, MS (2001-03). In this full-time position with Banner Medical, registered patients, assembled medical charts, analyzed medical information, and verified insurance using MEDIFAX.
- Transcribed doctors' orders and set up patient files and charts.
- Discharged patients; entered patients charges into system.
- Typed and maintained patient logs.
- Prepared nurses' reports; admitted patients to hospital; accepted patient payments.
- Utilized various office equipment including copier, fax, and credit card machines.

DATABASE TECHNICIAN. Department of Transportation, Senatobia, MS (1998-01). Reviewed documents such as identification and validated permits, out-of-state and out-of-country licenses. Assisted in the writing development of road and written tests. Also performed typing and data entry.
- Became skilled in all aspects of customer service and public relations.
- Utilized various office equipment including copier, fax, and credit card machines.

CUSTOMER SERVICE REPRESENTATIVE. Department of Transportation, Itta Bena, MS (1995-98). Verified and categorized documents; double checked previous day's work before mailing to Jackson; performed dealer work; operated phones and all office equipment while typing, performing data entry, conducting file searches, and collating documents.
- As Receptionist, provided information and answered multiline phones.

PERSONAL   Outstanding references. Interact well with others. Excellent problem solver. Fast learner. Strong communication skills. Natural leader. Strong analytical skills. Dedicated to company goals. Attention to detail. Team player. Highly motivated.

MEDICAL SECRETARY & TRANSCRIPTIONIST

Date

Exact Name of Person
Exact Title
Exact Name of Company
Address
City, State, Zip

MEDICAL SECRETARY & TRANSCRIPTIONIST
for a
children's
hospital
in
Tennessee

Dear Exact Name of Person (or Dear Sir or Madam if answering a blind ad):

I would appreciate an opportunity to talk with you soon about how I could contribute to your organization through my experience in medical administration and computer operations.

For the well-known children's hospital, I am a Medical Secretary and Transcriptionist. I have built a reputation as an articulate communicator with strong attention to detail along with the ability to handle multiple simultaneous responsibilities while managing office operations. I conduct training and staff development for new medical administrative personnel, and I schedule and coordinate meetings for staff members.

You will see that I have an Associate of Science degree in Business Administration from Bossier Parish Community College in Bossier City, LA. I am familiar with all office automation equipment including computers, photocopiers, facsimile machines, and multiline telephone systems. I proofread, edit, type, and prepare all outgoing correspondence for the office, and I analyze and interpret complex medical information in order to compile reports.

If you can use an articulate, personable, and mature professional, I hope you will call or write me soon to suggest a time when we might have a brief discussion of how I could contribute to your organization. I will provide excellent professional and personal references at the appropriate time.

Sincerely,

Adrianne C. Moore

ADRIANNE C. MOORE

1110½ Hay Street, Fayetteville, NC 28305 • preppub@aol.com • (910) 483-6611

OBJECTIVE   To benefit an organization that can use a motivated, experienced professional with exceptional communication and organizational skills who offers a background of excellence in positions of responsibility in administrative, office management, and customer service environments.

EDUCATION   **A.S., in Business Administration,** Bossier Parish Community College, Bossier City, LA, 2000.

COMPUTERS   Familiar with many of the most popular computer operating systems and software, including Microsoft Word, Access and Excel.

EXPERIENCE   **MEDICAL SECRETARY** and **TRANSCRIPTIONIST.** St. Jude's Medical Center, Memphis, TN (2004-present). For this well-known children's hospital in Memphis, provide administrative and clerical support at this busy teaching hospital; order prescriptions for patients.
- Built a reputation as an articulate communicator with a strong detail orientation and the ability to handle multiple simultaneous responsibilities while managing office operations.
- Conduct training and staff development for all new medical administrative personnel.
- Program meetings for staff members, coordinating schedules to avoid conflicts.
- Perform medical and administrative transcription from tapes recorded by physicians.
- Familiar with all office automation equipment, including computers, photocopiers, facsimile machines, and multiline telephone systems.
- Proofread, edit, type, and prepare all outgoing correspondence for the office; analyze and interpret complex medical information in order to compile reports.

ADMINISTRATIVE ASSISTANT. Shell-Oil, Inc., Cordova, TN (2002-04). Managed the workload for the office, assigning administrative and clerical duties to the appropriate employee as well as providing training to all new administrative and clerical personnel.
- Directed the work of three employees in the secretarial department, developing individual goals to ensure that the office completed all assigned tasks within deadlines.
- Read, interpreted, and analyzed highly technical data while proofreading, editing, and preparing reports and documents related to business development as well as government and private contracts.

With Leeson Electrical Systems, a high-tech firm selling electrical testing equipment, advanced in the following "track record" of increasing responsibilities, Bossier City, LA:
2002: **EXECUTIVE SECRETARY** to the **DIRECTOR OF GEAR MOTORS PRODUCTS.** Provided administrative support to the Products Department; performed all word processing, secretarial, and receptionist duties while overseeing the Director's personal and professional appointment schedule.

2001-02: **SALES DEPARTMENT SECRETARY.** Handled all written and verbal communications between the company and its customers while overseeing all office management and administrative support to the sales department staff. Made travel arrangements for sales department personnel.
- Scheduled, coordinated, and made all necessary preparations and arrangements for meetings involving the sales force and sales management staff.
- Proofread, edited, typed, and prepared memos, letters, reports, price quotes, and all other correspondence. Updated purchase order books; oversaw inventory control and ordered office supplies.

2001: **ASSISTANT** to the **EXECUTIVE SECRETARY.** Was personally responsible for the completion of several complex computer projects as well as day-to-day administrative tasks such as preparing for large meetings and telexing or telefaxing documents.

2000-01: **MAIL CLERK** and **RECEPTIONIST.** Sorted and disbursed mail, prepared regular and air mail for delivery, and ensured proper upkeep of the mail room and postage meter. Answered customer inquiries over the phone and in person; prepared employee time cards.

Other experience: Simultaneously with the above positions, excelled in a part-time customer service job with a Bossier City location of the Sam's Wholesale chain.

PERSONAL   Excellent personal and professional references are available upon request.

NEW LOAN DEPARTMENT COORDINATOR

Date

Exact Name of Person
Title or Position
Name of Company
Address (no., street)
Address (city, state, zip)

NEW LOAN DEPARTMENT COORDINATOR
for a mortgage company in Illinois

Dear Exact Name of Person: (or Dear Sir or Madam if answering a blind ad.)

I would appreciate an opportunity to talk with you soon about how I could contribute to your organization through my exceptionally strong office administration, sales, and secretarial skills.

As you will see from my resume, I offer a proven ability to excel in any job I take on. As a New Loan Department Coordinator and Payoff Clerk with CTX Mortgage Company, I have earned a reputation as a highly motivated "self starter" and enthusiastic hard worker while setting up new loans and calculating loan payoffs according to the investor, type of loan, and interest rate.

Because of my dedication to the company, I received a special bonus for not missing a single day of work in 2003 while excelling as the only professional in a fast-growing loan department. I have been commended for my speed and accuracy in working with numbers while working for this mortgage company servicing more than 200 investors. I have become respected for my ease in working with the public and I always try to put myself "in the customer's shoes."

I am in the process of relocating to Michigan to be with my husband, and I feel certain I could rapidly become a valuable part of an organization that seeks a skilled hard worker. I can provide outstanding references from all employers.

I hope you will welcome my call soon to arrange a brief meeting at your convenience to discuss your current and future needs and how I might serve them. Thank you in advance for your time.

Sincerely yours,

Linda M. Kirby

Alternate last paragraph:
I hope you will call or write me soon to suggest a time convenient for us to meet and discuss your current and future needs and how I might serve them. Thank you in advance for your time.

LINDA M. KIRBY

1110½ Hay Street, Fayetteville, NC 28305 • preppub@aol.com • (910) 483-6611

OBJECTIVE

To contribute to an organization that can use a cheerful, well organized young office support professional who offers versatile skills related to medical secretarial practices as well as banking and loan procedures.

TECHNICAL KNOWLEDGE & EQUIPMENT SKILLS

Computer software: Extensive data entry experience with Word, Excel and Access.
Medical skills: Knowledgeable of the following:

medical terminology	First Aid
admissions and discharge	nursing fundamentals
secretarial accounting	medical office practices

Other office equipment: Operate copiers and other office equipment such as:

l0-key by touch	microfiche	typewriter
fax machine	check writer	switchboard

EDUCATION & DIPLOMA

Excelled academically while studying medical office assisting practices and medical secretarial procedures, Morton College, Cicero, IL, 2000.
• Received a diploma as a Medical Office Assistant.
• Completed courses in time management and Quality Management, CTX Mortgage Company, 2004.

EXPERIENCE

NEW LOAN DEPARTMENT COORDINATOR and **PAYOFF CLERK.** CTX Mortgage Company, Cicero, IL (2002-present). Earned a reputation as a highly motivated "self starter" and enthusiastic hard worker while setting up new loans and calculating loan payoffs; reported to a bank vice president.

• **Payoffs:** Calculated payoffs according to the investor, type of loan, and interest rate; prepared documents according to investors' requirements.
• **New Loans:** Received a special bonus for not missing a single day of work in 2003 while excelling as the only professional in a fast-growing loan department; prepared and processed all new loans bought and loans acquired for servicing rights.
• **Finance:** Was commended for my speed and accuracy in working with numbers while working for this mortgage company servicing more than 200 investors.
• **Public Relations:** Became respected for my ease in working with the public; always try to put myself "in the customer's shoes."

DIET COUNSELOR (Part-time). HerbaLife Weight Loss Center, Cicero, IL (2001-present). In a part-time job on the weekends, teach clients the Dynamatrix diet. Provide information on several weight loss plans including lifetime maintenance, vitamin programs and injections/oral plans.

• Take blood pressure, weight, and body measurements.
• Monitor eating habits and make necessary adjustments.
• Monitor cholesterol and blood pressure.

PERSONAL

Am a positive person who finds it easy to motivate and persuade others.

OFFICE ADMINISTRATOR

Date

Exact Name of Person
Title or Position
Name of Company
Address (no., street)
Address (city, state, zip)

Dear Exact Name of Person: (or Dear Sir or Madam if answering a blind ad.)

I would appreciate an opportunity to talk with you soon about how I could contribute to your organization through my exceptionally strong office administration, sales, and secretarial skills. I have recently relocated to the Los Angeles area with my husband, and I am seeking an employer who can make use of my expert skills in all aspects of office operations.

As you will see from my resume, I offer a proven ability to excel in any job I take on. As an Office Administrator for Merrill Lynch, I supervised five employees and trained newly hired office workers while assuming responsibility for a wide range of financial transactions.

I began with my current employer as a sales person, was promoted to the corporate office, and then was selected as the Office Administrator. I played a key role in selecting a carrier for group medical insurance and became knowledgeable about how medical claims are processed. I have gained experience in determining the advertising media to be used in radio, TV, and print, and I am experienced in all aspects of direct mail. In addition, I was given an opportunity to write a commercial for a radio advertisement.

I feel certain I could rapidly become a valuable part of your organization. I can provide outstanding references from all employers, including from my current organization, which I would appreciate your not contacting until we meet.

I hope you will welcome my call soon to arrange a brief meeting at your convenience to discuss your current and future needs and how I might serve them. Thank you in advance for your time.

Sincerely yours,

Crystal Angelique Kirchen

Alternate last paragraph:
I hope you will call or write me soon to suggest a time convenient for us to meet and discuss your current and future needs and how I might serve them. Thank you in advance for your time.

CRYSTAL ANGELIQUE KIRCHEN

1110½ Hay Street, Fayetteville, NC 28305   •   preppub@aol.com   •   (910) 483-6611

OBJECTIVE

To contribute to an organization that can use a skilled office administrator who offers strong customer relations skills along with expert knowledge related to accounts payable, insurance, payroll, inventory control, and employment matters.

EXPERIENCE

OFFICE ADMINISTRATOR. Merrill Lynch, Easton, PA (1991-04). Supervised five employees and interviewed/trained all employees employed for office positions while assuming responsibility for a wide range of financial transactions; began as a sales person, was promoted to the corporate office and then was selected as the Office Administrator. Recently resigned from my position because I have relocated to California with my husband.

- *Accounts receivable*: Audited bills presented for payment and authorized all payments.
- *Workers compensation*: Investigated all claims made for workers compensation; authorized the inhouse payment of small claims and turned larger claims over to a third party for investigation.
- *Payroll administration*: Supervised the preparation and administration of payroll for 170 people; filed quarterly payroll reports.
- *Health insurance*: Played a key role in selecting a carrier for group medical insurance; became knowledgeable about how medical claims are processed.
- *Financial statements*: Compiled and generated financial statements.
- *Banking*: Handled bank deposits for payroll; transferred money from depository accounts to the main bank account.
- *Accounting*: Maintained records for pensions/profit sharing plans, and supplied data to CPA on employees qualified for vesting; issued 1099's for pension/profit-sharing distribution and supplied 1099's to individual landlords.
- *Employment administration*: Maintained liaison with state regulatory bodies overseeing employment; meticulously maintained employee records including records of sick leave.
- *Tax records*: Prepared yearly personal and business property listings for tax purposes.
- *Vehicle recordkeeping*: Maintained files on all vehicles; prepared annual reports to quote commercial insurance policies.
- *Reporting and communicating*: Conducted counseling sessions with employees; oversaw compilation of monthly statistics for discussion at managers' meetings.
- *Advertising*: Determined advertising media to be used and then placed advertising in radio, TV, and print while making skillful use of direct mail; once helped write a commercial for radio.

Highlights of accomplishments:
- On my own initiative, helped write and produce the company's first employee manual.
- Was commended for rapidly mastering and then training others on a new computer system introduced in 1998.
- When the corporation opened its second division in New York, was handpicked to help set up the accounting procedures and inventory tracking process.

EDUCATION

After excelling in high school and college, was identified as "management material" and was selected to attend numerous college-level professional seminars and workshops. Those courses refined my management and supervisory skills as well as enhance my technical knowledge of accounting, employment procedures, quality control, and computer operation.

PERSONAL

Am a professional and understand the "unspoken requirements" related to maintaining confidentiality and being discreet about all business matters. Am a fast learner who thrives on new challenges. Am a Notary Public. Excellent references upon request.

OFFICE ASSISTANT

Date

Exact Name of Person
Title or Position
Name of Company
Address (no., street)
Address (city, state, zip)

OFFICE ASSISTANT
for an emergency
medical center

Dear Exact Name of Person: (or Dear Sir or Madam if answering a blind ad.)

 With the enclosed resume, I would like to make you aware of my interest in the position of Office Assistant while acquainting you with my clerical skills and administrative experience.

 In my current job as Office Assistant for Emergency-Med Center, I efficiently handle a wide range of clerical and customer service functions. I am highly proficient at inputting technical data from forms, correspondence, and reports, and I offer exceptionally strong computer skills. I am familiar with many of the most popular computer operating systems and software including Word, Excel, Access, Works as well as Quicken and Corel Draw applications. A well-organized individual with excellent work habits, I have made many contributions to office efficiency and productivity through my personal initiative and natural problem-solving skills.

 You mention in your ad that dictation experience is "a plus," and I am skilled at taking dictation and performing transcription, which I have done in each of my last two positions.

 My current job is one in which I am continuously involved in customer service, and I have earned a reputation as a gracious, tactful, and well-mannered individual who professionally represents my employer to the public.

 I hope you will give me the opportunity to show you in person that I am the individual you are seeking. With a reputation as a dedicated hard worker, I pride myself on doing every job to the best of my ability, and I can assure you in advance that I could become a valuable member of your organization.

Sincerely,

Camille V. Jernigan

CAMILLE V. JERNIGAN

1110½ Hay Street, Fayetteville, NC 28305   •   preppub@aol.com   •   (910) 483-6611

OBJECTIVE   To benefit an organization that can use an articulate professional manager with exceptional communication and organizational skills who offers a background of excellence in office administration, customer service, computer operations, and clerical environments.

EDUCATION   Completed certification program in Office Automation, Marygrove College, Detroit, MI, 2000.
Finished six months of college-level course work, Madonna University, Detroit, MI, 1999.
Earned a Certificate of Completion from the Office Procedures Training program with Roper Care Alliance, Detroit, MI, 1998.

COMPUTERS   Am familiar with many of the most popular computer operating systems and software including Microsoft Word, Excel, Access, Works, Quicken and Corel Draw as well as Medic+, MedSoft, ABS, and other proprietary applications developed for use in medical office environments.

SPECIAL SKILLS   Skilled and knowledgeable in Medical Transcription, Medical Terminology, and ICD-9/CPT coding, as well as the operation of most common office equipment, including photocopiers, facsimile machines, 10-key calculators, and Pitney-Bowes postage meters.

EXPERIENCE   **OFFICE ASSISTANT.** Emergency-Med Center, Detroit, MI (2001-present). Provide a wide range of administrative, office automation, clerical, customer service, and receptionist support for this busy medical office.
- Take dictation, composing and preparing letters, memos, and other office correspondence; sort and distribute all incoming mail and process outgoing mail.
- Update and maintain the office filing system, ensuring that physical and computer files are current, accessible, and organized according to established office procedures.
- Receive a high volume of calls on a multiline phone system; route the caller to the appropriate person, taking messages or answering the inquiry, as appropriate.
- Answer customer inquiries over the phone and in person, resolving matters related to billing, scheduling, and service problems.
- Utilize Medic office management software for scheduling patient appointments and updating the calendar to reflect cancellations and changes.
- Check patients into the clinic, verifying insurance, inquiring about the nature of their symptoms, pulling their charts, and making notations in their patient histories.

OFFICE ASSISTANT. Roper Care Alliance, Detroit, MI (2001). For this neurology clinic, performed many of the same duties as in the above position, including medical transcription, receptionist, administrative and clerical duties; utilized the ABS proprietary medical history and patient information database system.

CERTIFIED NURSING ASSISTANT. Village Care, Detroit, MI (2000-01). For a long-term care organization, provided quality patient care to elderly and bedridden patients.

DESK CLERK/NIGHT AUDITOR. The Carriage House Inn, Detroit, MI (1998-99). For this cozy bed and breakfast, handled managerial responsibilities while supervising a housekeeping staff.

PERSONAL   Excellent personal and professional references are available upon request.

OFFICE ASSISTANT III

Date

Exact Name of Person
Title or Position
Name of Company
Address (no., street)
Address (city, state, zip)

Dear Exact Name of Person: (or Dear Sir or Madam if answering a blind ad.)

With the enclosed resume, I would like to make you aware of my interest in exploring employment opportunities with your organization.

In my current job as an Office Assistant III for Claremont County Disability Services, I provide clerical support to the clinical staff which includes transcribing clinical notes, progress notes, and evaluations. I maintain medical records and review charts to ensure that all documents are in compliance with county policies and procedures. In a previous temporary position with Canton Outreach, I provided support to the staff such as processing phone calls, taking messages, coordinating office supplies, greeting visitors, typing, performing medical record chart documentation, and maintaining administrative files. I earned a reputation as a gracious, tactful, and well-mannered individual who professionally represented my employer to the public.

Prior to my administrative work in the medical field, I excelled as a legal secretary for an attorney with a practice which included foreclosures, bankruptcies, and personal injury. While in that position, I greatly refined my ability to produce quality work under tight deadlines.

I hope you will give me the opportunity to show you in person that I am the individual you are seeking. With a reputation as a dedicated hard worker, I pride myself on doing every job to the best of my ability, and I can assure you in advance that I could become a valuable member of your organization.

Sincerely,

Paula White

PAULA WHITE

1110½ Hay Street, Fayetteville, NC 28305 • preppub@aol.com • (910) 483-6611

OBJECTIVE

I offer my clerical and secretarial skills to an organization that can use a hardworking young professional with exceptional public relations, planning, and organizing abilities.

EDUCATION

Successfully completed courses in Executive Secretary Skills and Business Administration, Lakeland Community College, Kirtland, OH and Malone College, Canton, OH, 2003.

- Take dictation and transcribe shorthand.
- Acquired expertise with this and other equipment: Microsoft Word, Excel, 10-key adding machines, and calculators.
- Developed business operations knowledge through courses in Business Law, Business Math, Economics, and Business English/Terminology.

EXPERIENCE

OFFICE ASSISTANT III (Medical Records). Claremont County Disability Services, Canton OH (2003-present). Provide clerical support to the clinical staff which includes performing transcription of clinical notes, progress notes, and evaluations.

- Maintain medical records; review and check charts to ensure that all documents and records are in compliance with policy and procedures.

LEAD WORKER III (Temporary). Canton Outreach, Canton, OH (2003). Provided clerical and administrative services to the staff including processing phone calls, taking messages, coordinating office resources, greeting clients/visitors, typing, performing medical record chart work and documentation, and maintaining administrative files.

- Calculated time sheets and set up appointments for supervisors.
- Performed reference checks on applicants and prepared, organized and maintained therapeutic records for the program.
- Typed performance work plans, job descriptions, IHP's, court reports, medical evaluations, treatment plans, admission assessments, and termination summaries.

LEGAL SECRETARY. Michael C. Hilliard, Attorney-at Law, Canton OH (1995-02). For this fast-paced legal office, answered a six-line phone system; processed accounts receivable statements; typed correspondence in addition to preparing various legal documents related to foreclosures, bankruptcies, and personal injury.

- Excelled in filing supplements in law library including OH General Statutes.
- Provided backup for other secretaries. Refined my communication skills and developed an excellent eye-for-detail.
- Scheduled appointments and kept up with deadlines. Performed monthly billings.

WAITRESS and **HOSTESS.** Little Caesars, Canton, OH (1993-95). Through my public relations skills and cheerful disposition, played a key role in producing satisfied customers and repeat business in a very competitive industry; greeted and served up to 120 customers daily.

- Was chosen for the special responsibility of opening and closing the restaurant and entrusted to account for daily revenues.

TELEMARKETING SPECIALIST. Tybee Resorts & Travel, Canton, OH (1993). Learned to organize persuasive sales presentations and learned valuable prospecting and sales techniques.

PERSONAL

Am a highly skilled organizer and achievement-oriented young professional.

OFFICE ASSISTANT & RECEPTIONIST

Date

Exact Name of Person
Title or Position
Name of Company
Address (no., street)
Address (city, state, zip)

OFFICE
ASSISTANT
&
RECEPTIONIST
for a position
with
city hall

Dear Exact Name of Person: (or Dear Sir or Madam if answering a blind ad.)

With the enclosed resume, I would like to make you aware of my interest in exploring employment opportunities with your organization.

In my current job as an Office Assistant with the City of Los Angeles, my exceptional customer service skills have led to continual advancement into positions of increasing responsibility. In my current position, I provide administrative, clerical, and receptionist support while serving as the initial point of contact for hundreds of visitors to our city offices on a daily basis. I receive, process, and alphabetize employment applications from prospective candidates and assemble processing packets for new employees. I have earned a reputation as a gracious, tactful, and well-mannered individual with outstanding interpersonal skills.

You will see from my resume that I have completed several years of college-level course work towards degree programs in Human Resource Management and General Education at Georgia Southern University. I have excelled in many training programs including a 232-hour course focusing on the development of administrative skills.

I hope you will give me the opportunity to show you in person that I am the individual you are seeking. With a reputation as a dedicated hard worker, I pride myself on doing every job to the best of my ability, and I can assure you in advance that I could become a valuable member of your organization.

Sincerely,

Joyce C. Meyers

JOYCE C. MEYERS

1110½ Hay Street, Fayetteville, NC 28305   •   preppub@aol.com   •   (910) 483-6611

OBJECTIVE

To benefit an organization that can use an articulate young professional with exceptional communication and organizational skills who offers a background of excellence in a variety of challenging customer service, administrative, and telecommunications environments.

EDUCATION

College: Have finished two years of college-level course work towards degree programs in Human Resource Management and General Education, Georgia Southern University, Statesboro, GA.
Administrative: Excelled in many employer-sponsored training programs including a 232-hour course focusing on the development of administrative skills, 1995.
Completed an Exceptional Customer Service course and a communication skills course sponsored by the City of Los Angeles.

LICENSES

Appointed a Notary Public for the state of California, my commission expires 05/15/05.

EXPERIENCE

With the City of Los Angeles, my exceptional customer service skills have led to continual advancement into positions of increasing responsibility:
2003-present: **OFFICE ASSISTANT** and **RECEPTIONIST.** Provide administrative, clerical, and receptionist support while serving as the initial point of contact for hundreds of visitors on a daily basis.
- Personally greet a heavy volume of visitors, giving directions to all city offices throughout Los Angeles.
- Answer a multiline telephone system, responding to numerous customer inquiries, routing calls, and taking messages when the requested party is unavailable.
- Receive, process, and alphabetize employment applications from prospective candidates; set up the orientation room for new employees.
- Control the Human Resource Department's form inventory; assemble applications and new employee orientation packets.

2000-03: **COURIER.** Received, sorted, and distributed incoming mail while collecting outgoing mail, sorting and processing outbound bulk mailings, and transporting mail to the post office.
- Transported a variety of time and content-sensitive documents and other materials between city departments and agencies in a timely and accurate manner.

1999-00: **BUS OPERATOR.** Provided exceptional customer service while operating a passenger bus for the L.A. Area Transit; maintained adherence with assigned routes and schedules.
- Enforced rules, regulations, codes, and policies; ensured that all customers behaved in a safe and orderly manner.
- Prepared and inspected assigned vehicle; performed minor preventive maintenance.

Highlights of earlier experience (1993-99): Excelled in customer service jobs as well as in administrative and telecommunication positions in the U.S. Air Force including:
- **CALL CENTER AGENT.** Baymont Inn & Suites, Los Angeles, CA. Received a large number of customer inquiries, providing price and availability information and booking reservation at various Baymont locations, using their computer network system.
- **SWITCHBOARD OPERATOR.** Radisson Hotel, Los Angeles, CA. Received and processed a high volume of incoming calls while conducting hourly checks on all communications circuits, maintaining a log of communications checks, and reporting any faulty circuits.
- **WIRE SYSTEMS INSTALLER.** U.S. Air Force, locations worldwide. Performed maintenance on cable lines servicing telephone substation equipment, test stations, voltage protection devices, repeaters, and restorers. Constructed tactical wire and cable phone lines.

PERSONAL

Excellent personal and professional references are available upon request.

OFFICE AUTOMATION CLERK

Date

Exact Name of Person
Exact Title
Exact Name of Company
Address
City, State, Zip

**OFFICE
AUTOMATION
CLERK**
for the archives
and records
administration

Dear Exact Name of Person (or Dear Sir or Madam if answering a blind ad):

I would appreciate an opportunity to talk with you soon about how I could contribute to your organization through my versatile office automation, personnel, and customer service skills.

As you will see from my enclosed resume, I am familiar with a variety of automation software such as Microsoft Word, Access, and Excel.

Currently as an Office Automation Clerk with the National Archives and Records Administration, I am displaying my versatility by handling multiple responsibilities in a training headquarters operation. The emphasis of this job is preparing narrative and tabular materials according to prescribed guidelines and forms, and I have earned respect for my excellent written communication skills and knowledge of grammar.

Earlier I excelled in positions as Administrative Assistant for an elementary school and as a Secretary and Assistant Accountant for a country club. I have become known as a reliable and honest professional who can be counted on to achieve quality results.

If you can use an experienced professional with strong skills in office operations, customer service, and human resources, I hope you will contact me to suggest a time when we might meet to discuss your needs. I can assure you in advance that I could rapidly become an asset to your organization.

Sincerely,

Juanita Pierson

JUANITA PIERSON

1110½ Hay Street, Fayetteville, NC 28305 • preppub@aol.com • (910) 483-6611

OBJECTIVE   To offer a versatile blend of office automation, personnel and human resources, and customer service skills to an organization that can use a dependable and personable professional.

SPECIAL SKILLS   *Computers:* Familiar with Microsoft Word, Excel, Access, and other software programs
Other: use typewriters, printers, all standard office equipment including multiline phones and fax

EXPERIENCE   **OFFICE AUTOMATION CLERK.** National Archives and Records Administration (NARA), Ft. Lauderdale, FL (2003-present). Handle office support functions for a training headquarters operation with an emphasis on using computers to prepare a variety of narrative and tabular material according to prepared formats that include form letters and standard paragraphs.
- Distribute mail and interoffice communication according to regulations and guidelines.
- Collect, consolidate, and manage credit card information for participants in a system which allows credit purchases of goods and services from outside the normal supply channels.
- Assist in producing periodic performance evaluations, narratives for awards and medals, and memorandums; schedule computer classes for organizational personnel.
- Maintain and update files and forms, including finance reports and personnel actions.
- Was selected for this job on the basis of my performance in a five-month temporary assignment with the NARA corporate office in Manhattan, NY: operate word processing computer equipment to update, revise, reformat, sort, calculate, and retrieve information.
- Described in a recent annual performance evaluation as "exceeding all expectations; performing at a level higher than warranted by position," was singled out as having natural leadership qualities and possessing sound judgment.

ADMINISTRATIVE ASSISTANT. Montclair Elementary School, Ft. Lauderdale, FL (2002-03). Quickly recognized by officials as a trustworthy and tactful professional, was entrusted with maintaining confidential files on kindergarten through fifth grade students while providing administrative support by answering phones, filing, typing, and preparing reports.
- Used software including Microsoft Word and Access while maintaining files containing information on medication, remediation, and behavioral disorders of students.
- Made a recommendation that the school purchase updated software: my suggestion was acted on and resulted in improving the capabilities of the recordkeeping systems.

SECRETARY, ASSISTANT ACCOUNTANT, AND CLERK. Creekside Country Club, Ft. Lauderdale, FL (2001-02). Became known for my flexibility in a busy meeting, social, and dining complex – handled activities which included exchanging currency and cashing checks, helping kitchen staff, and preparing profit and loss statements.
- Contributed planning and organizational skills during special celebration projects such as weddings, birthdays, and anniversary parties. Used Excel spreadsheets while compiling reports.

TELLER and **CUSTOMER SERVICE REPRESENTATIVE.** First Federal Bank, Ft. Lauderdale, FL (1998-01). Worked with computer systems on a daily basis while meeting goals of selling accounts.

EDUCATION   Studied Public Relations at Nova Southeastern University, Fort Lauderdale, FL.

PERSONAL   Exceptionally reliable – have missed only four days of work due to illness in a ten-year period.

OFFICE MANAGER

Date

Exact Name of Person
Exact Title
Exact Name of Company
Address
City, State, Zip

Dear Exact Name of Person (or Dear Sir or Madam if answering a blind ad):

With the enclosed resume, I would like to make you aware of my background in office operations and purchasing as well as the versatile computer skills I could put to work for you.

From my enclosed resume, you will see that I am employed as an Office Manager for the Trade Development Agency in Portland. I manage three clerical employees in a busy office providing personnel administration and human resource services supporting an organization with 75 employees. I expertly maintain an inventory of more than 330 personnel records while ensuring that all records are updated with changes related to training, job assignments, commendations for awards and disciplinary actions, and other matters. I use my excellent computer skills to upgrade the database used for recordkeeping.

I studied general subjects and prelaw at both the University of Oregon and Lane Community College, Eugene, OR and completed more than two years of college coursework in business administration, human resources, office management, bookkeeping, computer operations, and data entry.

If you can use a motivated, hardworking professional who could become a contributing member of your team, I hope you will contact me to suggest a time when we might meet in person to discuss your needs. I will bring excellent letters of reference with me, and I am certain I can excel in any type of testing your company administers. Thank you in advance for your time and courtesies.

Sincerely,

Wanda S. Collier

WANDA S. COLLIER

1110½ Hay Street, Fayetteville, NC 28305 • preppub@aol.com • (910) 483-6611

OBJECTIVE   I want to contribute to an organization that can use a young professional who offers excellent communication skills and computer software knowledge along with experience as an office manager, paralegal and legal assistant, customer service representative, and training manager.

COMPUTERS   Experienced in operating computers and skilled in using Microsoft Word, Excel, and Access.

EXPERIENCE   **OFFICE MANAGER.** Trade Development Agency, Portland, OR (2004-present). Was specially selected to manage three clerical employees in a busy office providing personnel administration and human resources services supporting an organization with 75 employees.
- Prepare paperwork related to promotions, job reassignments, awards, disciplinary actions, requests and assignments for training and schooling, job-related travel, and discharges.
- Utilize a computer to input a wide range of data used in spreadsheet analysis; author reports for top management identifying trends and problems.
- Was commended for my friendly yet professional manner when providing customer service.
- Expertly maintain an inventory of more than 330 personnel records.
- Used my excellent computer skills to upgrade the database used for recordkeeping.

Excelled in administrative positions with Tyco Automation Services, Portland, OR:
2001-04: TRAINING COORDINATOR. Was selected for promotion to the job above based on my excellent performance in this job which involved developing, implementing, and organizing a complete training program for more than 150 employees in multiple occupational areas.
- Developed concepts and operational details related to employee training, and then "sold" my ideas to top executives; after their approval, developed training schedules, purchased training supplies and equipment, managed training programs, and evaluated results.
- Implemented training programs that significantly improved the skill levels of employees.

1998-01: OFFICE MANAGER. Was promoted to supervise six employees involved in personnel administration in the central headquarters office of this 150-person organization.
- Maintained promotion packets and information for more than 400 people; updated these packets frequently with precise calculations which I prepared based on a point system in which numerical values were assigned to various activities.
- Prepared correspondence, memoranda, and reports to assist individuals in documenting key facts related to their promotion and selection for jobs.

Other experience:
PARALEGAL & LEGAL SPECIALIST. Lofton-Graham Law Offices, Eugene, OR (1996-98). Was quickly promoted to responsibilities related to research and client service because of my excellent communication and interpersonal skills. Acted as liaison with clients, agencies, courts, and attorneys.
- Drafted legal documents; analyzed, summarized, and indexed files.

EDUCATION   Studied general subjects and prelaw at both the University of Oregon and Lane Community College, Eugene, OR; have completed more than two years of college coursework in business administration, human resources, office management, bookkeeping, and computer operations.

PERSONAL   Can provide exceptionally strong references. Am known for my cheerful disposition and hardworking nature. Enjoy helping others, both customers and coworkers.

OFFICE MANAGER

Date

Exact Name of Person
Exact Title
Exact Name of Company
Address
City, State, Zip

Dear Exact Name of Person (or Dear Sir or Madam if answering a blind ad):

With the enclosed resume, I would like to make you aware of my background in office operations and purchasing as well as the versatile computer skills I could put to work for you.

From my enclosed resume, you will see that I am currently employed as an Office Manager for Weston, Inc. I began working for this heavy equipment distribution company and was rapidly promoted to handle increasing responsibilities for operations management. While working for the family-owned business, I made numerous suggestions which improved internal efficiency. For example, I made suggestions which were approved by the owners related to the automation of numerous functions which previously had been handled manually. The changes which we made led to vastly improved efficiency in ordering, purchasing, scheduling, and customer satisfaction.

You will also see that I graduated from Drew University with a Bachelor of Science degree in Office Technology. I excelled in course work such as accounting, bookkeeping, purchasing, advanced mathematics as well as typing, taking shorthand, data processing and business correspondence. I am highly proficient in utilizing computers to improve office efficiency and am skilled in using Microsoft Word, Excel, and proprietary office management programs for account management and distribution tracking.

If you can use a motivated, hardworking professional who could become a contributing member of your team, I hope you will contact me to suggest a time when we might meet in person to discuss your needs. I will bring excellent letters of reference with me, and I am certain I can excel in any type of testing your company administers. Thank you in advance for your time and courtesies.

Sincerely,

Leon M. Thomas

LEON M. THOMAS

1110½ Hay Street, Fayetteville, NC 28305   •   preppub@aol.com   •   (910) 483-6611

OBJECTIVE   I want to contribute to an organization that can use a hardworking young professional with extensive computer skills as well as experience in customer service, public relations, and purchasing, finance and accounting, as well as operations management.

EDUCATION &   **Bachelor of Science** degree in **Office Technology,** Drew University, Madison, NJ, 1996.
TRAINING
- Excelled in course work including accounting, bookkeeping, purchasing, marketing, advanced mathematics as well as typing, taking shorthand, data processing and business correspondence.

Completed numerous training courses related to Telephone Customer Service, Warranty Administration, and other areas.

COMPUTERS   Highly proficient in utilizing computer to improve office efficiency; skilled in using Microsoft Word, Excel, and proprietary office management programs for account management and tracking as well as heavy equipment distribution.

LANGUAGES   Fluent in Spanish; have acted as an interpreter for executives.

EXPERIENCE   **OFFICE MANAGER.** Weston, Inc., Newark, NJ (1999-present). Began working for this heavy equipment distribution company and was rapidly promoted to handle increasing responsibilities for operations management.
- Utilize my strong computer skills to continuously find new ways to automate, modernize, and improve internal procedures in order to increase efficiency, improve customer satisfaction, and facilitate decision making.
- Prepare orders related to building machines and accessories; draw up quotes; work out the costs of building machines as well as calculate the costs of financing and issuing the documents.
- Work daily on a computer, entering the machines into the EDP system and monitoring stocks of new and used machines; draw up different analyses such as inventory lists, calculations of machines, as well as recording and categorizing internal machine costs.
- Have become knowledgeable of company policies and requirements as I draw up delivery and export papers and prepare all necessary documentation.
- Solely responsible for all warranty administration; am also involved in vehicle rental administration.
- Perform as a liaison with foreign companies, and act as a translator between English-speaking and Spanish-speaking executives; am involved in numerous situations involving multimillion-dollar deals and have learned much about negotiating.
- Routinely interface with top-level managers within the company as well as with international executives, government officials, vendors, and customers.
- On my own initiative, made numerous suggestions which were approved by management which, after I implemented them, led to the transformation and modernization of the office procedures of this family business.
- Trained one assistant during her probation period, and am proud of the fact that she became a highly efficient coworker who made many contributions to office efficiency.

PURCHASING REPRESENTATIVE. Bennett Manufacturing, Newark, NJ (1996-99). Quickly became a valued employee of this organization while working in the purchasing department; handled order processing, coordinated the scheduling of shipments, and computerized records for the purchasing department.

PERSONAL   Excellent personal and professional references are available upon request.

OFFICE MANAGER (CAREER CHANGE)

Date

Mr. Paul Zabetos
Human Resources Manager
Delta Airlines
5511 Delta Airlines Road
Atlanta, GA 23300

Dear Mr. Zabetos:

OFFICE
MANAGER
seeking a
flight
attendant
position

With the enclosed resume describing my considerable public relations and customer service experience, I would like to formally initiate the process of applying for employment as a Flight Attendant.

As you will see from my resume, I have worked as an Office Manager for a highly regarded dentist who is retiring from private practice shortly. Although I am highly regarded by this employer and can provide excellent references at the appropriate time, I have decided to change careers and aggressively pursue a dream I have had for some time: to become a Flight Attendant.

My experience in managing the private practice of a busy dentist gave me many skills which would be useful in airline situations. I am extremely poised when dealing with the public, and I am known for my ability to serve the public with tact and grace. I work well with people at all organizational levels, and I have become accustomed to putting others at ease when external events are in flux. While working for the doctor, I have become his trusted personal advisor and have handled numerous personal matters for him.

In previous experience, I excelled briefly as a Certified Nursing Assistant and Teacher's Assistant. My communication skills are excellent, and I genuinely enjoy working with people individually and in groups. I feel confident that my medical knowledge, certification in CPR, and proven ability to remain calm in crises could be assets in flight situations where a calm head and prudent thinking are needed in emergencies.

I hope you will contact me to suggest the next step I should take in making formal application for employment as a Flight Attendant. I can assure you in advance that I have an excellent reputation, and I am confident that I could be a valuable asset to your organization.

Sincerely,

Bria D. Sullivan

BRIA D. SULLIVAN

1110½ Hay Street, Fayetteville, NC 28305   •   preppub@aol.com   •   (910) 483-6611

OBJECTIVE

To contribute to Delta Airlines as a Flight Attendant through my excellent communication skills, strong service orientation, proven public relations skills, and ability to motivate others to work as a team as well as through my ability to maintain a positive attitude under stress.

EDUCATION

Graduated from Armstrong Atlantic University, Savannah, GA, as **Certified Nursing Assistant**, 1995. Completed continuing education coursework: Insurance Reimbursement Update, Essential Verbal Skills, and Comprehensive Payment Strategies, 2003.

Graduated from Abercorn High School, Savannah, GA: participated in numerous activities and earned honors including:

- **Academic Excellence:** Ranked 124 in a class of 633 students.
- **German Language:** Was a member of the **German Club** and received the **"German Merit Certificate"** after being chosen to represent the school in a foreign language competition at Savannah State University.
- **Community Service:** Volunteered time in community service as a Candy Striper.

EXPERIENCE

OFFICE MANAGER. Jean Augustine, D.D.S., Savannah, GA (1998-present). Have become known for my positive and cheerful attitude as well as for my ability to interact graciously with the public while overseeing a wide variety of daily support activities in a busy and often hectic dental office.

- **Customer Service:** Demonstrate an "upbeat" manner while dealing with people who are in pain or scared and help them become comfortable with the situation.
- **Problem Solving:** Excel at motivating other staff members to work together to keep the office organized, pleasant, and friendly despite disruptions and emergencies.
- **Office Administration:** Handle a wide range of office activities from answering phones, to greeting patients, to scheduling appointments, to discussing treatment plans, to handling past due accounts.
- **Financial Administration:** Am in charge of financial support actions which include collecting and posting payments, filing insurance, and following through on unpaid claims; handle business and personal checking to include payroll checks, business expenses, Dr. Augustine's personal bills, Federal tax deposits, and Sales and Use Tax Reports. Balance daily transactions, order supplies, and make weekly bank deposits.
- **Outstanding Reputation:** Built a reputation as a thoroughly knowledgeable and dependable professional in this job.

CERTIFIED NURSING ASSISTANT (CNA). The Landings Retirement Homes, Savannah, GA (1995-98). Was known for my cheerful personality and compassionate nature displayed while providing daily care for patients with both mental and physical disabilities.

Highlights of earlier experience:
TEACHER'S ASSISTANT. Oakdale Elementary School, Savannah, GA (1992-95). Provided assistance to a classroom teacher while contributing an energetic manner.

PERSONAL

Enjoy traveling, seeing new places, and meeting new people. Am highly adaptable and able to handle stress, pressure, and change. Excellent references on request.

OFFICE MANAGER

Exact Name of Person
Title or Position
Name of Company
Address (no., street)
Address (city, state, zip)

OFFICE MANAGER for an orthopedic clinic

Dear Exact Name of Person: (or Dear Sir or Madam if answering a blind ad.)

I would appreciate an opportunity to talk with you soon about how I could contribute to your organization through my versatile skills related to medical office operations and financial services, as well as through my proven sales ability, initiative, and creativity oriented toward improving the "bottom line." My family and I have relocated to Phoenix, and I am seeking an employer who can use my expertise in office management.

As you will see from my resume, most recently I played a key role in the startup of a new orthopedics practice as an Office Manager. While developing office systems and office procedures "from scratch," including designing all forms, I used and trained other employees to use UNIX software and made valuable suggestions which the UNIX vendor applied to refine and upgrade the system. Skilled in bookkeeping and insurance claims administration, I have filed insurance claims and performed ICD-9 and CPT-4 coding. I also handled accounts payable/receivable and payroll and acted as Credit Manager. In my previous job at Wellesley Medical Center I was rapidly promoted to coordinate business office systems and supervised a large staff while acting as the "internal expert" on the computer system and software problems.

In earlier experience in the banking field, I was involved in loan administration, supervised teller transactions, and managed credit card accounts. I am skilled in dealing with the public.

I am confident you would find me in person to be a poised communicator and dynamic personality who enjoys solving technical and business problems. I have been told that I am a "natural" for sales, although I personally believe that the ability to sell a product has a lot to do with the salesperson's product knowledge. A fast learner with the ability to rapidly master new areas of knowledge, I am always eager to learn new things and accept new challenges.

I hope you will welcome my call soon to arrange a brief meeting at your convenience to discuss your current and future needs and how I might serve them. Thank you in advance for your time.

Sincerely yours,

Rachel T. Craig

Alternate last paragraph:
I hope you will call or write me soon to suggest a time convenient for us to meet and discuss your current and future needs and how I might best serve them. Thank you in advance for your time.

RACHEL T. CRAIG

1110½ Hay Street, Fayetteville, NC 28305 • preppub@aol.com • (910) 483-6611

OBJECTIVE To add value to a company that can use a creative professional and dynamic communicator who offers proficiency with computer software, expertise in managing offices and developing business systems, as well as knowledge of the medical and financial fields.

EXPERIENCE **OFFICE MANAGER.** Wellesley Orthopedic Care, Haverhill, MA (1997-04). Worked with UNIX software and made numerous suggestions which the UNIX vendor used to upgrade and refine the system; supervised six clerical employees in medical office operations and trained the entire staff in the operation of the computer system. Recently resigned from my position when my family decided to relocate to Phoenix.

- *Business development*: Joined this practice during its initial setup and played a key role in helping it become a profitable operation; developed office systems and internal procedures "from scratch" including designing all forms.
- *Insurance claims administration*: Filed insurance claims and performed ICD-9 and CPT-4 coding.
- *Customer service*: Acted as Patient Accounts Representative and Receptionist.
- *Accounting/bookkeeping*: Handled accounts payable/receivable and payroll and acted as Credit Manager.
- *Written communication*: Composed reports, memos, and correspondence.

BUSINESS OFFICE SYSTEM COORDINATOR. Wellesley Medical Center, Haverhill, MA (1993-97). Began with this hospital as a Patient Account Representative and was promoted to coordinate all systems in the business office; earned a reputation as a creative problem-solver who could develop efficient and simple new procedures and work flows.

- *Office systems coordination*: Supervised a large staff composed of insurance clerks, file room clerks, mail room personnel, cashiers, and switchboard operators; worked closely with the business manager to interview, hire, and train employees.
- *Customer service*: Supervised four people while overseeing the process of interviewing patients, determining sources of financial aid, collecting past due accounts, and filing insurance claims.
- *Computer consulting*: Acted as the internal expert/consultant on the operations of the computer system used to maintain patient information; performed keying and batching and continuously found innovative new ways of managing data.

PERSONAL BANKER. Omni National Bank, Haverhill, MA (1987-93). Began with this financial institution as a Sales Finance Secretary and earned rapid promotions in succession to Assistant to Installment Loan Manager, Senior Teller, and Personal Banker.
- *Loan administration*: Approved loan applications, conducted credit history investigations, sold and opened new accounts, and became skilled in solving a wide range of banking problems on behalf of customers.
- *Teller transactions*: Ordered currency and coin from the Federal Reserve, sold financial services, balanced vault and teller windows, trained tellers.
- *Credit card accounts*: Managed Ready Reserve and master charge accounts and computed terms for payment.

EDUCATION **Associate in Science** degree in **Business Administration,** Northern Essex Community College, Haverhill, MA, 1990.

PERSONAL Outstanding personal and professional references on request. Am an adaptable team player who works well under pressure. Am a creative person who welcomes new learning opportunities.

OFFICE MANAGER

Date

Exact Name of Person
Title or Position
Name of Company
Address (number and street)
Address (city, state, and zip)

OFFICE
MANAGER
for a
commercial
realty
company

Dear Exact Name of Person: (or Sir or Madam if answering a blind ad.)

With the enclosed resume, I would like to make you aware of my interest in exploring employment opportunities within your organization. My husband and I are in the process of relocating to Rochester, NY, because he is being transferred by his employer, and we are excited about our new home! We will be permanently living in the Rochester area by May 15, 2004.

As you will see from my resume, I offer considerable skills related to bookkeeping and accounting, office management, and computer operations which could be of value to your company. I have loyally served my most recent employer for 5 years, and the owners of the business will provide glowing references. I began my employment as a Receptionist in 1999, and I quickly became known for my enthusiastic style and intelligence. I was promoted to Office Manager, and I have made many major contributions to the firm's profitability. I provided the leadership which convinced the owners to purchase multiple computers for this real estate firm, and the firm is now operating in a state-of-the-art fashion with listings available on the Internet.

In addition to handling numerous administrative and management responsibilities, I am responsible for balancing checking accounts for five different companies. This includes handling sales escrow accounts, accounts payable and receivable, property management accounts, and tenant security accounts. Through my initiative in computerizing the construction company's bookkeeping, and through my leadership in computerizing rental income, we were able to free up precious time for management to engage in activities which improved the bottom line by 24%. I have also created numerous sales, production, and other reports which have allowed the owners to analyze multiple factors related to profitability and cash flow.

Highly proficient in operating computers and in training employees and managers to use them, I am skilled at using Microsoft Word and Works as well as Excel Communications and Spreadsheets. I am proficient in troubleshooting computer problems, and I can nearly always resolve computer problems without calling a hardware or software expert. I offer a proven ability to rapidly master new software and applications.

If you can use a vibrant communicator and enthusiastic hard worker, I hope you will contact me to suggest a time when we might meet to discuss your needs. You may feel free to contact me at the work number on my resume. I can assure you in advance that I could become a valuable asset to your organization.

Yours sincerely,

Lisa Ann Stanley

LISA ANN STANLEY

1110½ Hay Street, Fayetteville, NC 28305　•　preppub@aol.com　•　(910) 483-6611

OBJECTIVE　I want to contribute to an organization that can use my extensive background related to office management, computer operations, customer service, and public relations.

LICENSE　Obtained my real estate license, September 2001.

COMPUTERS　Highly proficient in operating and maintaining computers; utilize Microsoft Word and Works as well as Excel communications and spreadsheets.
Office equipment: Expertly utilize typewriters, calculators, scanners, copiers, fax machines

EXPERIENCE　**OFFICE MANAGER.** McDaniel Commercial Realty, Inc., Richland, VA (1999-present). Began as a Receptionist in May 1999 and was promoted to Office Manager in February 2000; have made many contributions to this business through my strong personal initiative, outstanding organizational skills, expertise in bookkeeping and accounting, and extensive computer knowledge.
Computer operations and administration:
- When I started with the firm, this real estate organization had two computers in the office; convinced the owners that multiple computers would result in more efficiency and boost profitability, and the company now has seven computers. By computerizing the rental department bookkeeping, we were able to free up the rental manager's time to put more rental properties under contract, with the result that rental income increased 25%.
- Have played a major role in assuring that the office is very up-to-date and efficient; all real estate agents are now on the internet, all the firm's listing are on line, and out-of-town sellers can pull up their houses listed on the Internet.
- Have become extremely skilled at troubleshooting computer problems, and can usually pinpoint a problem and fix it myself without calling in a computer expert.

Reports:
- On my own initiative, have compiled and created many different types of reports for my employers which they did not have before; these reports have allowed them to identify where excess money was being spent and where the most income was being generated, and they have praised me for enhancing their management decision-making process.
- Prepare payroll reports, production reports, sales reports, and other reports.

Accounting and bookkeeping:
- Balance checking accounts for five different companies including property management and tenant security deposit accounts and sales escrow account.
- Handle all accounts payable and receivable.

Customer service and public relations:
- Have expertly handled the public while answering a 15-line switchboard as a receptionist.
- Learned the Richland Area Board of Realtors Listings, and have provided highly professional support to the agents.

PROGRAM ASSISTANT. New Holland Farm Equipment, Richland, VA (1997-99). At a time when this office was receiving its first computers, I played a major role in fielding and implementing new equipment and software. Trained other employees. Made commodity loans; handled data entry.

ACCOUNTING CLERK. Cummins Diesel Engines, Richland, VA (1996-97). In my first experience with a computer, discovered that I have a knack for rapidly mastering new programs and applications; entered data into a computer, made journal entries, handled bank deposits, calculated parts and service invoices, computer payroll and maintained payroll records, and handled account receivable.

Other experience:
BOOKKEEPER & SECRETARY. For a real estate company and a semi-trucking company, computed payroll, handled accounts receivable/payable, and maintained inventory and parts records.

EDUCATION　Studied Real Estate Licensing Law, Richland Real Estate School, Richland, VA, 1997.
Studied Accounting, Southwest Virginia Community College, Richland, VA, 1994-96.

PERSONAL　Have a strong sense of loyalty to my employer, and always give more than 100% to my job. In my spare time, enjoy walking and jogging, cross stitching, and refinishing furniture with my husband.

OFFICE MANAGER

Date

Exact Name of Person
Exact Title
Exact Name of Company
Address
City, State, Zip

**OFFICE
MANAGER**
for a
beauty
salon
&
retail
center

Dear Exact Name of Person: (or Dear Sir or Madam if answering a blind ad):

With the enclosed resume, I would like to introduce you to my versatile skills related to office operations, computer operations and data entry, customer service, and telecommunications.

In my current job, I am excelling as the Office Manager for a beauty salon and retail center with two locations. In addition to scheduling appointments for the stylists and barber, I handle inventory control of a wide range of supplies and retail products while also handling financial recordkeeping and bookkeeping. I manage accounts receivable/payable, figure commissions, calculate payroll taxes and employee deductions, prepare quarterly taxes, compile financial statements, and handle numerous other responsibilities related to recordkeeping and financial control.

In a previous job for three years, I excelled in the telemarketing field, and I was handpicked by my employer to train new telemarketers. I have become very skilled at dealing with people on the telephone and in person, and I am known for my ability to handle the public with poise and tact.

In prior positions with Vause Equipment Co. and with the Department of the Treasury, I was involved in computer operations, data entry, and property management.

I offer a reputation as an enthusiastic self-starter, and I am known for my strong personal initiative as well as for my ability to rapidly master new tasks. If you can use my versatile skills and talents, I hope you will contact me to suggest a time when we might meet to discuss your needs.

Sincerely,

Heather B. Soffe

HEATHER B. SOFFE

1110½ Hay Street, Fayetteville, NC 28305   •   preppub@aol.com   •   (910) 483-6611

OBJECTIVE
To benefit an organization in need of a hardworking professional with experience in managing personnel and resources, administrative operations, and customer relations along with outstanding communication, planning, and organizational skills.

EDUCATION
Currently pursuing Associate of Science in Accounting with minor in Education and Business Management, Pacific Lutheran University, Tacoma, WA.

EXPERIENCE
OFFICE MANAGER. Dudley's Styling Center, Tacoma, WA (2000-present). Perform administrative, clerical, and receptionist duties for this busy local salon. Utilize my excellent communication and public relations abilities selling a variety of products to customers from diverse cultural and socioeconomic backgrounds; train new telemarketers.
- Schedule and manage appointments for seven stylists and one barber. Provide customer service for salon patrons, assisting them with purchase of hair care maintenance products.
- Handle inventory control of supplies; organize and control retail merchandise.
- Handle accounts payable/receivable and payroll; figure stylists' commissions; calculate payroll taxes and employee deductions; make daily deposits; handle petty cash.
- Prepare quarterly payroll taxes, financial statements, as well as monthly sales and use tax.

ADMINISTRATIVE ASSISTANT. Olsten Staffing, Tacoma, WA (1997-00). Handled temporary clerical positions, including secretarial, receptionist, bank teller, customer service representative, and medical records technician.
- Scheduled appointments, resolved customer-service problems, and performed office tasks.
- Handled accounting, bookkeeping, and records management procedures while analyzing, organizing, and evaluating patient medical records.
- Cashed checks, verified signatures, and maintained balance accuracy above 95%.

ADMINISTRATIVE ASSISTANT. Department of the Treasury, Tacoma, WA (1994-97). Handled general office duties, customer service, and office management functions. Assigned temporary hand-receipts for property issue or for short period loans, in addition to updated issued hand-receipts and coordinated all turn-ins and lateral transfers.
- Assisted in physical inventories, compared inventory with records; clarified discrepancies.
- Utilized the standard property book system and redesigned the installation/table of distribution and allowances, maintaining a 95% accuracy rate.
- Maintained records and processed organization's documents on a daily basis.
- Completed monthly reports for presentation to top-level management.
- Prepared cash collection vouchers, fiscal reports; reconciled all accounts payable/receivable.
- Typed correspondence and messages for transmittal overseas.

DATA ENTRY OPERATOR. Vause Equipment Co., Vancouver, WA (1992-94). Operated online terminals off the main computer system from the postal service.

COMPUTERS
Familiar with most popular computer operating systems and software including Microsoft Word, Excel, and PowerPoint; operate facsimile machines, 10-key calculators, photocopiers, digital cameras, multiline phones, and other office automation equipment.

PERSONAL
Dedicated professional who enjoys challenges, problem-solving, and decision-making.

OFFICE MANAGER

Exact Name of Person
Title or Position
Name of Company
Address (no., street)
Address (city, state, zip)

OFFICE
MANAGER
for a
retail
equipment
company

Dear Exact Name of Person: (or Dear Sir or Madam if answering a blind ad.)

With the enclosed resume, I would like to make you aware of my interest in the job of User Support Technician which you recently advertised. I can provide outstanding personal and professional references at the appropriate time.

As you will see from my resume, I hold an Associate's Degree and possess the strong computer knowledge which your ad requests. In my job as Office Manager of Async, Inc., I have played a key role in computerizing many manual functions. Since our company provides rental equipment for large industrial clients, I work with our corporate clients to handle all kinds of matters related to billing and service issues.

With a reputation as a self-starter and resourceful problem solver, I am highly computer literate and offer a proven ability to rapidly master new software and applications.

I hope you will contact me to suggest a time when we might meet in person to further discuss the details of the job in which you advertised. I feel certain that I could quickly become a valuable resource to you.

Sincerely,

Tisha E. Wainwright

TISHA E. WAINWRIGHT

1110½ Hay Street, Fayetteville, NC 28305 • preppub@aol.com • (910) 483-6611

OBJECTIVE

To offer my experience with word processing, spreadsheets, and database programs along with my proven skills in office management to an organization that can use a hardworking self-starter known for excellent problem-solving and troubleshooting abilities.

EDUCATION

Associate of Science degree in **Secretarial Sciences,** Topeka Community College, Topeka, KS, 2002. Completed this degree in my spare time while excelling in my full-time job.
Extensive formal and hands-on training in computer operations, word processing, spreadsheet, and databases.

COMPUTERS

Proficient with Microsoft Word, Excel, and Access as well as Pagemaker, Adobe Photoshop, and QuarkXpress. Utilize QuickBooks and Quicken.

EXPERIENCE

OFFICE MANAGER. Async, Inc., Topeka, KS (2004-present). Efficiently handle a wide variety of office management and secretarial functions which include handling accounts payable and receivable, collections, payroll, typing, filing, and answering telephones for this company which provides rental equipment to large industrial plants.
- Played a key role in helping this company move from a manual billing and purchase order system to a computerized system which now handles those functions as well as work orders.
- Am known for my excellent customer service skills in working with large corporate clients.

SECRETARY. Keyser, Inc., Topeka, KS (2003-04). As a member of the Safety, Health, & Environmental Department, performed secretarial duties for the Manager, Safety Specialist, and Fire Marshal; my responsibilities included typing, answering telephones, relaying messages, distributing mail, and copying documents.
- Frequently acted as the "right arm" to busy executives, and was commended for my gracious style of serving the public.
- Typed safety procedures, monthly reports, memorandums, and letters using Microsoft Word, Excel, and Access.

INVENTORY CONTROL OPERATOR. Peterson Light Co., Topeka, KS (2000-03). As a member of the Physical Distribution Department, performed data entry in order to produce a bill of lading for shipment of fixtures using mainframe computer system.
- Provided customer service while handling a busy telephone system.
- Typed letters as well as bills of lading for the Traffic Analyst.
- Provided shipping information.

TECHNICAL AIDE. Cauldwell Power Inc., Topeka, KS (1994-00).
1998-00: As part of the Procurement Engineering Department, operated a computer system using Microsoft software in order to track the procurement of parts, generate reports, and create charts used for analysis and decision making.
- Prepared memorandums and letters.
1994-98: As part of the Regulatory Compliance Department, operated a computer system to track periodic testing of equipment.
- Produced schedules and reports for groups performing tests.

PERSONAL

Can provide outstanding personal and professional references.

OFFICE MANAGER & BOOKKEEPER

Date

Exact Name of Person
Exact Title
Exact Name of Company
Address
City, State, Zip

**OFFICE
MANAGER
&
BOOKKEEPER**
for a retailer
of
motorcycles
&
marine
products

Dear Exact Name of Person (or Dear Sir or Madam if answering a blind ad):

With the enclosed resume, I would like to make you aware of my background in office operations and purchasing as well as the versatile computer skills I could put to work for you.

From my enclosed resume, you will see that I am currently employed as an Office Manager and Bookkeeper for Cresswell Recreation Sales. I have become highly adept at balancing numerous areas of responsibility and functional operations simultaneously in this retail business. I have earned a reputation for my ability to provide customers with information and services in a business which sells big-ticket items such as motorcycles, marine products, and accessories for both types of products. I ensure that customers are treated well which has helped build a strong repeat customer base. I have been entrusted with the responsibility of accepting applications from prospective buyers and preparing contracts for purchases. I have gained experience in training new office employees and am known for my ability to establish warm working relationships with others.

I completed an Associate's degree in Data Processing from Lexington Community College, where I excelled in course work such as accounting, bookkeeping, and mathematics as well as typing, shorthand, data processing, and business correspondence. Highly proficient in utilizing computers to improve office efficiency, I am skilled in using Microsoft Word, Excel, and PowerPoint.

If you can use a motivated, hardworking professional who could become a contributing member of your team, I hope you will contact me to suggest a time when we might meet in person to discuss your needs. I will bring excellent letters of reference with me, and I am certain I can excel in any type of testing your company administers. Thank you in advance for your time and courtesies.

Sincerely,

Mary J. Stubbs

MARY J. STUBBS

1110½ Hay Street, Fayetteville, NC 28305   •   preppub@aol.com   •   (910) 483-6611

OBJECTIVE

To offer my versatile skills and strong background in all functional areas of office operations and administration to include bookkeeping, making financial decisions, sales, and computer operations to an organization in need of a customer service professional.

EXPERIENCE

OFFICE MANAGER and **BOOKKEEPER.** Cresswell Recreation Sales, Lexington, KY (2001-present). Have become highly adept at balancing numerous areas of responsibility and functional operations simultaneously in this retail business.

- Earned a reputation for my ability to provide customers with information and services in a business which sells big-ticket items such as motorcycles, marine products, and accessories for both types of product.
- Ensure that customers are treated fairly and honestly which helps build a strong repeat customer base.
- Accept applications from prospective buyers and prepare contracts documenting their purchases.
- Process payroll and prepare state and federal tax returns as well as complete W-2s for an average of 20 employees each fiscal year.
- Control daily receipts and bank transactions as well as reconcile bank statements and disbursement ledgers.
- Prepare warranty claims for customers and submit them to manufacturers for payment using automated systems for processing.
- Manage the inventory control process from ordering, through stocking, to the final sale of parts and accessories.
- Maintain accurate and up-to-date computerized records of the inventory figures.
- Answer phone and in-person inquiries and direct customers to the correct department and person to assist them.
- Train parts department employees and new office employees.
- Was the only on-site Notary Public which allowed me to document title work for customers and make the process easier and quicker for them.

ADMINISTRATIVE ASSISTANT. Moncks Corner Honda Sales, Lexington, KY (1999-01). Handled a wide range of sales support and administrative activities for this business which merged with Cresswell Motors in 2004. Controlled daily receipts, bank reconciliations, and disbursements.

- Processed payroll and payroll taxes as well as corporate state and federal tax returns and employees' W-2 forms each fiscal year.
- Assisted customers in completing applications and prepared contracts used to request financing for purchases.
- Prepared documents needed to obtain titles to vehicles and notarized documents for customers. Set up a system of vehicle inventory ledgers.

Highlights of other experience: Took service orders from customers by phone and then filed and posted them as well as ordering parts for Hines Heating & Air, Lexington, KY.

COMPUTERS

Use Macintosh and IBM operating system for inventory and documentation purposes. Familiar with several types of software programs such as Microsoft Word, Excel, and PowerPoint.

EDUCATION

Earned an Associate's degree in Data Processing from University of Kentucky Lexington Community College, KY, 2002.

PERSONAL

Am detail-oriented and conscientious. Offer a track record of dedication to excellence and the ability to adapt to new procedures and methods. Excellent references on request.

OFFICE MANAGER

Date

Exact Name of Person
Title or Position
Name of Company
Address (number and street)
Address (city, state, and zip)

**OFFICE
MANAGER
&
CUSTOMER
SERVICE
COORDINATOR**
for a metal &
construction
company

Dear Exact Name of Person: (or Sir or Madam if answering a blind ad.)

With the enclosed resume, I would like to make you aware of my background in accounts management, personnel supervision, and customer service as well as my strong organizational, interpersonal, and communication skills.

While recently completing my Bachelor of Science degree, I excelled academically and was named to the Dean's List seven times. Prior to earning my degree, I excelled in both military and civilian environments. From 1992 to 1996, I served my country and was promoted rapidly ahead of my peers to Administrative Assistant and Supply Manager.

In one job in Illinois, I began as a Receptionist answering a 30-line phone system for a 1100-employee company which provided online computer services. I rapidly advanced to Accounts Manager and Shift Supervisor, which placed me in charge of eight people. In that job, I made hundreds of decisions daily which involved committing the company's technical resources. In addition to dispatching technicians and managing liaison with companies such as The Omni National Bank, Chase Bank, and K-Mart, I was authorized to commit company resources valued at up to $500,000 in the form of kits.

My husband and I are eager to replant our roots in Indiana, and I am seeking employment with a company that can use a highly motivated hard worker who is known for excellent decision-making, problem-solving, and organizational skills.

If you can use a resourceful and versatile individual with administrative and computer skills, I hope you will contact me to suggest a time when we can discuss your present and future needs and how I might meet them. I can provide outstanding personal and professional references, and I thank you in advance for your time and consideration.

Sincerely,

Carmen C. Blige

CARMEN C. BLIGE

1110½ Hay Street, Fayetteville, NC 28305 • preppub@aol.com • (910) 483-6611

OBJECTIVE   To contribute to an organization that can use a highly motivated young professional who offers strong administrative abilities, computer operations skills, as well as a reputation as a resourceful problem solver, decision maker, and organizer.

EDUCATION   **Bachelor of Science** degree in **Government and History** (double major), Northern Illinois University, DeKalb, IL, 2004. Earned a place on the Dean's List seven times.

EXPERIENCE   **OFFICE MANAGER** and **CUSTOMER SERVICE COORDINATOR.** Highland Metal & Construction, DeKalb, IL (2004-present). Manage this busy office of a company which erects metal buildings and garages.
- Prepare local, state, and federal payroll reports. Resolve a wide range of problems while overseeing office supplies and maintaining communication with customers.

ADMINISTRATIVE ASSISTANT. Northern Illinois University, DeKalb, IL (2003-04). While completing my college degree, worked in the Graduate School program preparing teaching packets for submission to the Education Department of Illinois.
- Computerized complete program on 200 graduate students.
- Personally created the layout of the school's catalogue of approximately 100 pages.

ACCOUNTS MANAGER & SHIFT SUPERVISOR. DataCom, Inc., DeKalb, IL (2000-02). Began as a Receptionist answering a 30-line phone system for this 1100-employee company which provided online computer support services; was promoted to a supervisory position and acted as the liaison with major accounts including the Chase Bank, Omni National Bank, K-Mart, and others; managed eight people on the second shift.
- Was granted extensive authority to commit the company's resources; for example, authorized the supply to customers of kits which ranged in valued from $10,000 to $500,000.
- Functioned as a Dispatcher, handling as many as 400 calls which required me to dispatch technicians to companies. Was frequently commended for my resourceful problem-solving style and for my tact when dealing with anxious customers experiencing technical difficulties.

CREDIT CLERK, CASHIER, SALES CLERK. Terre Haute and Indianapolis, IN (1996-00). While moving frequently with my husband who was in the military, excelled in jobs as a retail Layaway Clerk for Marshalls, Cashier for K-Mart, and Sales Clerk for Cracker Barrel.

Other military experience:
ADMINISTRATIVE ASSISTANT & SUPPLY MANAGER. U.S. Army, Ft. Knox, KY (1992-96). Was promoted ahead of my peers to the rank of E-5 while serving my country in the U.S. Army.
- As a Supply Manager, ordered and managed the distribution of office supplies and equipment.

COMPUTERS   Proficient with Microsoft Word, Excel and PowerPoint software programs.
While serving in the U.S. Army, completed numerous technical training programs related to these and other areas: supply management, office administration, human resources.

PERSONAL   Very well organized individual who offers a proven ability to manage multiple priorities and produce excellent results in numerous areas under tight deadlines. Offer excellent written and oral communication skills along with strong research and analytical abilities. Excellent references.

OFFICE MANAGER & LICENSED REPRESENTATIVE

Date

Exact Name of Person
Title or Position
Name of Company
Address (no., street)
Address (city, state, zip)

**OFFICE MANAGER
& LICENSED
REPRESENTATIVE**
for an
insurance
and
financial
services
company

Dear Exact Name of Person: (or Dear Sir or Madam if answering a blind ad.)

   With the enclosed resume, I would like to make you aware of my interest in the position of Office Manager while also acquainting you with my strong clerical and management skills and experience related to this job.

   In my current job I am excelling as Office Manager & Licensed Office Representative for Nationwide Insurance & Financial Services. I became employed by my father's insurance agency shortly after graduating from high school and have become a Licensed Insurance Agent while also acting as Office Manager. I quote and write insurance applications for Auto, Life, Health and Fire coverage including homeowners, renters, boatowners, personal liability umbrella, inland marine, and commercial.

   I have become skilled in all aspects of managing an insurance agency, including the necessity of re-underwriting our book of business in order to remain a profitable agency. I have also learned how to operate a multiline single-line business in order to maintain a quality book of business and have gained expert understanding of Nationwide policies, procedures, and practices. I prospect for new customers and work with existing clients to determine their need for certain products and to tailor those products to their particular needs and situations.

   You will also see on the resume that I have completed a Bachelor of Science degree in Education at the University of Wyoming in Laramie. I completed this degree in my spare time while excelling in my full-time job. I excelled academically and graduated magna cum laude.

   I hope you will give me the opportunity to show you in person that I am the individual you are seeking. With a reputation as a dedicated hard worker, I pride myself on doing every job to the best of my ability, and I can assure you in advance that I could become a valuable member of your organization.

Sincerely,

Felicia S. Mouzone

FELICIA S. MOUZONE

1110½ Hay Street, Fayetteville, NC 28305 • preppub@aol.com • (910) 483-6611

OBJECTIVE

To contribute to an organization that can use a dedicated hard worker who excels in establishing and maintaining effective working relationships while providing excellent personal service and applying my expert knowledge of insurance.

EDUCATION

Completed a **Bachelor of Science degree in Education**, University of Wyoming, Laramie, WY, 2001.
- Completed this degree in my spare time while excelling in my full-time job.
- Excelled academically; graduated **magna cum laude.**

LICENSE

Licensed Insurance Agent, Property and Casualty as well as Life, Accident, and Health with the State of Wyoming.

TRAINING

Extensive training in all aspects of quoting and writing insurance applications for Auto; Fire (Homeowners, Renters, Boatowners, Personal Liability Umbrella, Inland Marine, and Commercial); Life and Health.

EXPERIENCE

OFFICE MANAGER & LICENSED OFFICE REPRESENTATIVE. Nationwide Insurance & Financial Services, Cheyenne, WY (1998-present). Became employed by my father's insurance agency shortly after graduating from high school; have become a Licensed Insurance Agent while also acting as Office Manager.

- Quote and write insurance applications for Auto; Life and Health; and Fire coverage including homeowners, renters, boatowners, personal liability umbrella, inland marine, and commercial.
- Have become skilled in all aspects of managing an insurance agency, including the necessity of re-underwriting our book of business in order to remain a profitable agency; have also learned how to operate a multiline business in order to maintain a quality book of business.
- Have gained expert understanding of Nationwide policies, procedures, and practices.
- Prospect for new customers and work with existing clients to determine their need for certain products and to tailor those products to their particular needs and situations.
- Although I am working in my father's office, have gained the respect and loyalty of the customers we service because of my sincere concern for their well being and my professional approach to serving their needs.
- Have learned that the insurance business is a relationship business, and have established warm relationships with all of our policyholders.
- Have a great respect for my supervisor and the way he does business; have played a key role in his being named a Top 100 Agent.

PERSONAL

Have grown up in the insurance business and consider it "home." My career goal is to operate my own insurance agency. I am confident that I could be successful in this highly competitive business which I thoroughly enjoy. Derive much personal satisfaction from identifying and selling insurance products for specific situations.

OPERATIONS CLERK

Date

Exact Name of Person
Title or Position
Name of Company
Address (no., street)
Address (city, state, zip)

Dear Exact Name of Person: (or Dear Sir or Madam if answering a blind ad.)

With the enclosed resume, I would like to make you aware of my strong desire to become permanently employed by Nextel in a role in which I could benefit the company through my computer knowledge, sales skills, and customer service experience.

As you will see from my resume, I am currently excelling as an Operations Clerk working for Nextel in Providence, where I am employed in a temporary full-time position through Olsten Staffing. In this job I am involved in a wide range of activities involving computer operations, customer service, and administrative support. I have become proficient in using Eudora Mail, in utilizing the LAN system, and in researching and coordinating service orders in the most efficient manner while applying my knowledge of Nextel's telecommunications operations.

In my previous job in Providence as an Administrative Aide, I became a valuable employee and was entrusted with many complex responsibilities because of my demonstrated initiative, intelligence, and customer service skills. Since I am bilingual in Spanish and English, I conducted new hires of employees in both languages and frequently translated communication between production workers and office personnel.

My computer skills are excellent and I enjoy learning new software. While in my previous job I completed a major project in which I computerized data entry for all production workers' payroll. I am knowledgeable of software including Microsoft Word, Excel, and PowerPoint.

Please consider me for a position within Nextel which can utilize my excellent communication, problem solving, and decision making skills. I can provide outstanding personal and professional references including very strong references from Nextel personnel in the regional and district office with whom I work.

Sincerely,

Tiffany K. Mitchell

TIFFANY K. MITCHELL

1110½ Hay Street, Fayetteville, NC 28305 • preppub@aol.com • (910) 483-6611

OBJECTIVE
To offer my experience in sales, marketing, and customer service to an organization that would benefit from my gracious style of developing customer relationships, my computer operations skills, as well as my excellent communication skills including fluency in Spanish.

LANGUAGE
Fluently speak, read, and write Spanish

COMPUTERS
Knowledgeable of software including Microsoft Word, Excel, and PowerPoint

TRAINING
Completed Telecommunications Training, Rhode Island College, Providence, RI, 2002.

EXPERIENCE
OPERATIONS CLERK. Nextel Communications, Providence, RI (2002-present). In a temporary assignment through Olsten Staffing, am involved in a wide range of activities related to customer service and operations support; am now knowledgeable of Nextel's internal policies and procedures, and have earned a reputation as a hard worker known for my tactful and gracious style of interacting with others as well as my excellent planning and organizational skills.
- Have become proficient in using Eudora Mail, in utilizing the LAN system, and in researching and coordinating service orders while becoming knowledgeable of Nextel's telecommunications operations.
- Process Providence district contractor invoices through CLMRS; process vendor invoices.
- Perform follow up communication with the accounting department related to past due bills and delinquent payments in order to verify receipt and payments.
- Utilizing communication received through a LAN, process information related to problem accounts and transmit to appropriate supervisors for action; coordinate with supervisors and then present supervisors' replies to the manager for decision making; transmit manager's remarks via LAN to the regional office.
- Maintain files; receive information from service technician prior to calling in request to drop placement and prior to entering information into data logs.
- Consolidate President's Report information received from supervisors into the District report and send the report via LAN to regional office by specified dates.
- Maintain personnel files with up-to-date address changes, transfers, and other data; transmit information via LAN to regional office.
- Receive, review, and distribute mail.
- Provide customer service while answering the telephone and handling questions.

ADMINISTRATIVE AIDE & SPANISH INTERPRETER. Culbreathe Linen, Providence, RI (1995-02). Became a valuable employee and was entrusted with many complex responsibilities because of my demonstrated initiative, intelligence, and customer service skills.
- Conducted new hires of employees in both English and Spanish.
- Acted as a translator between office staff and Spanish-speaking applicants.
- On my own initiative and while working numerous extra hours, completed a major project in which I computerized data entry for all production associates' payroll.
- Handled extensive computer data entry including inputting data into computer to figure poundage processed for the plant and for each production associate.
- Composed and compiled numerous reports including observation report for production employees.
- Handled a busy switchboard; answered calls from clients and prospective employees.
- Ordered all office supplies.

PERSONAL
Can provide excellent references. Known for absolute reliability, honesty, and dedication.

PARALEGAL CLERK

Date

Exact Name of Person
Title or Position
Name of Company
Address (number and street)
Address (city, state, and zip)

**PARALEGAL
CLERK**
for a
local
judge's
office

Dear Exact Name of Person: (or Sir or Madam if answering a blind ad.)

With the enclosed resume, I would like to acquaint you with my background as an office clerk, secretary, and receptionist while also making you aware of the strong organizational, interpersonal, and communication skills I could offer your organization. I have recently moved to the Detroit area, and I am seeking employment with an organization that can use a hardworking young professional with a proven ability to make significant contributions to efficiency and profitability.

As you will see from my resume, I offer more than ten years of office experience and have demonstrated my ability to excel in various environments including the real estate and legal fields. Most recently I worked for a Circuit Court Judge and played a key role in collecting delinquent child support payments. Prior to that, I was promoted by a prominent real estate firm from Receptionist to head Secretary.

A skilled communicator, I have earned a reputation for having a talent for dealing effectively with people. I believe my hardworking nature and ability to work with little or no supervision have been the keys to my success.

If you can use a motivated professional with strong office and computer operations skills, I hope you will contact me to suggest a time when we can discuss your present and future needs, and how I might meet them. I can provide outstanding personal and professional references, and I thank you in advance for your time and consideration.

Sincerely,

Rolanda A. Junot

ROLANDA A. JUNOT

1110½ Hay Street, Fayetteville, NC 28305 • preppub@aol.com • (910) 483-6611

OBJECTIVE   To benefit an organization that can use an experienced secretary, office clerk, and receptionist with exceptional organizational, communication and interpersonal skills.

COMPUTERS   Proficient with Microsoft Word, Access, Excel and PowerPoint

EDUCATION   Graduated from The School of Paralegal Technology, Grand Rapids, MI, 2001.
Graduated from the School for Secretaries, Grand Rapids, MI, 1994.
Graduated from Grand Rapids High School, Grand Rapids, MI, 1992.

EXPERIENCE   **Promoted twice while employed for Circuit Court Judge Andrew W. Lawson's Office, Grand Rapids, MI:**
2002-04: PARALEGAL CLERK. Demonstrated excellent organizational and time-management skills, effectively handling collection of money owed to clients in child support cases. Recently resigned from my position when my family moved to Detroit.
*   Through my persistence and attention to detail, played a key role in reducing the percentage of delinquent payments and improving recovery figures. Wrote demands to ensure the recovery of client monies and prepared weekly and monthly reports on collections. Coordinated with numerous court officials.

2000-02: RECEPTIONIST. Performed a variety of secretarial and clerical office tasks while refining my knowledge of legal and office practices.
*   Received special recognition commending my efforts from Judge Lawson.
*   Operated a multiline phone system, answering and directing phone calls and taking messages. Typed business letters and other correspondence.
*   Handled scheduling of appointments and contacted clients.
*   Tracked inventory and maintained appropriate stock levels of all office supplies.

Excelled in two promotions while employed with Aquinas Realty, Grand Rapids, MI:
1997-00: HEAD SECRETARY. As Head Secretary, managed the production of other office workers and secretarial staff. Communicated with clients and agents, scheduling and maintaining the appointment calendar for a busy real estate office.
*   Wrote and typed newspaper advertisements, letters, and memos.
*   Familiarized myself with local real estate market in order to better serve customers and agents. Made travel arrangements, such as hotel and airline reservations.

1994-97: RECEPTIONIST. Performed general office duties for a busy realty office; developed excellent telephone and customer service skills.
*   Operated a multiline phone system, answering and directing calls and taking messages.
*   Served as liaison between the agency and the customer, answering customer inquiries for information on specific properties and requesting listing information from clients; photocopied and filed letters and other documents.

Other experience:
APPRENTICE. Davenport College of Business, Grand Rapids, MI (1992-94). Worked a secretarial apprenticeship while studying at the School for Secretaries. Learned basic skills of letter writing, shorthand, proper telephone etiquette, written and verbal communication, and presenting a professional appearance.

PERSONAL   Excellent personal and professional references are available upon request.

PARALEGAL SPECIALIST

Date

Exact Name of Person
Title or Position
Name of Company
Address (no., street)
Address (city, state, zip)

**PARALEGAL
SPECIALIST**
for the
Department
of
Transportation

Dear Sir or Madam:

Can you use a hardworking young professional who has excelled as a paralegal and legal secretary?

I will be moving to Fayetteville to join my husband, a military professional who expects to be stationed there for several more years. I can provide outstanding personal and professional references from current and previous employers who would describe me, I am certain, as a cheerful and adaptable office professional who can be counted on to meet tight deadlines and produce quality work under pressure.

In my current job I work with a 15-person staff of attorneys, paralegals, and secretaries with the Department of Transportation in Florida. Since the department's primary mission is to continue building Florida's network of roads and superhighways, we deal routinely with contractors who are in the field valuing real estate that the Transportation Department might want to buy. I use the dictaphone routinely and work with several popular software programs while also functioning as an executive secretary, organizing and scheduling meetings among the contractors and legal staff.

You would find me to be an intelligent person who is good at problem solving in office environments. In my paralegal studies, I excelled academically and achieved a 3.9 GPA.

I hope you will call or write me soon to suggest a time convenient for us to meet and discuss your current and future needs and how I might serve them. Thank you in advance for your time.

Sincerely yours,

Janet Llaneta

JANET LLANETA

1110½ Hay Street, Fayetteville, NC 28305 • preppub@aol.com • (910) 483-6611

OBJECTIVE   To contribute to an organization that can use a poised young professional who offers specialized training and experience as a paralegal and legal receptionist.

EDUCATION   **Associate of Paralegal** degree, Tampa College, FL, 2001.
- Excelled academically with a 3.9 GPA based on a 4.0 scale.

Fields of study included the following:

Civil Litigation	Legal Research I & II
Legal Document Writing	Torts
Real Estate	Criminal Law
Legal Vocabulary	Business Law
Computer Applications	Accounting I, II, and III
Eminent Domain	

COMPUTERS
- Familiar with Microsoft Word and Excel
- Offer proven ability to rapidly master interoffice software packages
- Experienced in using e-mail

EXPERIENCE   **PARALEGAL SPECIALIST.** State of Florida Department of Transportation, Tampa, FL (2003-present). Earned a reputation as a cheerful worker who readily adapts to new working environments as needed while working within a department that is primarily concerned with the mission of building roads throughout Florida; interface regularly with contractors who are "in the field" valuing properties that the department might want to purchase in order to continue Florida's highway transportation system.

- Work with a 15-person staff of attorneys, paralegals, and secretaries.
- Routinely utilize software including Microsoft Word, Excel, CICS, and Samas.
- Develop expertise in the area of preparing legal documents.
- Prepare expert witness contracts as well as discovery requests, orders, and letters.
- For several months, was assigned to operate a busy three-line switchboard and became known for my telephone etiquette.
- Use the dictaphone on a daily basis in the process of transcribing communication of attorneys.
- Functioned frequently in the capacity of an **Executive Secretary** as I organized and scheduled meetings among attorneys and contractors so they could meet face-to-face over matters of land valuation.

SALES ASSISTANT. Thom McAn, Tampa, FL (2002-03). Became skilled in working with customers in a retail environment while assisting people with shoe selection; was entrusted with the responsibility of opening and closing the store.

- Won the respect of management because of my attention to detail when handling financial transactions and accounting for cash.
- Helped the store cement its relationships with previous customers through my warm personality and customer service skills.

WAITRESS/HOSTESS. Pizza Hut, Tampa, FL (1999-02). Was rapidly promoted to greater responsibility related to handling cash and receipts in this popular "fast-food" restaurant.

PERSONAL   Known as a conscientious, professional young person who excels in dealing with people.

PAYROLL ADMINISTRATOR

Date

Exact Name of Person
Exact Title
Exact Name of Company
Address
City, State, Zip

Dear Exact Name of Person (or Dear Sir or Madam if answering a blind ad):

Can you use an experienced Payroll Manager with exceptional supervisory, organizational, and communication skills as well as a background in payroll and benefits administration, accounts receivable/payable, and payroll tax regulations in multi-state and multiunit environments?

As you will see, I am excelling as Payroll Administrator for the manufacturing division of Berringer Wholesale company, where I manage a $52 million annual payroll for three facilities employing more than 550 personnel. I create, update, and maintain employee files, entering new hires into the system. In addition, I act as a liaison between the employees and the garnishment trustees of various organizations, such as tax officials and bankruptcy courts, and I interact with Social Services and lending institutions regarding various issues related to the verification of employment, child support, and salary information.

In a previous position with Hunter Golf Courses, Inc., I managed a $1.5 million annual payroll for 150-350 employees. I prepared daily sales recaps, state/federal payroll taxes, quarterly/annual tax forms, and monthly sales tax reports for a multi-course, multi-state operation. Earlier, as a Supervising Accounting Clerk for Dyncorp, Inc., I supervised five accounting clerks and prepared financial statements for the corporation.

I have completed nearly three years of college in Pre-Law Government at Texas Wesleyan University, where I was awarded the President's Scholarship. I maintained a 3.9 GPA throughout my academic career while working full-time. Through training and experience, I am skilled in operating popular accounting and office-related software including the ADP payroll software, Microsoft Word, Access, Excel, QuickBooks, and Adobe PageMaker.

If you can use a self-motivated and experienced Payroll Manager with extensive payroll and benefits administration experience, I look forward to hearing from you soon to arrange a time when we might meet and discuss your needs. I assure you in advance that I have an outstanding reputation and could quickly become a valuable asset to your organization.

Sincerely,

Stephanie P. McNeill

STEPHANIE P. McNEILL

1110½ Hay Street, Fayetteville, NC 28305   •   preppub@aol.com   •   (910) 483-6611

OBJECTIVE

To benefit an organization that can use an experienced accounting professional and payroll manager with exceptional communication and organizational skills along with a background in multi-state, corporate, and manufacturing environments.

COMPUTERS

Skilled in the operation of most common accounting and office software, including these: ADP Payroll, Microsoft Access, Excel, Word, QuickBooks, and Adobe PageMaker.

EXPERIENCE

PAYROLL ADMINISTRATOR. Bessingers Wholesale Co., Fort Worth, TX (2003-present). Oversee all aspects of a $52 million payroll and benefits administration for three factories employing 550 personnel.

- Create, update, and maintain employee files accurately, entering all new employees into the system.
- Process credit union payroll deductions for employees while coordinating and integrating charitable donations into the payroll deduction system.
- Create various human resources reports, tracking and monitoring employee insurance, 401-K, garnishments, and credit union deductions and deposits.
- Prepare and produce monthly statistics and reports as requested for the Employment Security Commission. Work closely with human resource managers for each of the three factories and assist them when an employee has a question concerning benefits.

OFFICE MANAGER. El Pancho, Inc., Fort Worth, TX (2001-02). Managed all office operations for this family-owned business that manufactured salsa for sale to food service distributors and vendors. Managed accounts receivable, accounts payable, payroll administration, and billing.

- Negotiated contracts with vendors and other food brokers.
- Scheduled, attended, and set up demonstrations in addition to food trade shows.
- Planned, developed, and implemented innovative and creative marketing programs, sales promotions, and strategies.
- Assisted in the updating and maintenance of the company's new web site store.
- Interacted closely with store managers to ensure that customers were receiving the highest possible levels of customer service.
- Coordinated advertising and acted as liaison with media and sales representatives.

ASSISTANT BOOKKEEPER. Hunter Golf Courses, Inc., Fort Worth, TX (1999-01). Managed an annual payroll of $1.5 million for 150-350 employees. Reconciled bank accounts for 20 franchises nationwide. Handled accounts payable and receivable for several subsidiary companies.

- Prepared daily sales recaps and monthly sales tax reports for courses in multiple states.
- Processed state and federal payroll taxes in addition to federal and state quarterly and annual tax forms. Administered and developed a census program for the 401-K plan.

ACCOUNTING CLERK. Dyncorp, Fort Worth, TX (1994-1999). Performed a variety of payroll administration and accounting duties while supervising five accounting clerks; duties were essentially the same as those in the above position. Prepared financial statements.

EDUCATION

Completed nearly three years of college in Pre-Law Government at Texas Wesleyan University. Maintained a 3.9 GPA while working full-time.

PROCESSING ASSISTANT

Date

Exact Name of Person
Title or Position
Name of Company
Address (number and street)
Address (city, state, and zip)

**PROCESSING
ASSISTANT**
for a DMV in
Alabama

Dear Exact Name of Person: (or Sir or Madam if answering a blind ad.)

With the enclosed resume, I would like to make you aware of my background as a motivated young professional with exceptional communication and organizational skills who offers a track record of success in office administration, customer service, computer operation, and data entry.

As you will see from my enclosed resume, I am currently employed as a Processing Assistant for the State of Alabama's Department of Motor Vehicles in Tuscaloosa. I have been employed in a full-time position for this organization for the past three years. I perform a variety of clerical and administrative support duties which require me to be proficient in every aspect of office operations. I handle extensive public contact including handling incoming calls and professionally taking messages for supervisors, inspectors, and process officers. I communicate with the public regarding proper fees for various classifications of license plates, and I also communicate with taxpayers, insurance companies, and law enforcement agencies in receiving and transmitting information.

In addition, I perform a variety of activities pertaining to receiving investigative reports and records and entering data into a computer as well as filing and maintaining reports. Responsible for payroll worksheets turned in to me biweekly, I compose letters, memorandums, reports, spreadsheets, graphs, and other correspondence.

You would find me to be a dedicated, highly motivated professional who understands the importance of skillful customer service and who enjoys working with others. I am always glad to share my extensive knowledge of personnel recordkeeping and reporting with colleagues, and I pride myself on my ability to produce consistently perfect work. You would also find that I am highly effective in using the telephone, and I offer familiarity with the full range of office equipment.

I hope you will call or write soon to suggest a time convenient for us to meet and discuss your current and future needs and how I might serve them. Thank you in advance for your time.

Sincerely yours,

Marilyn Scott

MARILYN SCOTT

1110½ Hay Street, Fayetteville, NC 28305   •   preppub@aol.com   •   (910) 483-6611

OBJECTIVE

To contribute to an organization that can use a hard worker and fast learner with extensive computer operations experience, proven skills in customer service and public relations, along with a reputation as a dependable hard worker known for reliability and dependability.

COMPUTERS

Proficient with Microsoft Word, Excel, and Access

EDUCATION

Completed approximately 80 college credits toward a Criminal Justice Curriculum, Southern Union State Community College, Wadley, AL, 2001-03.
Completed my high school degree through Southern Union State Community College, 1999.

EXPERIENCE

PROCESSING ASSISTANT IV. State of Alabama Department of Motor Vehicles, Tuscaloosa, AL (2002-present). Have been employed full-time with the DMV for the past three years. Perform a clerical and administrative support duties which require me to be proficient in every aspect of office operations.

- **Public relations:** Handle extensive public contact including incoming calls and professionally taking messages for supervisors, inspectors, and process officers; communicate with the public regarding proper fees for various classifications of license plates; communicate with taxpayers, insurance companies, and law enforcement agencies in receiving and transmitting information.
- **Record and reports:** Perform a variety of activities pertaining to receiving investigative reports and records and entering data into a computer; file and maintain files of reports.
- **Payroll:** Compile data from payroll worksheets turned in to me biweekly.
- **Written communication:** Compose letters, memorandums, reports, spreadsheets, graphs, and correspondence.
- **Office operations:** On a daily basis, operate a wide variety of equipment including personal computers, printers, calculators, fax, copy machines, and pagers.
- **Files:** Maintain files related to thefts, bad checks, motor vehicle dealers, notice and storage, registration, odometer violations, special investigations, safety inspection stations, thefts of motor vehicles, tax assessments, and tax warrants.
- **Collections and other responsibilities:** Handle collections almost daily for safety inspection certificates, tax assessments, dealer and salesmen licenses, civil penalties, temporary transporter plates, registration and motor carrier application fees, overweight penalties, IRP registration fees and trip permits, temporary registration permits, as well as registration process and civil penalties.
- In my job, I demonstrate knowledge of the duties of an Inspector, VEO-I Process Officer, and Weight Officer along with knowledge of the dealer and manufacturers licensing laws, safety inspection regulations, notice and storage/mechanic's laws, weight enforcement laws, and motor carrier regulations.

STUDENT. Southern Union State Community College, Wadley, AL (2000-02). Attended college enrolled in the Criminal Justice curriculum.

CREDIT CLERK. Precision Tune, Wadley, AL (1998-00). Gained experience in working with the public while accepting payments, posting payments into a computer, preparing contracts, filing court documents, answering phones, and handling collections.

Other experience:
CASHIER. For two Piggly Wiggly grocery stores in Wadley, became a valuable employee while operating cash register, stocking groceries, and serving the public.

PERSONAL

Can provide professional and personal references at any time. Am a resourceful individual with a proven ability to optimize efficiency and maximize profit. Excellent references on request.

PROJECT SECRETARY

Date

Exact Name of Person
Title or Position
Name of Company
Address (no., street)
Address (city, state, zip)

PROJECT
SECRETARY
for an
offshore
drilling
company

Dear Exact Name of Person: (or Dear Sir or Madam if answering a blind ad.)

Can you use an energetic and highly motivated young professional who offers a background of excellent performance in office automation and clerical support activities?

As you will see from my enclosed resume, I offer a broad base of experience as a Project Secretary for Senco, Inc. I have provided outstanding administrative support, customer service, organizational ability, and clerical skills to upper-level executives of this busy corporation which manufactures construction components for offshore oil drilling platforms. I work closely with the president, vice-president, and owners of the company, preparing all executive-level correspondence and scheduling appointments as well as plan and organize meetings between corporate executives and clients, making travel arrangements, airline and hotel reservations. I also communicate directly with domestic and foreign contractors and subcontractors about clients' facility requirements while serving as purchasing agent for office supplies, computers, and office equipment.

I have completed five semesters of college course work in Administrative Technology at Glendale Community College, Glendale, AZ, and completed a number of training programs sponsored by my employers.

With a strong technical background in word processing, I have experience in using multiline phone systems, typewriters, and all of the commonly used office equipment.

I hope you will welcome my call soon to arrange a brief meeting at your convenience to discuss your current and future needs and how I might serve them. Thank you in advance for your time.

Sincerely yours,

Shelby C. Rogers

Alternate last paragraph:
I hope you will call or write soon to suggest a time convenient for us to meet and discuss your current and future needs and how I might serve them. Thank you in advance for your time.

SHELBY C. ROGERS

1110½ Hay Street, Fayetteville, NC 28305 • preppub@aol.com • (910) 483-6611

OBJECTIVE
To benefit an organization that can use an experienced project secretary and administrative assistant with strong communication skills who offers a background in commercial construction and finance environments along with a reputation as a motivated and resourceful team player.

EDUCATION
Finished five semesters of college course work in Administrative Technology at Glendale Community College, Glendale, AZ, 2004.
Completed a number of training programs with courses in the following: Executive Office Training, Microsoft Office Suite and workplace safety sponsored by Senco, Inc. Also completed a course on Inter-Office Relations sponsored by BB&T Bank.

COMPUTERS
Familiar with popular computer software packages and operating systems including:
Microsoft Word   Works   Excel   Access

EXPERIENCE
PROJECT SECRETARY. Senco, Inc., Glendale, AZ (2003-present). Provide outstanding administrative support, customer service, organizational ability, and clerical skills to upper-level executives of this busy corporation that manufactures construction components for offshore oil drilling platforms.

- Work closely with the president, vice-president, and owners of the company, preparing all executive-level correspondence and scheduling appointments.
- Plan and organize meetings between corporate executives and clients, making travel arrangements, airline and hotel reservations, etc.
- Communicate directly with domestic and foreign contractors and subcontractors about clients' facility requirements while also serving as purchasing agent for office supplies, computers, and office equipment.
- Act as liaison between clients and equipment suppliers, phone services, and other companies, ensuring quick and efficient setup of the client's office.
- Update and maintain the office filing system, ensuring that bid letters, contracts, and other important documents are organized, complete, and accurate.
- Record the minutes of meetings between Project Managers, upper-level management, and clients.
- Operate various types of office equipment, including fax machines, copiers, intercom systems, paging systems, answering machines, voice mail, and CB radios.
- Type bid letters, contracts, memos, and other executive correspondence.
- Answer a multiline phone system, directing calls to the appropriate person and taking messages when they are not available.

SECRETARY and **RECEPTIONIST.** BB&T Bank of Glendale, AZ (2000-03). Performed a variety of administrative, clerical, and receptionist duties as well as providing support and assistance to the loan department for this busy financial institution.

- Provided administrative support to commercial lenders, commercial development officers, and loan assistants; provided support to real estate and construction/perm departments.
- Assisted office manager, setting up new offices, ordering supplies, and coordinating telephone service.
- Typed letters, memos, commitment bank letters, and other correspondence.
- Demonstrated exceptional verbal communication skills through direct contact with commercial bank clients, retail customers, administrative staff, and executives.

PERSONAL
Excellent personal and professional references are available upon request.

RECORDS MANAGER

Date

Exact Name of Person
Title or Position
Name of Company
Address (number and street)
Address (city, state, and zip)

RECORDS MANAGER
for the
Federal
Labor
Relations
Authority

Dear Exact Name of Person: (or Sir or Madam if answering a blind ad.)

I am responding to your advertisement for a Records Management/Human Resources Coordinator. I feel that my background and personal qualities are ideally suited to the job you are seeking to fill, and I would welcome the opportunity to learn more about your organization and your needs.

As you will see from my enclosed resume, I offer you a reputation—acquired through hard work and relentless attention to detail—as a records management "expert." On several occasions I have been singled out to receive respected awards because of my error-free work in processing a variety of human resource records/documents under tight deadlines. I have become an excellent writer, and I have become respected for my ability to assure top-notch quality control of written products.

You would find me to be a dedicated, highly motivated professional who understands the importance of skillful customer service and who enjoys working with others. I am always glad to share my extensive knowledge of personnel record keeping and reporting with colleagues, and I pride myself on my ability to produce consistently perfect work.

You would find that I am highly effective in using the telephone, and I offer familiarity with the full range of office equipment.

I hope you will call or write soon to suggest a time convenient for us to meet and discuss your current and future needs and how I might serve them. Thank you in advance for your time.

Sincerely yours,

Lonnie Baker

LONNIE BAKER

1110½ Hay Street, Fayetteville, NC 28305   •   preppub@aol.com   •   (910) 483-6611

OBJECTIVE

To benefit an organization that can use a hardworking and innovative professional who offers strong administrative abilities including office management skills, computer operations know-how, customer service experience, and recordkeeping expertise.

EDUCATION

Associate of Science, Business Management, Riverland Community College, Austin, MN, 2000. Excelled in extensive training in administrative, leadership, and clerical areas with the U.S. Army.
- Was cited as distinguished Graduate from Advanced Individualized Training (A.I.T.).

CIVILIAN EXPERIENCE

Excelled in a track record of promotion with Federal Labor Relations Authority, Los Angeles, CA:

2003-present: RECORDS MANAGER and **ASSISTANT OFFICE MANAGER.** Train and supervise three employees, including establishing work priorities and organizing work schedules, while maintaining hundreds of personnel records and personally handling the processing of employees in transition to new work locations.
- Improved customer satisfaction and reduced administrative costs. Developed and implemented a new system of employee outprocessing which dramatically streamlined personnel administration.

2002-03: ADMINISTRATIVE ASSISTANT. Excelled in all aspects of a job which involved performing administrative, clerical, and typing duties, and answering a heavy volume of telephone calls while preparing correspondence, message orders, special and recurring reports, requisitions, forms, standard operating procedures, and other materials.
- Was entrusted to be custodian of classified documents; received, logged, inventoried, filed, and secured such documents.

2000-02: PERSONNEL CLERK. Oversaw the in-processing of new employees in a central location and supervised the transfer of personnel records to appropriate organizational locations.

Other civilian experience:
- At Langston Manufacturing Co., Austin, MO (1998-00). Prepared invoices, checked orders, and handled customer service.
- At Austin's Communications, Inc., Austin, MO (1997-98). Worked as a switchboard operator.
- At A-1 Installations, Inc., Austin, MO (1995-97). Tested chemicals and other materials.

MILITARY EXPERIENCE

PERSONNEL RECORDS SPECIALIST. U.S. Army, Fort Carson, CO (1994-95). Received a prestigious award award for achieving 100% accuracy in maintaining and supervising personnel records for more than 1,500 people; expertly maintained an extensive filing system while continuously monitoring consistency with a wide range of highly specific office procedures.

PERSONNEL SPECIALIST/ASSISTANT TEAM CHIEF. U.S. Army, Fort Benning, GA (1992-94). Was singled out to receive a respected award for my error-free work in maintaining more than 500 personnel records; assured quality control of written products.

PERSONAL

Always dedicate myself to my job. Am highly motivated and try to motivate others. Feel I am an expert in maximizing the effectiveness of the telephone. Enjoy customer service.

SECRETARY

Date

Exact Name of Person
Title or Position
Name of Company
Address (no., street)
Address (city, state, zip)

SECRETARY

for a
church
in
New
York
City

Dear Exact Name of Person: (or Dear Sir or Madam if answering a blind ad.)

With the enclosed resume, I would like to make you aware of my interest in discussing the position of Administrative Aide for your organization. As you will see from my resume, I have worked as Personal Assistant and Church Secretary to a Baptist minister for the past two years, and I can provide outstanding references at the appropriate time. I have read the "position description" of the job you are seeking to fill, and I feel that I am ideally suited to your needs.

I offer strong technical competencies in computer operations, bookkeeping, and office operations, and I am known for my strong command of the English language. I have made numerous contributions to productivity and efficiency during my employment with Joshua Baptist Church, and church members have often told me that I have been a key factor in the amazing growth of the church. I will always be proud that I played a role in helping the church to grow to the point that it could dedicate a new church building.

You will see from my resume that I previously worked for several government organizations as well as for other Christian organizations. I pride myself on my ability to interact graciously with others and to handle people and information with tact and sensitivity.

I would deeply appreciate your considering me for the opening, and I would be delighted to make myself available to you for a personal interview at your convenience. I know that the position you have in mind is one in which the personal relationship between you and the Administrative Aide must "work," and I would enjoy the opportunity to talk with you to see if there could be a fit between your needs and my considerable talents and gifts.

Yours sincerely,

Tori K. Gamble

TORI K. GAMBLE

1110½ Hay Street, Fayetteville, NC 28305 • preppub@aol.com • (910) 483-6611

OBJECTIVE

I want to contribute to an organization that can use an experienced secretary and administrative support professional who thrives on the challenge of increasing productivity and efficiency.

EXPERIENCE

SECRETARY. Joshua Baptist Church, New York City, NY (2003-present). Began with this church as a volunteer and became the first full-time paid secretary; have worked as the personal assistant and secretary to Pastor Anthony L. Perry throughout these years.

- **Office automation:** Played a key role in the automation of numerous manual tasks; routinely utilize computers to word process the pastor's sermons, create letters and mailings for members, and create databases used for various purposes.
- **Writing:** Have been commended for my strong written communication skills, and am considered a top-notch speller. Routinely use my analytical and research abilities to create documents and papers used for decision making purposes by church officials.
- **Bookkeeping and Tax documents:** Am involved in controlling expenses, accounting for church funds, and keeping books. Prepare 1099s for paid church workers, post contributions from church envelopes and maintain records of church contributions, and prepare individual giving statements for members on an annual basis.
- **Office management:** Maintain an inventory of supplies needed for office operations, including supplies used for special events such as Vacation Bible Study.
- **Church relations and "customer service":** Am constantly involved in assisting church members with a variety of matters, and have earned a reputation as a gracious and cordial individual with a true "helping instinct." Have been told by numerous individuals that my friendly and professional manner has been a key reason why church membership has more than doubled to the point that the church is on the eve of dedicating a new church building.

Highlights of other experience:

SECRETARY. Department of the Interior, New York City, NY. Excelled in a job as the Secretary to the Director of Development; took dictation and prepared copy in final form. Attended meetings and conferences, received visitors, and controlled public access to key officials.

SECRETARY & STENOGRAPHER. National Labor Relations Board, Houston, TX. Performed a variety of clerical, stenographic and human resource duties for the Labor Relations Board.

PROCUREMENT TECHNICIAN. Department of Defense, Houston, TX. At the Supply Division, typed purchase orders and blanket purchase agreements, reimbursement vouchers, and other procurement paperwork.

PURCHASING AGENT. Coast Guard, Jacksonville, FL. Received requests for materials, prioritized requests, and then solicited quotes and selected sources of supply after analyzing bids.

SECRETARY, WORLD EVANGELISM. Worked as a Volunteer Secretary to the President of World Evangelism. Took and transcribed dictation, performed general office work, distributed mail, maintained files, and prepared correspondence.

SECRETARY, LIGHTHOUSE MINISTRIES. Worked as a Volunteer Secretary to the Pastor of Lighthouse Ministries; took dictation, used word processing equipment, and handled visitors.

EDUCATION

Completed more than two years of college courses at Florida Community College, Jacksonville, FL. Completed numerous courses related to bookkeeping, office management, computer operations.

COMPUTERS

Proficient with Word, Excel, Access, and other customized programs.

SENIOR SECRETARY

Date

Exact Name of Person
Title or Position
Name of Company
Address (no., street)
Address (city, state, zip)

**SENIOR
SECRETARY**
for a
county
hospital
in
New
Mexico

Dear Exact Name of Person: (or Dear Sir or Madam if answering a blind ad.)

Can you use an energetic and highly motivated young professional who offers a background of excellent performance in office automation and clerical support activities?

As you will see from my enclosed resume, I offer a broad base of experience with the Dona Ana County Memorial Hospital. I have been singled out on several occasions to handle and prepare sensitive reports and other materials for management personnel in medical support and other service facilities.

I received a Bachelor of Science degree in Business Management with a concentration in International Studies from the New Mexico State University in 2004. While graduating with honors, I refined my time management and organizational skills in the process of completing a college degree and excelling in a full-time job.

With a strong technical background in word processing and graphic applications, I have experience in using multiline phone systems, typewriters, and all of the commonly used office equipment.

I hope you will welcome my call soon to arrange a brief meeting at your convenience to discuss your current and future needs and how I might serve them. Thank you in advance for your time.

Sincerely yours,

Brennie F. Hertz

Alternate last paragraph:
I hope you will call or write soon to suggest a time convenient for us to meet and discuss your current and future needs and how I might serve them. Thank you in advance for your time.

BRENNIE F. HERTZ

1110½ Hay Street, Fayetteville, NC 28305 • preppub@aol.com • (910) 483-6611

OBJECTIVE

To apply my diverse talents related to data processing, computer programming, and office administration to an organization that can use an adaptable and mature young professional with outstanding problem-solving, motivational, and communication skills.

EDUCATION

Bachelor of Science degree in **Business Management and International Studies**, New Mexico State University, Las Cruces, NM, 2004. Graduated with honors; **3.9 GPA.**

EXPERIENCE

Refined my time management skills attending college and excelling in my full-time job while employed by the Dona Ana County Memorial Hospital, Las Cruces, NM:

2003-present: SENIOR SECRETARY. Provide the Directorate for Nursing Services at DACMH with office automation and clerical support.

- Receive, screen, and distribute incoming correspondence and reports and then maintain records of actions taken and responses when made.
- Schedule and coordinate meetings and appointments for the director and assistant director; brief them on matters to be discussed and provide necessary background.
- Handpicked as the only secretary for a sensitive assignment, prepare and submit performance reports on nurses.

2001-03: ADMINISTRATIVE ASSISTANT. Handled the day-to-day office administration for a twelve-person staff in the Neurology Department.

- Enhanced my computer and clerical skills while inputting data using word processing and graphics software to produce materials including letters, reports, and manuals.
- Used my fluent Spanish language skills to act as liaison and translator between physicians, nurses and patients.
- Received special recognition for my talents in multiple roles.

1999-01: PATIENT REGISTRATION CLERK. Created, updated, and maintained the database of information on the medical history of patients. Registered patients for in- and out-patient services.

- Polished my typing and data entry skills while preparing documents, reports, and work requests.

Other experience:
CLERK/TYPIST and **SOCIAL SERVICES SPECIALIST**. Department of Social Services, Las Cruces, NM (1997-99). Was commended for my professionalism in juggling the demands of two main areas: maintaining, typing, and proofreading office files/records/documents; and represented the Department of Social Services at community workshops and local job fairs.

- Set up and oversaw a library of social service organizations throughout the state of New Mexico. Delivered two newcomer orientation briefings a month and conducted tours.

SPECIAL SKILLS

Through training and experience, am familiar with a variety of word processing and graphics applications.
Proficient with Microsoft Word, Excel, Access and PageMaker for desktop publishing duties.
Speak, read, and write Spanish fluently; am skilled as a translator.

PERSONAL

Have received training in subjects including time management and customer service skills. Can provide outstanding professional and personal references at any time.

SERVICE CENTER ASSISTANT

Date

Exact Name of Person
Title or Position
Name of Company
Address (no., street)
Address (city, state, zip)

SERVICE CENTER ASSISTANT for a telephone company

Dear Exact Name of Person: (or Dear Sir or Madam if answering a blind ad.)

I would appreciate an opportunity to talk with you soon about how I could contribute to your organization through my experience related to secretarial skills as well as my sales and customer service experience.

As you will see from my enclosed resume, I am a Service Center Assistant for BellSouth and have advanced to positions of increasing responsibility, providing direct assistance via telephone to service technicians. I process a large number of inbound service orders and repair requests, dispatching service technicians to job sites and assisting them with wiring and installation information. I act as a liaison, developing and maintaining effective relationships with various other internal departments such as the central office, facility assignors, and business office. I also work closely with officials involved in the implementation of the E-911 initiative, providing correct addresses so that emergency personnel can locate numbered street addresses.

With a reputation as a fast learner with an energetic and enthusiastic manner, I feel that among my greatest strengths are my flexibility and adaptability. Known as a good listener, I am very effective at developing a sense of teamwork among employees and motivating them to provide high quality services. In every company I have worked for, I have been effective in finding ways to contribute to the success of services and increased productivity.

I hope you will welcome my call soon to arrange a brief meeting at your convenience to discuss your current and future needs and how I might serve them. Thank you in advance for your time.

Sincerely yours,

Ophelia Clemmons

Alternate last paragraph:
I hope you will call or write me soon to suggest a time convenient for us to meet and discuss your current and future needs and how I might serve them. Thank you in advance for your time.

OPHELIA CLEMMONS

1110½ Hay Street, Fayetteville, NC 28305   •   preppub@aol.com   •   (910) 483-6611

OBJECTIVE   To benefit an organization that can use a hardworking professional with exceptional communication and organizational skills who offers a background in providing technical, clerical, and administrative support to service centers and office environments.

COMPUTERS   Familiar with many of the most popular computer operating systems and software including Microsoft Word, PowerPoint, Excel and Corel Draw.

EXPERIENCE   *With BellSouth in Savannah, GA, have advanced to positions of increasing responsibility, providing direct assistance via telephone to service technicians:*
2003-present: **SERVICE CENTER ASSISTANT.** Process a large number of inbound service orders and repair requests, dispatching service technicians to job sites and assisting them with wiring and installation information.

- Assign service orders to a "field team" of service technicians, providing assistance with repair, installation, and documentation of work orders.
- Manually access the customer loop assignment system when necessary, confirming service order assignments are completed in an accurate and timely manner.
- Perform liaison, developing and maintaining effective relationships with various other internal departments such as the central office, facility assignors, and business office.
- Work closely with officials involved in implementation of the E-911 initiative, providing correct addresses so that emergency personnel can locate numbered street addresses.
- Process all service orders and outages in a prompt and thorough manner to ensure that residential and commercial telephone service is restored as quickly as possible.

2002-03: **COLLECTIONS REPRESENTATIVE.** (through Adecco Staffing) Before advancing to a permanent position with BellSouth, excelled in this busy collections environment and became known as an articulate communicator with a talent for defusing tense situations and handling irate customers with tact and diplomacy. Called on a large volume of delinquent residential accounts, setting up payment arrangements to assist customers in satisfying their obligation.

Other experience:
SENIOR CLERK. Housing Authority of Savannah, Savannah, GA (1996-02). Assisted housing counselors with collecting case files and other documentation containing client financial history and housing needs; maintained and updated records related to payment history. Performed routine walk-through inspections to ensure that each client adheres to housing regulations.

- Ensured that all necessary legal documents were fully and accurately prepared before they were submitted to law officials for delinquent accounts.
- Entered the analysis and notes into a computer database after each inspection.

DATA ENTRY CLERK. Blue Cross/Blue Shield, Savannah, GA (1994-1996). Prioritized and distributed daily assignments to data entry clerks while performing data entry and formatting of medical claims received from doctor's offices and hospitals in this production-intensive data entry environment.

EDUCATION   Graduated from Middleground High School, Savannah, GA, 1990.

PERSONAL   Offer exceptional administrative and clerical skills; type 50 words per minute. Excellent references.

SERVICE COORDINATOR & HOUSING CONSULTANT

Date

Exact Name of Person
Exact Title
Exact Name of Company
Address
City, State, Zip

**SERVICE
COORDINATOR
&
HOUSING
CONSULTANT**
for a
mobile
home
dealer

Dear Exact Name of Person: (or Dear Sir or Madam if answering a blind ad):

With the enclosed resume, I would like to make you aware of my background as an articulate young professional with a "track record" of accomplishments in customer service, sales, finance, and office automation.

Recently I excelled as a Service Coordinator and Housing Consultant for James Merritt Mobile Homes in Santa Clara, where I became known for my strong customer focus and ability to interact effectively with individuals from diverse backgrounds. My outgoing personality and natural salesmanship led to my promotion to additional responsibilities for assisting customers in completing credit applications and closing paperwork. On my own initiative, I created and implemented a customer satisfaction survey to ensure that exceptional service is provided at all stages of the purchasing process.

Earlier as Office Manager for The Mobile Home Outlet, I oversaw the automation of accounting and clerical procedures for the office, transferring all accounting data into QuickBooks accounting software. I performed accounts payable and accounts receivable, processed the biweekly payroll, and prepared state and federal withholding taxes while administering the company's benefits plan.

Although I was highly regarded by my previous employer and can provide outstanding references at the appropriate time, I am interested in exploring career opportunities in the San Francisco area, and I feel that there might be a good "fit" between my skills and your organization's needs.

If you can use an enthusiastic young professional whose versatile skills have been tested in challenging situations, I hope you will write or call me soon to suggest a time when we might meet to discuss your needs and goals and how my background might serve them.

Sincerely,

Maria C. Gonzalez

MARIA C. GONZALEZ

1110½ Hay Street, Fayetteville, NC 28305 • preppub@aol.com • (910) 483-6611

OBJECTIVE

To benefit an organization that can use a motivated young professional with exceptional communication and organizational skills. Offer a background of excellence in office automation, sales, finance, and customer service environments.

EDUCATION

Bachelor of Arts degree in **History** with a minor in **Sociology**, Santa Clara University, Santa Clara, CA, 2002.
Associate of Arts in General Studies, College of the Canyon, Santa Clara, CA, 2000.

COMPUTERS

Familiar with the operation of many popular computer operating systems and software including Microsoft Word, Excel and QuickBooks.

EXPERIENCE

SERVICE COORDINATOR and **HOUSING CONSULTANT.** James Merritt Mobile Homes, Santa Clara, CA (2004-present). Provide sales, customer service, and operational support for one of California's largest independent mobile home dealers.
- Design and implement a customer relations program involving pre-sale and post-sale surveys to insure customer satisfaction and exceptional service throughout the purchasing process.
- Inspect customer home sites, coordinate delivery of mobile homes, and arrange examination by the building inspector.
- Prepare work orders and schedule contractors to make necessary repairs required by the building inspector or due to damage that occur during transportation and set up.
- Interview customers purchasing new homes to obtain needed information for credit applications; process completed applications and obtain loan approvals.
- Interact with attorneys to process paperwork for closing land/home deals, as well as preparing mortgage documentation and applications for bank officials.

OFFICE MANAGER. The Mobile Home Outlet, Santa Clara, CA (2001-04). Performed office automation, accounting, clerical, and customer service duties for this local company providing delivery and set up to local mobile home sales outlets.
- Oversaw the automation of all office accounting and clerical procedures, implementing the installation of new computer hardware and software.
- Transferred all accounting data for the company from outdated programs into QuickBooks accounting software.
- Oversaw human resources, from interviewing and hiring, to administering the employee benefits program to eligible employees.
- Processed biweekly payroll, accounts payable, and accounts receivable; prepared state and federal withholding taxes; and handled deductions from employee paychecks.
- Renegotiated contracts with established vendors and contractors to reduce company setup and delivery expenditures and maximize profit.
- Prepared Department of Transportation (DOT) mileage logs for all delivery drivers to ensure that all drivers maintained compliance with DOT regulations and guidelines concerning maximum number of miles driven in a single day.

AFFILIATIONS

Donated my time as a volunteer for numerous civic and charitable organizations including the United Way, Easter Seals of California, Hope Harbor Christian Missions, Abney Chapel of Community Service, and the Homeless Women with Children; served as a volunteer tutor for an after school program in Santa Clara.

PERSONAL

Excellent personal and professional references are available upon request.

STENOGRAPHER & TRANSCRIBER

Date

Exact Name of Person
Exact Title
Exact Name of Company
Address
City, State, Zip

Dear Exact Name of Person (or Dear Sir or Madam if answering a blind ad):

With the enclosed resume, I would like to make you aware of my stenographic skills and background in office administration. I have recently relocated to Trenton, NJ, and am seeking an employer who can utilize my top-notch stenographic skills.

As a Stenographer, Court Reporter, and Transcriber for Collier Legal Services in Newark, I performed a variety of stenography and clerical duties for a busy local company which produced legal transcripts for use in court proceedings. I recorded testimonies of witnesses and utilized a stenography mask and transcriber while producing typed transcripts of depositions, sealing and notarizing the original for delivery to the judge presiding over the case. I am accustomed to working under extremely tight deadlines.

I worked closely with attorneys throughout New Jersey and used my authority as a Notary Public to swear in witnesses before taking their depositions. After completing a Medical Terminology course, I was able to facilitate transcriptions of depositions in personal injury and other medical-related cases. I strived to learn different types of computer software programs and have also applied my written and oral communication skills in preparing correspondence and presentations.

If you can use a motivated, hardworking professional who is dedicated to providing quality services in environments requiring attention to detail, I look forward to hearing from you soon. I assure you in advance that I have an excellent reputation and could quickly become an asset to your organization.

Sincerely,

Edna T. Fleetwood

EDNA T. FLEETWOOD

1110½ Hay Street, Fayetteville, NC 28305   •   preppub@aol.com   •   (910) 483-6611

OBJECTIVE

I want to contribute to an organization that can use a hardworking young professional who takes pride in my exceptional customer service, communication, and sales skills.

LICENSES

Licensed Notary Public for the state of New Jersey.

EXPERIENCE

STENOGRAPHER, COURT REPORTER, and **TRANSCRIBER.** Collier Legal Services, Newark, NJ (2003-04). Performed a variety of stenography and clerical duties for this busy local company which produces legal transcripts for use in court proceedings.
- Recorded testimony of witnesses, utilizing a stenography mask and transcriber.
- Produced typed transcripts of depositions, sealing and notarizing the original for delivery to the judge presiding over the case.
- Worked closely with attorneys throughout New Jersey; used my authority as a notary public to swear in witnesses before taking their depositions.
- Completed a Medical Terminology course to facilitate transcriptions of depositions in personal injury and other medical-related cases.
- Performed additional duties as receptionist, answering a multiline phone system and scheduling appointments with clients.

ASSISTANT BOOKKEEPER & COLLECTOR. Quality Finance, Newark, NJ (1997-03). During my final year in high school, began working for this finance company part-time as a Customer Service Representative and was immediately hired full-time upon high school graduation.
- Was entrusted with the responsibility of opening and closing the office.
- Worked with customers taking payments, clearing applications, and processing loans.
- Performed collections, mostly by telephone but sometimes outside collections as well, of 30, 60, and 90 day accounts receivable.
- Became skilled in checking credit by CBI, Equifax, and TRW.
- Handled every type of office task including typing, filing, and operating a computer.
- Increasingly promoted into responsibilities related to bookkeeping; handled the end-of-month close out and assisted the manager in various accounting tasks.
- Became knowledgeable of all aspects of finance company operations, and was commended for attention to detail in handling bookkeeping and accounting activities.
- Can provide an outstanding reference from my employer, who frequently commended me for my gracious manner of dealing with the public as well as for my personal qualities of reliability, dependability, and loyalty to the company.

EDUCATION

Completed a Medical Terminology I course at Essex County College, Newark, NJ, 2004.
Completed numerous technical and management training programs sponsored by Quality Finance.
Graduated from Northeastern High School, Newark, NJ, 1997.

COMPUTERS

Proficient using computers with a variety of software, including proprietary and commercial programs; familiar with Microsoft Word, Excel and PowerPoint.

PERSONAL

Am a very creative, energetic, and highly motivated individual. In my spare time, enjoy painting, sculpting, fishing, and exercising. During and after high school, was active with the Newark Theater and was a cast member in plays including The Lion King.

UTILITY ACCOUNTS SPECIALIST

Date

Exact Name of Person
Title or Position
Name of Company
Address (no., street)
Address (city, state, zip)

UTILITY
ACCOUNTS
SPECIALIST
for a
county
school system

Dear Exact Name of Person: (or Dear Sir or Madam if answering a blind ad.)

I would appreciate an opportunity to talk with you soon about how I could contribute to your organization through my experience in payroll administration and accounts payable administration within the unique environment of a school system.

As you will see from my resume, I have excelled since 1996 in working for the Roanoke County School System. From 1996-03 I administered payroll for 130 employees involved in plant operations and facilities maintenance, and I was asked to handle a wide variety of other duties because of my excellent computer operations skills and background in purchasing and quality control. Highly proficient in computer operations, I am extremely knowledgeable of software including Microsoft Word, Excel, PowerPoint, and Access. A quick learner, I offer a proven ability to rapidly master new programs.

Most recently I was promoted to Utility Accounts Specialist and currently am in charge of authorizing payment of all utility bills for all schools in Bladen County. As part of this job I manage a fuel oil program, coordinate with vendors, and maintain an extensive database for all school locations while cheerfully assisting with other projects as needed.

You would find me in person to be a congenial professional who prides myself on my ability to work well with people at all levels.

I hope you will call or write me soon to suggest a time when we might meet to discuss your current and future needs and how I might serve them. Thank you in advance for you time.

Sincerely yours,

Christina Zwaga

Alternate last paragraph:
I hope you will welcome my call soon to arrange a brief meeting at your convenience to discuss your current and future needs and how I might serve them. Thank you in advance for your time.

CHRISTINA ZWAGA

1110½ Hay Street, Fayetteville, NC 28305 • preppub@aol.com • (910) 483-6611

OBJECTIVE
To contribute to an organization that can use my excellent skills in office administration and computer operations as well as my specialized expertise in payroll administration, accounts payable, purchasing, inventory control and quality control, and customer service.

EDUCATION
Completed 48 credit hours in Business Administration, Roanoke Technical Community College, and 12 credit hours in Business Administration, Richmond University.
• Excelled in these college courses at night while working full-time in demanding jobs.
Graduated from Roanoke Senior High School, Roanoke, VA.

TECHNICAL SKILLS
• Offer the ability to expertly operate every kind of office machinery; am a Notary Public.
• Operate word processors including IBM, Zenith, and Wang Mini Computers.
• Proficient in using 10-key machine.
• Knowledgeable of computerized purchasing, sales, shipping and inventory control.
• Extremely knowledgeable of Microsoft Word, Excel, PowerPoint, and Access.
• Skilled in technical library maintenance. Expert in the operation of various telephone switchboards

EXPERIENCE
Have excelled in the following track record of advancement with the Roanoke County School System, Roanoke, VA, 1996-present:
2003-present: UTILITY ACCOUNTS SPECIALIST. Was recently promoted to this job in which I authorize payment of every utility bill for all the schools in Bladen County including gas and electric bills.
• Manage a fuel oil program including reporting, ordering, transfers, and compliance with statutory requirements on Underground Storage Tanks (USTs) including Tier II report forms.
• Monitor the cost of fuel oil and make projections based on current market conditions and past price history.
• Receive and review utility bills for accuracy using data entry techniques; solve problems in the case of questionable bills.
• Maintain telephone equipment database for all school locations; order equipment.
• Review telephone bills for accuracy and process using data entry.
• Maintain utility vendor files and energy reports.
• Maintain safety database to include Employee and Student Accident Records and Safety Training Records.
• Maintain fire drill reports and emergency weather list.
• Cheerfully assist with other duties as needed, including special project research, newsletters, and publications.

1996-03: PAYROLL ADMINISTRATOR/SECRETARY III. Administered payroll for 130 employees involved in plant operations and facilities maintenance.
• Established and maintained personnel files and set up new employees on payroll; logged all days which employees used as sick leave, annual leave, and no-pay days, and keyed absences into the Kronos payroll system.
• Prepared weekly punch detail reports, month ending reports, end-of-payroll reports, and a payroll schedule.
• Abide by state regulations with regard to Workman's Compensation.
• Oversee the work order system including assigning the job to the proper department, assisting schools with problems, and closing work order when job was complete.
• Produced daily reports for the department foreman.
• Maintained certifications for the State Inspections Department in reference to the operation of all boilers; issued work orders for the inspections and also issued work orders for new boilers, pressure vessels, water tanks, air rec, cast irons, and fire tubes.

PERSONAL
Can provide outstanding letters of recommendation. Am known for my positive attitude and willingness to help other coworkers. Dependable hard worker who produces quality work.

PART THREE:

Federal Resumes & KSAs for Administrative Support, Office & Secretarial Jobs

You may already realize that applying for a federal government position requires some patience and persistence in order to complete rather tedious forms and get them in on time. Depending on what type of federal job you are seeking, you may need to prepare an application such as the SF 171 or OF 612, or you may need to use a Federal Resume, sometimes called a "Resumix," to apply for a federal job. But that may not be the only paperwork you need.

Many Position Vacancy Announcements or job bulletins for a specific job also tell you that, in order to be considered for the job you want, you must also demonstrate certain knowledge, skills, or abilities. In other words, you need to also submit written narrative statements which microscopically focus on your particular knowledge, skill, or ability in a certain area. The next few pages are filled with examples of excellent KSAs. If you wish to see many other examples of KSAs, you may look for another book published by PREP: "Real KSAs--Knowledge, Skills & Abilities--for Government Jobs."

Although you will be able to use the Federal Resume you prepare in order to apply for all sorts of jobs in the federal government, the KSAs you write are particular to a specific job and you may be able to use the KSAs you write only one time. If you get into the Civil Service system, however, you will discover that many KSAs tend to appear on lots of different job announcement bulletins. For example, "Ability to communicate orally and in writing" is a frequently requested KSA. This means that you would be able to use and re-use this KSA for any job bulletin which requests you to give evidence of your ability in this area.

What does "Screen Out" mean? If you see that a KSA is requested and the words "Screen out" are mentioned beside the KSA, this means that this KSA is of vital importance in "getting you in the door." If the individuals who review your application feel that your screen-out KSA does not establish your strengths in this area, you will not be considered as a candidate for the job. You need to make sure that any screen-out KSA is especially well-written and comprehensive.

How long can a KSA be? A job vacancy announcement bulletin may specify a length for the KSAs it requests. Sometimes KSAs can be 1-2 pages long each, but sometimes you are asked to submit several KSAs within a maximum of two pages. Remember that the purpose of a KSA is to microscopically examine your level of competence in a specific area, so you need to be extremely detailed and comprehensive. Give examples and details wherever possible. For example, your written communication skills might appear more credible if you provide the details of the kinds of reports and paperwork you prepared.

KSAs are extremely important in "getting you in the door" for a federal government job. If you are working under a tight deadline in preparing your paperwork for a federal government position, don't spend all your time preparing the Federal Resume if you also have KSAs to do. Create "blockbuster" KSAs as well!

ADMINISTRATIVE ASSISTANT

LAURA C. BRYANT
Address: 1110 1/2 Hay Street, Fayetteville, NC 28305
Home number: (111) 111-1111
SSN: 000-00-0000
E-mail: preppub@aol.com

Position, Title, Series, Grade: Human Resources Coordinator, GS-05
Announcement Number: DN-00-000

EDUCATION	Currently pursuing a **Bachelor of Arts degree in Human Resources,** Essex County College, Trenton, NJ. • Am only one Economics course short of completing my degree. Completed two-year program at Mercer County Community College, Trenton, NJ, 1996. Graduated from E.A. Burnes High School, Trenton NJ, 1994.

ADMINISTRATIVE ASSISTANT

Here you see a resumix of a woman who is seeking a position in the human resources field.

EXPERIENCE

ADMINISTRATIVE ASSISTANT. Maxwell Properties, 698 Wallace Trail, Trenton NJ 66666 (07/2004-present). Salary: $23,000. Supervisor: Thomas Deaver, Executive Manager: (222) 222-2222. Provide administrative support to four top-selling real estate executives.

- Manage finances for a staff of more than 25 members.
- Act as the Human Resources representative for personnel pay, travel, and recruitment issues.
- Manage a $100,000 travel budget for real estate executives traveling on business to company property in various national locations.
- Manage financial, administrative, and travel records while coordinating with our home office in New York.
- On formal performance evaluations, was evaluated as "a hard charger who is willing to do whatever it takes to get the job done;" and "an individual with unique ability to coordinate group efforts toward common goal in any given situation" and as "an individual whose advice and technical knowledge is regularly sought by subordinates, peers, and superiors alike."
- Routinely write and deliver press releases which have been praised for their articulate and concise style; communicate via e-mail and the Internet while also communicating extensively through telephone, meetings, and written correspondence.
- Utilize computers regularly, and apply my specialized expertise with Excel while using that program to manage the monthly supplied budget. Am skilled in database management.
- Maintain daily statistical records for annual reports.
- Continuously seek new methods of improving internal efficiency while maintaining administrative and personnel files.

ADMINISTRATIVE ASSISTANT. Wachovia Bank, 6644 Garner Road, Baltimore, MD 29845 (04/2001-07/2004) Salary: $20,000. Supervisor: Allison Malone, Bank Manager: (333) 333-3333. In this administrative position, performed support activities for the Human Resources Department.

- Reviewed and corrected evaluation reports.
- Prepared reports related to personnel strength, promotions, branch transfers, staff actions, evaluation reports, and various banking personnel assignments.
- Assisted in preparing, coordinating, and monitoring personnel strength levels at numerous locations of Wachovia.

ADMINISTRATIVE ASSISTANT. Department of Defense, 1548 Faxton Avenue, Baltimore, MD 29887 (05/1999-04/2001). Salary: $18,000. Supervisor: Carlton M. Busch: (444) 444-4444. Assisted 3 managers supporting 45 staff members; was involved in managing the full range of personnel administration activities.

- Typed military and nonmilitary correspondence used notes, drafts, verbal instructions, or other courses to prepare documents.
- Prepared suspense control documents and maintained suspense files.

ADMINISTRATIVE ASSISTANT

- In an ongoing process once a month, acted as supervisor in charge of training and managing employees in administrative duties; developed lesson plans and gave formal classes; counseled employees about personnel matters.
- Researched, prepared, and processed retirement packets, reclassification packets, early out request packets, and other specialty actions.
- Acted as Customer Service Representative for outside organizations.
- Analyzed and resolved minor problems that employees were experiencing related to promotions, awards, personnel records, and financial matters.
- Handled duties that included filing, writing, and preparing reports and documents.
- Utilized computers for word processing and statistical analysis, and became skilled in database management. Played a role in organizing humanitarian aid and disaster relief for victims of Hurricane Floyd and received the Humanitarian Service Award.

CLERK TYPIST. Jones & Martin Law, 1168 Cool Springs St., Baltimore, MD 13546 (11/1996-05/1999). Salary: $15,000. Supervisor: Carolyn Heyward: (555) 555-5555. Processed legal documents; performed transcription and dictation duties for memorandums and managed records of oral briefings and conversational notes.

- Maintained database of client evidence, court records, and hearing documentation; distributed copies to lawyers, clients and court attendees. Conducted briefings which included question-and-answer sessions which refined my ability to "think on my feet."
- Used computer databases, files, typed, prepared training reports and documents, and maintained statistical information and records used to compile annual reports.
- Named Employee of the Month for September 1997.

COMPUTERS   Highly proficient in utilizing a variety of software and operating systems.
- Used Microsoft Office including Word, Excel, Access, and PowerPoint.
- Used Adobe Acrobat Reader when dealing with Internet and HTML software.
- Have automated thousands of files; produced numerous graphics for briefing presentations; produced and maintained administrative files and databases; wrote and produced hundreds of written reports of oral briefings and conversational notes.

TRAINING   Management Development and Leadership Course, May 2003
Business Management Course Phase I, February 2003
Business Finance Course Phase II, July 2002
Administrative Specialist Course, September 2001

CLEARANCE   Hold Secret security clearance

HONORS &   Achievement Awards (2), Humanitarian Award; Good Conduct Medal, Joint Meritorious Unit Award,
AWARDS   Certificate of Appreciation.

PERSONAL   Outstanding personal and professional references upon request. Strong work ethic.

ADMINISTRATIVE ASSISTANT

BRYAN TIMOTHY
SSN: 000-00-0000
1110 1/2 Hay Street
Fayetteville, NC 28305

Home: (999) 999-9999
Work: (888) 888-8888
E-mail address: preppub@aol.com
Position, Title, Series, Grade: Administrative Assistant, GS-05
Announcement Number: DN-00-000
Veteran's Preference:

SUMMARY of SKILLS	Knowledge of several administrative operations and automated data processing as well as strong motivational, leadership, and counseling skills.

ADMINISTRATIVE ASSISTANT & DATA PROCESSOR
This military veteran has a 10-point preference derived from his military service.

EXPERIENCE

ADMINISTRATIVE ASSISTANT and **DATA PROCESSOR.** Tacoma Medical Center, 11635 Long Branch Road, Tacoma, WA 88987-9611 (December 2003-present).
Supervisor: Julian Stephenson (777) 777-7777
Pay grade: **Hours worked per week:** 40
Duties: Provide clerical and logistics support for chaplains at a major medical center; assist in programs which provide for the free exercise of religion; administer to the spiritual, moral, and ethical needs of patients, their families, and staff members.
Accomplishments:

- Described as a highly resourceful professional, was cited for my contributions during a ten-day training exercise designed to prepare medical students for field duty; provided support for the religious program and in other functional areas.
- Was awarded the Employee of the Month during the month of August 2003 and August 2004 and selected for special training in providing instruction, technical writing, and blueprint reading.

ADMINISTRATIVE ASSISTANT TO THE MAYOR. Mayor's Office, 3654 Grimble Circle, Tacoma, WA 88265 (Feb 2001-Dec 2003).
Supervisor: Mayor Terrence Herriott (666) 666-6666
Pay grade: **Hours worked per week:** 40
Duties: Supported city officials and other mayoral personnel and attended councilmen meetings, and handled the processing of regular performance reports and other administrative actions.

Other experience gained in the U.S. Navy:
SENIOR ADMINISTRATIVE ASSISTANT TO THE CHIEF OF CHAPLAINS. U.S. Navy, USS Garrett #535, Jackson, MS, 56775-4688 (May 1998-February 2001).
Supervisor: Commander Fredrick Ranalli (555) 555-5555
Pay grade: **Hours worked per week:** 40
Duties: Learned administrative skills in the fast-paced, multi-task environment of the office of the Chief of Naval Operations.
Accomplishments:

- Was awarded a Navy Achievement Medal for my contributions which included coordinating the reorganization of office work space for increased productivity. Handled multiple responsibilities in ADP security, training, and career counseling.
- Was entrusted with numerous functional duties ranging from trainer to ADP system security specialist, to career counselor, to financial counselor.
- Held the additional special duty assignments as Career Counselor, member of the quality assurance/quality control board, and member of the Command Assessment Team.

ADMINISTRATIVE ASSISTANT

MATHEMATICS STUDENT. U.S. Navy, USS Garrett #535, Jackson, MS, 56775-4688 (July 1995-May 1998).
Supervisor: Captain Jeffrey V. Quimby (444) 444-4444
Pay grade: RP2   **Hours worked per week:** 40
Duties: Earned an A.S. in Mathematics in a military-sponsored education program for active duty personnel–
the Academic Advancement Program.
Accomplishments:

- Volunteered as a tutor for students at a high school for math and science.
- Was accepted for membership in the Honor Society with a 3.7 GPA.

ADMINISTRATIVE ASSISTANT TO THE CHAPLAIN. U.S. Navy, USS Carter, Naval Operations,
Okinawa, Japan, FPO AE 77684-4644 (September 1992-July 1995).
Supervisor: LTC Matthew L. O'Connor (333) 333-3333
Pay grade: RP 1   **Hours worked per week:** 40
Duties: Was cited for numerous contributions to the effectiveness of the ship's religious programs and support
for personnel requiring counseling and support services during crisis and emergency situations.
Accomplishments:

- Was described in official performance evaluations as "intelligent, impressively articulate, and
  refreshingly conscientious."
- On my own initiative, developed a cross-training program.
- Utilized my computer skills to create a database of all books and video tapes as well as a tracking
  system for library materials.

EDUCATION   **Associate of Science** degree in **Mathematics**, Tacoma Community College, Tacoma, WA, 1997.

TRAINING   Attended US Navy training schools which included basic infantry and basic administration as well as the
                      "Class A and Class F" career courses.
                      Completed nonresident training courses which included the following subjects:

religious program operations	inventory control
safety	customer service
human behavior	administrative assistance
engineering administration	electricity/electronics
computer programming	educational services

CLEARANCE   Was entrusted with a Secret security clearance.

COMPUTERS   Experienced with FORTRAN, C++, Microsoft Word, Excel, Access, and PageMaker.

EXECUTIVE ASSISTANT

MICHELLE A. HOFFMAN
1110 1/2 Hay Street
Fayetteville, NC 28305
111-111-1111 **HOME**
222-222-2222 **CELL**
SSN: 000-00-0000

Source: EXTERNAL
Highest Grade Held: N/A
Vacancy Announcement Number:
Position Title:

EXECUTIVE ASSISTANT for a human resources office with the government

EXPERIENCE

2002-present. **EXECUTIVE ASSISTANT.** Office of Government Ethics, Human Resources Division, 43984 Mixson Hwy, Washington, DC 20023. Salary: $20,000. Oscar E. Allen, 333-333-3333. Assigned to the Personnel Administration office with over 125 employees total. Handle administrative duties for all of the organization's personnel. Supervise three other administrative assistants, and conduct seminars for human resources attended by 400 people annually. Maintain employee qualifications and training records for 125 individuals. Coordinate course registration with numerous outside organizations. Serve as an Training Instructor for new hires, and have earned a reputation as an articulate and enthusiastic communicator who genuinely cared for the well-being and success of all personnel.
Accomplishments:
On my own initiative, developed and implemented filing system for the organization's records, and also developed a tracking system using ORACLE database used by qualified personnel. Played an active role in the development of eight training programs of instruction and seminar schedules. Evaluated as a "dedicated administrator willing to go out of her way for others."

2000-02. **ADMINISTRATIVE ASSISTANT.** Environmental Protection Agency, 488 Pinckney Blvd, Washington, DC 20561. Salary: $18.000. Howard Millington, 555-555-5555. Managed personnel administration support which included processing financial transactions, coordinating personnel evaluations including human resource benefit packages, and preparing extensive paperwork. Trained and managed four employees, and incorporated risk assessment and safety awareness in all training sessions. On a formal performance evaluation of my work, was described as one who "instilled motivated in her department by her willingness to listen."

1999-00. **ADMINISTRATIVE ASSISTANT.** Berkshire Hathaway, 867 Tallaway Street Chicago, IL 45410. Salary: $17,000. Simon Jackson, 444-444-4444. Performed office duties in support of a 30-person organization. Created filing systems. Developed and maintained recordkeeping systems. Was specially selected by the General Sales Manager to serve as his Administrative Assistant, and prepared correspondence for the signature of executives.

Experience in the US Army:
1998-99. **NONCOMMISSIONED OFFICER IN CHARGE.** 24TH Mission Support Squadron, Fort Drum, NY. Salary: $25,000. Supervisor: CSM Thomas Haigler, 999-999-9999. Was selected for a position as the Change of Command Coordinator for a 240-person Group. Ensured that employees' promotion proceedings were accurately monitored in order to assure appropriate advancement to the next rank. Supervised financial support provided to 395 soldiers in nine units, and assured that payroll processing was accurate and timely.

1995-98. **HEAVY WHEELED VEHICLE DRIVER.** US Army, 742nd Airlift Squadron, Fort Shafter, Hawaii. Salary: $20,000. Supervisor: SFC Bryan K. Pete, 666-666-6666. In a medium truck company in Honolulu, was responsible for the delivery of U.S. mail, the air line of communication, and general cargo administration throughout Hawaii. Prepared all documentation and paperwork associated with operating one M915A1 14-ton tractor. Was selected over 26 other Sergeants as Motor Pool NCO, and on the citation for the Army Commendation Medal which I received,

EXECUTIVE ASSISTANT

I was praised for "initiative and expertise which were instrumental in the development of the Motor Pool Standard Operating Procedures which the organization still uses today." Was Acting Squad Leader in charge of seven people during the recovery phase for a 30 day field exercise. On a written performance evaluation, was described as a supervisor who "inspired the confidence of subordinates."

1992-95. SENIOR WHEEL VEHICLE OPERATOR AND ACTING SQUAD LEADER. US Army, 85th Transportation Company 95th BN VHC, Fort Carson, CO 84456. Salary: $17,000. Supervisor: Matthew S. Baker, 777-777-7777. Supervised five employees in an airborne light/medium truck company supporting the army airfield in Fort Carson. Received a respected Army Achievement Medal for my exceptional performance and "can do attitude." Transported more than 2,500 soldiers in support of the Special Forces Assessment and Selection Committee. On a formal evaluation was praised for "a safety first attitude which contributed to the platoon's achieving 75,000 accident-free miles in six months."

1989-92. WHEEL VEHICLE OPERATOR. US Army, 20th Regiment Battalion, Fort Benning, GA 12884. Salary: $16,000. Supervisor: Terrell L. Donaldson, 888-888-8888. Conducted local and limited line haul operations of personnel and equipment in support of the Aviation Training facility (an M35A2).

EDUCATION

Associate of Arts degree in **Business Technology** at Central Texas College, Fort Drum, NY, 1999.

SPECIALIZED TRAINING, LICENSES & CERTIFICATES

Convoy Operations and Winter Driving, Combat Maneuver Training Center. 1999, Bus Training Course, Fort Drum Support Battalion. 1998, Emergency Lifesaver, Army Education Center. 1998, Bus Driver Course, Training Integration Branch. 1997, Primary Leadership Development Course, NCO Academy. 1997, Equal Opportunity Representative Course, Fort Benning. 1996, Total Army Recruiting and Retention School. 1996, 88M Motor Transport Operator Course, Fort Shafter. 1995, Parachute Rigger Course. Licensed to operate military vehicles and light wheel vehicles.

AWARDS

Numerous medals including Army Achievement Medals (two), Army Service Ribbon, Army Lapel Button, National Defense Service Medal, Good Conduct Medals, and numerous letters of appreciation from supervisors and commanders praising my outstanding results.

COMPUTERS & EQUIPMENT

Operate PCs with software including Word and Excel; Operate all office equipment including copier, fax, switchboards, radios, and other equipment.

CLEARANCE

Secret security clearance

MEDICAL CLERK

SHANNON R. TROY
1110 1/2 Hay Street
Fayetteville, NC 28305
Home: (888) 888-8888
Work: (999) 999-9999

ANNOUNCEMENT NUMBER: 00-000-00
POSITION TITLE: Safety and Occupational Health Specialist
GRADE: GS-07
SOCIAL SECURITY NUMBER: 000-00-0000
CITIZENSHIP: U.S.
VETERAN'S PREFERENCE: 10%

MEDICAL CLERK
for a hospital's emergency room

OBJECTIVE

I want to offer my knowledge of Safety and Occupational Health, knowledge of automation (software and operating systems), as well as my ability to communicate orally and in writing.

EDUCATION & TRAINING

Associate of Science degree in **General Studies, 1998.**
Associate of Science degree in **Laboratory and X-ray Technology, 1996.**
Basic Medical Specialist Course, eight weeks, 2004.
Race Relations/Equal Opportunity Course, four weeks, 2004.
Occupational Health and Safety Seminar, four weeks, 2003.

COMPUTERS

Knowledgeable of software including: Microsoft Word, Excel, Access, and numerous specialized software programs related to the medical field.

HONORS

Have been singled out for numerous honors and awards including the Good Conduct Medal, Meritorious Service Medal, three U.S. Army Commendation Medals; Peacetime Service Medal from duty in Panama; Humanitarian Service Medal, and eight Army Achievement Medals; National Defense Service Medal; US Army Training Ribbon; Noncommissioned Officer's Professional Development Ribbon; Army Service Ribbon; US Army Longevity Service Medal.

EXPERIENCE

MEDICAL CLERK. Lake County Medical Hospital, 6584 Southern Avenue, Grayslake, IL 41847 (2003-present). Hours per week: 40+. Salary: $21,000. Supervisor: Katherine Swanson, phone: 777-777-7777. Handle a variety of responsibilities in this administrative position which requires me to apply my extensive knowledge of safety and health program elements while continuously applying safety and occupational health standards, regulations, practices, and procedures to eliminate or control potential hazards.
Front desk duties: When patients arrive at the Emergency Room, process them and direct them to appropriate personnel, usually the Triage Nurse or the fast-track process.
Monitoring public health and safety: Provide oversight of cleaning crews and alert them to the need to immediately clean and disinfect rooms after patients with communicable diseases have been treated; most recently meningitis has been a problem.

SALES ASSOCIATE. Books-A-Million, Grayslake Mall, 2574 Habertown Road, Grayslake, IL 41836 (2002-03). Hours per week: 40+. Salary: $9.00 per hour. Supervisor: Allison Kindred, phone: 666-666-6666. Assisted customers in selection and purchase of books. Audited inventory for reorders.

Experience in the U. S. Army:
COMMUNICATIONS MANAGER. 437th Medical Group, Fort Stewart, GA (1999-2002). Hours per week: 40. Salary: E-7. Supervisor: Colonel Earl Borris, phone: 444-444-4444. For the Medical Group, was responsible for the procurement, storage, and security of automation, communications, and security equipment. Played a key role in the supervision of the brigade security force which protected sensitive signal sites. Was directly responsible for communication equipment utilized by all medical units on the southeast coast including Hawaii and by the Winn Army Hospital. Maintained constant liaison with all departments and clinics to ensure

adequate signal support. Applied safety and occupational health standards and regulations in controlling potential hazards.

SECURITY MANAGER & COMMUNICATIONS NCO. U.S. Army, 83rd Med Comm, Fort Sam Houston, TX (1996-1999). Salary: E-6. Supervisor: Lt. Montrell C. Jordan, phone: 333-333-3333. Was Security Manager and Communications NCO for the 2,900-person battalion. Supervised installation and operation of all signal support systems to include local area networks (LANs), tactical radios, records management, an audiovisual system support and automation. Personally purchased $315,000 in computers and communications equipment.

Highlights of other U.S. Army experience:
Military Intelligence: During the Gulf War, served as an Intelligence Analyst and was responsible for the supervision of 75 personnel in installing and setting up all communications equipment wiring during Operation Desert Shield. Interfaced with foreign allied authorities in the setup and operation of equipment.

Military Police: Served in various security assignments including performing duty as monitor for joint intrusion detection systems for 30 high-security sites storing classified documents and weapons storage facilities at Fort Benning, GA. Also performed as Access Control Guard for high-level officer training courses; maintained accountability and security related to badges and access control devices. Maintained accountability of keys. Enforced physical security policies. Performed military police patrol duties and enforced military laws. Maintained statistical data for the Lieutenant Commander, and assisted in the crime prevention program.

Nursing and Occupational Health and Safety: Because of my strong management skills, was selected to take control of a disorganized medical facility at Ft. Rucker, AL which was experiencing a variety of control problems, including problems related to public safety and occupational health. Trained employees, rewrote Standard Operating Procedures (SOPs), and managed 25 people operating a medical outpatient facility serving a population of 1,250.

MILITARY TRAINING	Advanced Noncommissioned Officer Course, 19 weeks, 1998.
	Battalion Training Management Course, 3 weeks, 1998.
	Communications Security Course, two weeks, 1997.
	Health and Safety Course, two weeks, 1996.
	Instructor Training, two weeks, 1995.
	US Army Computer Science School, Local Area Network Training, 10 weeks, 1994.
	Telecommunications Center Operator Course, 10 weeks, 1993.
CLEARANCE	Was entrusted with a **Top Secret** security clearance.

OFFICE MANAGER

CARLA V. DALE
SSN: 000-00-0000
1110 1/2 Hay Street
Fayetteville, NC 28305
Home Phone: (111) 111-1111
Work Phone: (222) 222-2222

Highest Federal Civilian grade held, job series, and dates of employment in grade:
Vacancy Announcement Number: BC-000-00-0000
Position Title and Grade: Nurse, GS-09

**OFFICE
MANAGER**
for a
commercial
cleaning
company

**SUMMARY
OF SKILLS**

Over ten years of experience in office management and personnel management, customer service and public relations, as well as computer operations and office equipment operation. Extensive knowledge of specialized terminology needed to type correspondence, reports, and memoranda along with knowledge of grammar, spelling, capitalization, and punctuation. Ability to type 55 words per minute.

EXPERIENCE

2003-present. 40 hours per week. **OFFICE MANAGER.** Merrimac Commercial Cleaning, 3524 Douglass Road, Jonesboro, AR 40025. Salary: $25,000. Supervisor: Warren Simmons (333) 333-3333. Manage office operations, customer service, and the organization of accounting information for the company accountant. Type correspondence, memoranda, and reports in final form. Utilize my excellent knowledge of functions, procedures, and policies of the office.
* Have become known for my gracious manner when answering the phone. Utilize my communication skills while speaking with potential customers as well as existing clients by phone and in person to answer their technical questions about the company's cleaning services.
* Manage both commercial and residential accounts. Schedule appointments for company services and determine correct prices.
* Handle a wide range of bookkeeping functions; investigate and analyze previous invoices in order to attach them to current work orders.
* Have been commended for my ability to deal graciously with the public and have been credited with increasing company revenue through my public relations and customer service skills.

2001-03. 40 hours a week. **PERSONNEL ADMINISTRATIVE SPECIALIST.** Department of Veterans Affairs, 213 Third Street, Lexington, KY 39754. Salary: $23,000. Supervisor: Camden Washington (444) 444-4444. Expertly performed a wide range of office duties. Coordinated benefit packets for discharged and retired veterans.
* Utilized a computer with Microsoft Office for word processing.
* Handled personnel administration activities which included processing hundreds of discharged and retired veterans in and out of our 325-person organization.
* Performed clerical support functions related to the preparation of personnel reports as well as documents pertaining to personnel assignments. Typed personnel evaluations including achievement awards as a part of our job placement assistance program.
* Proofread documents, reports, and communication.
* Arranged and scheduled appointments for personnel to obtain official documentation including IDs as well as financial information for veteran and personnel documents.

1999-01. 40 hours per week. **OFFICE MANAGER.** Baker-Reynolds & Associates, 8327 Barnard Avenue, Lawton, OK 65448 (555) 555-5555.
* Supervised one administrative assistant and up to five technicians involved in legal services. Handled accounts payable and receivable and performed bookkeeping functions.
* Prepared payroll for all company employees.
* Organized all accounting records for the company's accountant.

- Designed and coordinated marketing activities and advertising programs.
- Operated a computer, utilized a typewriter to type forms, and prepared correspondence.

Experience in the US Army:

1995-99. 40 hours a week. **PERSONNEL ADMINISTRATION SPECIALIST & UNIT CLERK.** US Army, 3912 Armory Street, Fort Sill, OK 68741. Salary: E-6. SSG Alexander W. Graham, 888-888-8888. Utilized my skills in office procedures while excelling in a job as a Unit Clerk (1995-97) and then as a Personnel Administration Specialist (1997-99) within the same organization.

- Received a special award for my leadership as Unit Clerk in reducing a large backlog of personnel documents to zero – our unit was the first one to achieve that goal within a one year period in 1999. The citation for the Army Achievement Medal which I received praised my efforts in "reducing 295 critical data blanks using Microsoft Access, allowing Headquarters Company to become the first of 21 units to reach this target."

1993-95. 40 hours a week. **ADMINISTRATIVE SPECIALIST & PERSONNEL SPECIALIST.** US Army, 22nd Signal Battalion, Camp Casey, Korea APO AP 30139. Salary: E-5. Supervisor: MSG Frederick S. Keller 666-666-6666. Excelled in a job as a Clerk Typist and advanced to handle more complex office administration duties because of my cheerful attitude and ability to handle large volumes of work which had to be performed accurately and quickly.

TRAINING

Certificate, USAR Unit Administration Basic Course, 1999.
Certificate, Administrative Specialist Course, U.S. Army, 1999.
Certificate, Primary Leadership Course, U.S. Army, 1998.
Certificate of Training, Battalion Training Management Course, U.S. Army, 1998.
Certificate of Training, Maintenance Management Course, 1997.
Certificate of Completion, Clerk-Typist Course, U.S. Army, 1997.
Certificate, Unit Administration Basic Course, U.S. Army, three weeks, 1996.
Certificate, Administrative Specialist Course, U.S. Army, 33 credit hours, 1996.
Certificate, Primary Leadership Development Course, U.S. Army, two weeks, 1995.
Certificate, Battalion Training Management Course, U.S. Army, two days, 1993.
Certificate of Training, Maintenance Management Course, two days, 1993.
Certificate of Completion, Clerk-Typist Course, U.S. Army, eight weeks, 1993.

CLEARANCE

While in military service, held a Secret clearance.

OFFICE SKILLS

Proficient with all office equipment: computers, typewriters, copiers, fax machines.

MEDALS & AWARDS

While in military service, received numerous awards and medals including the Army Service Ribbon, Army Reserve Components Overseas (Korea) Training Ribbon, Army Achievement Medal, NCO Professional Development Ribbon, Army Good Conduct Medal.

SECRETARY

STUART B. INGRAM
1110 1/2 Hay Street
Fayetteville, NC 28305
999-999-9999 **Home** 888-888-8888 **Work**

Country of citizenship: U.S.A.
SSN: 000-00-0000
Source: EXT
Highest Grade Held: N/A
Vacancy Announcement Number:
Position Title:

SECRETARY
for the Federal Reserve
System

EXPERIENCE

CHIEF SECRETARY. GS-08.
Start and End Date: Apr 2003-present. **Hours worked per week:** 40+.
Starting Salary: $12.00 per hour; **Ending Salary:** $14.00 per hour. **Employer's Name and Address:** Federal Reserve System/Board of Governors, 09894 Parsonage Street, Plymouth, NH, 00905-0446. **Supervisor's Name & Phone Number:** Major Darren Coles, 777-777-7777.
Review and reconcile biweekly payroll reports, and perform extensive problem solving related to pay and benefits. Respond to customer problems orally and in writing. Review and complete forms for input into a national database, and observe an extensive set of rules, regulations, and policies governing federal pay issues. Receive and direct telephone calls to appropriate officials. Interview callers and obtain information related to their background and problems. Implement supervisor's instructions, and advise colleagues on office procedures.
Simultaneous volunteer work: Counselor Intern (Part-time, 20 hours per week).
Jun 2003-Mar 2004. Continuing Education Center for Hesser College campus known as English Cove. Coordinate, analyze, and evaluate fee waivers for eligible senior-citizen students in order to determine eligibility for both part-time and full-time admittance utilizing payment plans including installment payments. Created health awareness seminars under the supervision of professional advisors. Created a career opportunity board listing all current jobs. Gained professional counseling skills while counseling students on social, psychological, and political issues presented by the global economy.

REGISTRATION TECHNICIAN. GS-07.
Start and End Dates: Sep 2001-Apr 2003. **Hours worked per week:** 40+.
Current Salary: $11.00 per hr. **Employer's Name and Address:** Department of Social Services, 4357 Seaford Drive, Suite 100, Manchester, NH, 00912. **Supervisor's Name & Phone Number:** Randall Howard, 666-666-6666.
Manage the registration function and represent the DSS on all registration matters; serve as the primary point of contact with the public and various government agencies. Receive and review applications for Registration from low income clients, adoption agencies, and foster parents and homes. Examine referrals from state on licenses which have been revoked, investigated, or placed on probation by the state. Verify DSS registration information pertaining to social services and state license inquiries. Work with DSS investigators.
Simultaneous volunteer work: Counselor's Aide (Part-time, 20 hours per week). Mar 2002-Feb 2003. St. Luke's Cathedral. Assisted in the coordination of the food distribution program. Conducted visits to local area rest homes in order to conduct seminar for seniors. Utilized special counseling techniques to assist seniors in dealing with their problems and in bringing closure to the counseling process. Managed a series of group discussions on matters pertaining to life after retirement.

ASSISTANT TRAINING COORDINATOR. GS-06.
Start and End Dates: Feb 1999-Sep 2001. **Hours worked per week:** 40+.
Salary: $10.50 per hour. **Employer's Name & Address:** Merit Systems Protection Board, 4554 Manor Court, Manchester, NH 00902-8532. **Supervisor's Name & Phone Number:** Julian Capers, 555-555-5555.
Managed a computer database which collected the training history of 12 personnel members in the Performance Enhancement Division. Maintained strict attention

to detail as I observed the need for accuracy and timeliness of information. Became proficient in database sorting, indexing, and manipulation to provide selective criteria listings. Expertly operated a locally created computer application which contained information on training courses and personnel in those courses. Notified personnel accepted for classes. Maintained training files. Reserved classrooms for training. Maintained course schedules pertaining to 13 courses. Acted as division control point for correction action reports, and reviewed performance reports. Coordinated approvals for courses.

CLERK TYPIST. GS-05.
Start and End Dates: Apr 1996-Feb 1999. **Hours worked per week:** 40+. **Salary:** $9.75 per hour. **Employer's Name & Address:** Social Security Administration, 9045 Ridge Avenue, Durham, NH 00152-4301. **Supervisor's Name and Phone Number:** Graham Washington, 444-444-4444.
Prepared correspondence including reports and charts, and maintained an extensive filing system. Operated word processors. Logged in incoming and outgoing messages.

CLERK TYPIST/OFFICE MANAGEMENT. GS-05.
Start and End Dates: Jan 1993-Apr 1996. **Hours per week:** 40+. **Salary:** $8.00 per hour. **Employer's Name & Address:** Montgomery County Court House, Immigration and Naturalization Division, 5330 Linden Road, Huntington Valley, PA 10312. Supervisor's Name & Phone Number: Arthur Cummings, 333-333-3333.
Determined the suitability of noncitizens for admission to the U.S. while examining passports and visas. Examined applications and supporting documents for proof of citizenship. Identified instances of false identity and untruthful statements. Maintained liaison with passport officers for various cases.

CLAIMS DEVELOPMENT CLERK. GS-05.
Start and End Dates: Nov 1990-Jan 1993. **Hours per week:** 40+. **Salary:** $7.56 per hour. **Employer's Name & Address:** New York Life, 1847 Adolphus Avenue, Huntington Valley, PA 10312. **Supervisor's Name and Phone Number:** Charles Hannahan, 222-222-2222.
Established a tally system for new accounts which improved the efficiency of claims handling. Assisted the Claims Representative in handling processing related to overpayment and underpayment.

EDUCATION

Master's Degree, Gerontology Option, Plymouth State College of the University System of New Hampshire, Plymouth, NH, 2004.
Bachelor of Liberal Arts, Hesser College, Manchester, NH, 2002.
Associate of Arts, Hesser College, Manchester, NH, 2000.

COMPUTERS

Extensive training related to computer operations including PageMaker, Microsoft Word, Windows, Microsoft PowerPoint, Microsoft Outlook, Excel, and Access.

SECRETARY TYPIST

LATOYA E. HESS
Mailing address:
1110 1/2 Hay Street
Fayetteville, NC 28305
Home phone: (111) 111-1111
Work phone: (222) 222-2222
Social security number: 000-00-0000

**SECRETARY
TYPIST**
for the Central
Intelligence
Agency

**SUMMARY
OF SKILLS**

Word processing and data entry, typing, answering multiline phones, filing, English-German translation, taking shorthand, ensuring an office runs smoothly and efficiently while working as an administrative assistant or office manager, providing proficiency with the Internet and e-mail systems as well as Microsoft Word, Excel, Access and PowerPoint software.

EXPERIENCE

SECRETARY/TYPIST. Central Intelligence Agency (CIA), Recruitment Center, PO Box 4090, Reston, VA 20195-7034 (2/03-present). Supervisor: Mr. Marvin Blackwell; Hours worked per week: 40; Grade: GS-04-08. As secretary to the Foreign Area Specialist (FAS), relieve him of many administrative and clerical duties and functions. Was selected for this permanent position because I was considered the most qualified individual in the office to handle the wide range of responsibilities.

- Receive and screen all incoming phone calls; greet and direct visitors to the proper person to assist them; handle routine requests for information and refer those requiring technical information to the appropriate action officer or section.
- Review reports on a daily basis to obtain information on foreign and domestic disturbances and then maintain an automated log as a record of such incidents; check on whether it was a first, second, or third offense. Write a letter to the individual involved and send it with accompanying backup material to the Foreign Area Specialist for his signature.
- Keep the Foreign Area Specialist and his staff informed of regular and special meetings, events, and projects; during the FAS's absence, make appointments and commitments for him; act as his liaison with other staff sections.
- Use discretion when answering and referring calls from higher headquarters and other staff agencies. Place and receive calls to other staff members and organizations as well as other government agencies.
- Compose draft correspondence from brief verbal instructions/rough handwritten drafts and notes and ensure correspondence is in the proper format using correct grammar, sentence structure, spelling, punctuation, and capitalization; ensure correspondence conforms with CIA regulations and check to be sure that background material or enclosures are included.
- Complete typing of administrative reports, letters and correspondence from verbal instructions, handwritten drafts and notes, or my own composition; routinely prepare such material for executives.
- Have a password and am able to access the office LAN (Local Area Network) terminal, retrieve, type, and transmit messages to the appropriate staff office.
- Serve as a source of information for supervisors and employees regarding personnel actions and procedures; coordinate personnel and financial action with appropriate personnel in the Personnel, Finance and Accounting Offices.
- Collect, maintain, and review time and attendance cards for 29 CIA employees.

CLERK/TYPIST. Central Intelligence Agency (CIA), CST Division, PO Box 4605, Reston, VA 20195-7048 (1/98-3/03). Supervisor: Mr. Jason Thomas; Hours worked per week: 40; Grade: GS-04-05. For the CST Division, performed a wide range of clerical duties including using the IBM computer to input, edit, and retrieve statistical data on traffic accidents and compile traffic reports as well as to maintain daily logs of all administrative paperwork and applicable suspense dates.

- Typed narrative and tabular material such as correspondence, messages, rosters, statistical reports, work orders, awards, forms, and charts in final form.

- Prepared typed documentation with nonspecialized terminology provided in a variety of formats while assuring proper form, style, and spacing.
- Typed statistical or other tabular material using my judgment to ensure proper form and arrangement on the page to allow for numerous columns and headings.
- Selected, rearranged, and consolidated data from a number of source documents based on general instructions which described the end product but gave me responsibility for typographical accuracy, capitalization, punctuation, grammar, and spelling. Checked references to supporting data and assembled material in the proper order for signature.
- Served as a Notary Public in cases involving alcohol when chemical analysis was conducted and to support the section in cases where applications for citizenship, name changes on birth certificates, and odometer readings had to be notarized.
- Filled in for the Statistician's secretary as described in my current job and was selected for a permanent assignment as the Foreign Area Specialist's secretary when that position became vacant.

CLERK/TYPIST. Department of Defense, 8772 Constitution Avenue Suite 935, Washington, DC 22507-6500 (11/95-4/98). Supervisor: Mr. Richard Fields; Hours worked per week: 40; Grade: GS-04-04. Typed a wide range of official correspondence using Microsoft Word according to prescribed formats as well as using Excel to prepare spreadsheets as well as charts and graphs.
- Received visitors and phone calls and furnished the callers with information they requested or referred them to the proper person.
- Took messages; filed documents; typed unemployment insurance forms in response to inquiries from the Employment Security Commission of Washington, DC.

SECRETARY/TYPIST. Camden Elementary School, 3489 Rockford Drive, Fort Polk, LA 77854-5845 (7/92-6/95). Supervisor: Mrs. Patricia Ryan; Hours worked per week: 40; Grade: GS-04-03. As secretary to the school principal, handled office functions including typing, filing, taking shorthand, taking messages, providing callers and visitors with information, and setting up appointments and meetings.
- Utilized Microsoft Word and Excel to prepare correspondence and documentation.
- Greeted and assisted dignitaries and visitors. Prepared time cards and trained new personnel.
- Typed training schedules, student rosters, and new lessons for Instructors.

CLERK/TYPIST. Civilian Personnel Office, 4389 English Oaks Road, Fort Polk, LA 77514-5445 (9/89-11/92). Supervisor: Mr. Carroll Delmar; Hours worked per week: 40; Grade: GS-04-02. Assigned to the office of the Personnel Manager, directed visitors, answered phone and in-person inquiries, and took messages for all assigned personnel.
- Assisted in training and instructing clerical personnel on established policies and procedures used and proper formats for correspondence.
- Received and processed distribution from the administrative offices of the operations center.
- Posted pen and ink changes and revisions to materials in the reference library.
- Typed all correspondence and other related military and civilian material in final form to include proofreading and making corrections of any typographical, grammatical, spelling, and format errors.
- Filed documents according to the then-existing U.S. Army regulations/guidelines.

WARD CLERK. Cravens Medical Center, 8569 Medical Boulevard, Cravens, LA 76447-1744 (2/79-5/83). Supervisor: N/A; Hours worked per week: 40 to 60; Grade: N/A. Maintained patient medical charts; answered phones and directed calls; took and distributed messages; learned basic nursing assistant skills (taking blood pressure/pulses and giving injections).

TRAINING

Central Intelligence Agency (CIA) Certificate of Training — MS-DOS Computer Training — 5/7-8/03
Beyond Secretary: The Growing Role of the Administrative Assistant 5/20/03 Certificate of Completion
Central Intelligence Agency (CIA) Preparing and Managing Correspondence Course — 11/9/03
Central Intelligence Agency (CIA) Record Keeping System — 7/5/02
Subcourse FIO63 — Office Management — 2002
Subcourse AGO123 — Punctuation — 2001
Subcourse AGO0043 — Files Maintenance and Disposition Procedures — 2000
Subcourse AGO122 — Spelling, Abbreviation, and Capitalization — 2000

AWARDS

Exceptional Central Intelligence Agency (CIA) Performance Appraisal—2002
Special Act or Service Award — 2002

TELECOMMUNICATIONS COORDINATOR

SHIRLEY HENDREN
SSN: 000-00-0000
1110 1/2 Hay Street
Fayetteville, NC 28305
Home: (111) 111-1111 or (222) 222-2222
Work: (333) 333-3333
E-mail: preppub@aol.com

Vacancy Announcement #: DN-00-000
Source Code: External
Country of Citizenship: U.S.A.
Veteran's Preference: N/A
Reinstatement Eligibility: Yes
Highest Federal Grade Held: GS-00-07

TELECOMMUNICATIONS COORDINATOR for the Homeland Security Information Services	**SUMMARY**	Skilled in performing various communications, office automation, administrative, and accounting functions; known for my attention to detail and ability to perform complex tasks in a timely and accurate manner; possess exceptional communication and organizational skills.

EXPERIENCE

TELECOMMUNICATIONS COORDINATOR. Department of Homeland Security, Washington, DC 77777-7777 (2002-present).
Supervisor: SFC Aaron Maddox, (444) 444-4444
Pay Grade: GS-07
Hours worked per week: 40
Duties: Process a large volume of incoming calls, operating two separate communications, consoles for receiving and routing both secure and non-secure calls. Handle high priority local, calls occurring in a Top Secret environment. These include complex and extremely sensitive calls for general officers assigned to the Chief of Staff, the Inspector General, and the Division Signal Office as well as major military commands.

Highly skilled in the application of specialized procedures required for operating various circuits or networks. Provide service over a variety of secure and non-secure communications networks and switches without compromising system security. Complete numerous difficult calls such as connecting one or both parties to facilitate complicated conference calls as well as making difficult overseas connections to third world countries, which require alternate calls and routing through other countries and operators.

Coordinate with the appropriate organization or contractor in the event of a communications outage, receiving and documenting the initial report of a system or circuit outage and communicating this information when placing the service or repair call. Monitor progress of repairs and perform any necessary follow-up actions to ensure that the communications system is fully functional with the least possible loss of service. Operate the command alerting system, which is comprised of two different paging networks. Update and maintain the pager listing and recall roster on a daily basis, using an automated data system to enter changes into the database.

Entrusted with responsibility for the issue and receipt of cellular phones, dial-up pagers, and other communications equipment worth thousands of dollars. Perform operational checks on communications equipment prior to issue and instruct user in the proper use of the cellular phones and dial-up pagers. Maintain issue and turn-in documentation to preserve accountability for all equipment. Hold additional responsibility for the vehicle assigned to the Chief of Staff. Maintain control logs, issue keys, and keep maintenance logs for the vehicle up-to-date. Open, sort, log and route incoming correspondence. Sign for certified and registered mail. Prepare, receive, file, dispatch, and safeguard classified documents.
- Demonstrated the maturity, stability, and self-confidence required to overcome the stress and anxiety of working in a high pressure, Top Secret environment.

TELECOMMUNICATIONS COORDINATOR

VOUCHER EXAMINER. US Army, 34th Protocol Office, Fort Meade, MD 66666-6666 (1998-02).
Supervisor: SFC Katherine Brandon, (555) 555-5555
Pay Grade: GS-00-05
Hours worked per week: 40
Duties: Audited travel vouchers and other documentation related to travel, transportation, and relocation expenses for the operation and control of personnel and cargo movement by air, rail, motor transport and water. Supervised subordinates performing duties of the motor operator, traffic management coordinator, and terminal operations coordinator. Provided assistance to the Operations sections of the transportation battalion and higher level headquarters. Verified travel and transportation expense claims matched up with official orders and dates. Processed all categories of travel and transportation vouchers, including family member travel, delayed travel, invitational travel, and shipment/storage of personal effects. Verified information related to requests for allowances or entitlements, such as claimant status, individual or group travel, and purpose of travel. Interviewed individuals in person, by telephone, and through correspondence to obtain additional information or clarify information previously provided. Reviewed all supporting documents for accuracy and validity, performing mathematical computations of time and distance as well as converting expense amounts from foreign currencies.

Processed travel vouchers, operating an automated data system that used a proprietary software system designed by the Executive Officer of Finance and Accounting. Once a voucher was fully researched and documented, posted advance payments, collections, and outstanding amounts to the claimant's travel record cards. Composed letters to individuals who owed money to the government to collect overpayment of travel and transportation expenses. Referred any cases that appeared to be fraudulent to my supervisor.

QUALITY INSPECTION ASSISTANT. US Army, Lockheed Martin, 321st Aviation Battalion, Korea APO AP 44444-4444 (1995-98).
Supervisor: SSG Geraldine Walsh, (777) 777-7777
Pay Grade: $1,355 per month
Hours worked per week: 40
Duties: Conducted physical inspections of schools, day care centers, and office buildings to monitor performance of cleaning crews assigned to these locations and ensuring that all facilities under company contract are cleaned properly. Verified quality and quantity of cleaning materials to assure that merchandise delivered matches what was ordered and all materials are used on the job for which they were ordered. Composed and prepared correspondence for the Lockheed Martin Quality Assurance Specialist to report any incidences or discrepancies which require corrective action. Reviewed Quality Assurance provisions of procurement documents for accuracy and compliance with regulations. Operated an automated data system to maintain and update files related to condition codes as well as to file reports of any discrepancies according to established policies, practices, regulations or procedures.

MEDICAL FILES CLERK. Department of Veterans Affairs, 2898 McArthur Road, Easton, PA 33333-3333 (1991-95).
Supervisor: Mr. Eric Stokes, (888) 888-8888
Pay Grade: N/A (Volunteer)
Hours worked per week: 25
Duties: Used an automated data system to retrieve records needed for admissions, as well as for scheduling clinic appointments and laboratory testing. Located printed copies of records that had been removed to perpetual storage or retired to the Data Storage Center. Before returning printed records to the file room, screened all documents to ensure that they were updated and ready for filing, returning any records containing incomplete information to the appropriate area for updating prior to returning them to the files. Returned completed, up-to-date records to their appropriate location according to the terminal digit filing system.

EDUCATION & TRAINING	Completed **Associate of Science** degree in Medical **Technology,** LaFayette College, LaFayette, PA, 1995. Completed four weeks of college-level training in computer operation, focusing on Windows XP and ME, Microsoft Word, and Microsoft Excel.
CERTIFICATIONS	Certification in Community CPR (adult, child, and infant) from Easton Medical Center expires 12/05.
HONORS	Was awarded several cash incentives for exemplary performance in civilian service from the Department of Veterans Affairs, as well as a cash award from Cedar Valley Nursing Care.
CLEARANCE	Hold a current **Top Secret** security clearance.

CLERK SUPERVISOR

LYDIA MICHELLE HINDEMITH

SSN: 000-00-0000

CLERK SUPERVISOR , GS-05 ANNOUNCEMENT #XYZ123

KSA #1: Knowledge of grammar, spelling, capitalization, and punctuation.

In my current position as Office Manager for the Federal Reserve System, I work essentially without supervision and therefore must rely on my own excellent knowledge of grammar, spelling, capitalization and punctuation. I type correspondence, reports, and memoranda in final form and without supervision. As Office Manager, I control all documents for the office, assuring that all deadlines are met. I take great pride in the fact that my knowledge of grammar, spelling, capitalization and punctuation allow us to present a very polished and professional look in all written communication.

In my previous job as Personnel Administrative Specialist, I was selected to serve as Rear Detachment S-1 NCOIC as a Specialist E-4, even though this position usually was reserved for an individual at the rank of SFC (E-7). This special selection was partially in recognition of my superior knowledge of grammar, spelling, capitalization and punctuation which I continually used to type correspondence, reports, and memoranda in final. I was extremely knowledgeable of the written forms, documents, and paperwork used in the personnel administration field as I typed personnel evaluations such as NCOERs, prepared finance documents related to employee payroll, and proofread documents, reports, and other written communication. I prepared written communication for the signature of executives.

In my job as Personnel Administration Specialist and Unit Clerk from 1999-02, I received respected awards in recognition of my excellent knowledge of spelling, punctuation, capitalization, and grammar as I prepared reports, correspondence, and memoranda. As Unit Clerk, I received the Army Achievement Medal for my efforts in reducing critical data blanks on the SIDPERS System, which allowed my organization to become one of the first units within 2d Army to reach the goal of "zero backlog" of personnel documents. This accomplishment was due in large part to my excellent spelling and grammar as well as my command of the rules of punctuation and capitalization while accurately and quickly completing reports, memoranda, and correspondence.

In my jobs from 1995-99 as Administration Specialist, I prepared both military and nonmilitary correspondence in final form while also handling a variety of complex office management duties. I became known for excellent spelling, capitalization, grammar, and punctuation.

You'll see this KSA
required for many office
administration jobs.

Education and Training related to this KSA:
More than two years of college-level training related to this KSA:
USAR Unit Administration Basic Course, three weeks, 2002
Administrative Specialist Course, 33 credit hours, 2001
Primary Leadership Development Course, two weeks, 2000
Battalion Training Management Course, two days, 2000
Maintenance Management Course, two days, 1998
Clerk-Typist Course, eight weeks, 1996

CLERK SUPERVISOR

LYDIA MICHELLE HINDEMITH

SSN: 000-00-0000

CLERK SUPERVISOR, GS-05 ANNOUNCEMENT #XYZ123

KSA #2: Knowledge of format and clerical procedures used in typing a variety of materials.

In my current position as Office Manager for the Federal Reserve System, I am the resident expert on the knowledge of format and clerical procedures used in typing a variety of materials for a company which provides services to commercial, industrial, and residential customers. I type correspondence, reports, and memoranda in final form and without supervision. I maintain files such as chronological, time and attendance, personnel, and other files, and I apply my knowledge of format and clerical procedures in ordering materials using a variety of written communication forms. I work usually without supervision in my current job, and I must continually rely on my resourcefulness and analytical skills as a constantly add to my knowledge of specialized terminology used in this business. As Office Manager, I control all documents for the office, assuring that all deadlines are met.

In my previous job as Personnel Administrative Specialist, I was selected to serve as Rear Detachment S-1 NCOIC as a Specialist E-4, even though this position usually was reserved for an individual at the rank of SFC (E-7). This special selection was due to my demonstrated knowledge of format and clerical procedures used in typing a variety of materials including correspondence, reports, and memoranda. I was extremely knowledgeable of the format and clerical procedures used in the personnel administration field as I typed personnel evaluations such as NCOERs, prepared finance documents related to employee payroll, and proofread documents, reports, and other written communication.

In my job as Personnel Administration Specialist and Unit Clerk from 1999-02, I received respected awards in recognition of my excellent knowledge of the format and clerical procedures involved in preparing reports, correspondence, and memoranda. As Unit Clerk, I received the Army Achievement Medal for my efforts in reducing critical data blanks on the SIDPERS System, which allowed my organization to become the one of the first units within 2d Army to reach the goal of "zero backlog" of personnel documents. This accomplishment was due in large part to my knowledge of the format and clerical procedures used in order to quickly and accurately complete reports, memoranda, and correspondence in final form. In my jobs from 1995-99 as Administration Specialist, I prepared both military and nonmilitary correspondence in final form.

Education and Training related to this KSA:
USAR Unit Administration Basic Course, three weeks, 2002
Administrative Specialist Course, 33 credit hours, 2001
Primary Leadership Development Course, two weeks, 2000
Battalion Training Management Course, two days, 2000
Maintenance Management Course, two days, 1998
Clerk-Typist Course, eight weeks, 1996

**Clerk Supervisor,
GS-05
Announcement #XYZ123
KSA #2**

Focus on the precise procedures you are knowledgeable of in this type of KSA.

FIELD OFFICE COORDINATOR

MELANIE T. EUBANKS

SSN: 000-00-0000

FIELD OFFICE COORDINATOR, GS-09 ANNOUNCEMENT #XYZ123

KSA #1: Ability to edit written material.

In my most recent position as a Field Office Assistant for the Department of Defense, I composed and prepared initial drafts of all correspondence for the office. Carefully proofread and edited this initial draft, making necessary changes to ensure precision of language, correct grammatical usage, and compliance with the appropriate format under the rules and regulations of correspondence. Also prepared all personnel actions for the office to include editing, proofreading, and preparing final drafts of performance appraisals and incentive awards. Used style manuals, technical and nontechnical dictionaries, and other references to ensure correctness of grammar and usage as well as precision of language. This position involved writing, editing, proofreading, and final printing of a large volume of letters, memos, reports, and other correspondence, as I posted transactions for over 35 contractors and more than 150 subcontractors. Was known for my sound judgment, exceptional communication and organizational abilities, and attention to detail.

In earlier positions as the Secretary and stenographer to the Chiefs of the Plans and Operations Division and Logistics Communication, I edited and proofread all office correspondence, including letters, memos, reports, and personnel actions, using style manuals, technical and nontechnical dictionaries, and other reference materials to ensure correctness of grammar and usage, precision of language, and adherence to proper formats according to the rules and regulations of correspondence. I composed and prepared initial drafts of all correspondence, proofread and edited the initial draft, made necessary changes and prepared the final documents. As I worked closely with a senior rater, this position involved editing, proofreading, and final preparation of a heavy volume of personnel actions, including OERs, EPRs, recommendations for military awards, and civilian employee appraisals (DA-7223). Performed stenography duties, recording minutes of weekly staff meeting and other information which I then compiled, edited, and modified for use in memos, reports, letters, and other correspondence.

Education and Training related to this KSA:
Graduated from the Central Florida Community College with an Associate of Arts degree in General Studies, Jensen Beach, FL, 2004.
- Correspondence English Usage, Kessler AFB, Mississippi, 2003.
- Programmed English Usage, Kessler AFB, Mississippi. 2002.
- United States Message Text Formats (MTF), Andrews AFB, Maryland, 2001.
- Building a Professional Image, Andrews AFB, Maryland, 2000.

FIELD OFFICE COORDINATOR

MELANIE T. EUBANKS

SSN: 000-00-0000

FIELD OFFICE COORDINATOR, GS-09 ANNOUNCEMENT #XYZ123

KSA #2: Skill in interpersonal relations.

In my most recent position as Field Office Assistant to the Department of Defense, I demonstrated my skill in interpersonal relations on a daily basis while interacting on a personal and professional level with military and civilian personnel of diverse ranks and backgrounds. Dealt with a heavy volume of office traffic, tactfully and diplomatically fielding questions and complaints from contractors, subcontractors, military personnel, and office visitors both in person and over the telephone and radio. Referred civilian contractors to Lockheed Martin, and provided contractors with information regarding the location of supplies ordered for their job sites. Performed liaison between civilian contractors, engineers, and warehouse personnel, relaying important information or taking messages if I could not resolve a problem or answer an inquiry. Frequently received calls from contractors who were angry or upset due to supply problems or other delays; handled these calls expertly, using tact and diplomacy to defuse the situation, then presenting the contractors concerns to the appropriate person in order to efficiently resolve the conflict. Answered multiline phones in a courteous and professional manner, routing incoming calls to the appropriate person, taking telephone messages, and providing callers with information over the phone.

In earlier positions as Secretary to the Chiefs of the Plans and Operations Division and of the Logistics Communication Division, I interacted daily with a large number of people, both on the phone and in person. I recorded telephone messages and answered multiline phones, effectively communicating with callers in order to ascertain the purpose of their call. Responded to caller inquiries, furnishing information and resolving their problems when possible and directing calls to the supervisor or appropriate personnel when I was unable to assist them. Maintained lines of communication and developed strong working relationships with higher, lateral, and subordinate counterparts at military headquarters in order to facilitate the exchange of information concerning each division's affairs.

Education and Training Related to This KSA:
Graduated from the Central Florida Community College with an Associate of Arts degree in General Studies, Jensen Beach, FL, 2004.
- Correspondence English Usage, Kessler AFB, Mississippi, 2003.
- Programmed English Usage, Kessler AFB, Mississippi, 2002.
- United States Message Text Formats (MTF), Andrews AFB, Maryland, 2001.
- Building a Professional Image, Andrews AFB, Maryland, 2000.

FINANCE OFFICE CLERK

PAIGE L. FORBES
SSN: 000-00-0000
FINANCE OFFICE CLERK, GS-05 ANNOUNCEMENT #XYZ123

KSA #1: Ability to use computer systems and related software.

Overview of my work experience: In the job described below, I have received a Certificate of Outstanding Performance every year and have been cited each year for performing all duties in an outstanding manner. I have been commended on numerous occasions for my expertise in utilizing computer systems and related software as well as for my ability to rapidly master new tasks, new knowledge, and new projects. I have earned a reputation as a self-starter known for attention to detail and follow-through in every aspect of my job.

In my current position as Supply Clerk, NF-2, I review, analyze, and prepare a wide variety of documentation and paperwork while assuring that paperwork is always within guidelines established by regulatory authorities and other authorities. While maintaining, updating, and utilizing a variety of data systems and using personal computers, I operate a GTA computer with WordPerfect software, Time Management Labor System software, Microsoft Office software to include Word, Excel, PowerPoint, and Access. I type all correspondence for the Supply and Warehouse Section using the WordPerfect and Word software. One of my responsibilities is to maintain the internal supply budget on Excel software and prepare flyers for the MWR Auction on PowerPoint. Furthermore, I maintain and prepare all NAF time cards using the Time Management Labor System software. In addition to maintaining the annual budget for the Supply & Warehouse and the Recycling Section, I use the internal software (NAF Financial Management Budget System). My knowledge of the computer and programs enables me to type all performance appraisals for all employees within the section, to type memoranda for the Chief, Technical Services Branch, to maintain and print all NAF time cards, to maintain annual budget for the Supply and Warehouse and Recycling Section and Forward to Budget Office. I have operated a Zenith Data System computer with ADEPT and WordPerfect software to maintain the NAF property book, adding property when received, deleting property whenever it is turned in or missing.

In my previous position, as Personnel Clerk for the Civilian Personnel Office at Ft. Hood, I prepared all NAF job announcements, contacted all eligible applications for interviews, and coordinated with activity managers for interviews while also preparing referrals. I informed selected applicants of their selection, I typed non-selection letters, and I also maintained files for applications and referrals.

Knowledge and Training related to this KSA:
- In 2003, I completed a Microsoft Office course at Galveston Technical Community College. This course enabled me to use Word, Excel, PowerPoint, and Access to type a variety of material and documents for the Supply and Warehouse Section.
- In 2001, I took 116 hours of IBM Operations at Western Texas Technical College.
- In 2000, I took a NAF Financial Management Budget System Course at Ft. Hood, TX. This course gave me the knowledge, skills and ability to maintain the NAF budget for Supply and Warehouse, and the Recycling Section.

This supply clerk seeks a job in a finance office.

FINANCE OFFICE CLERK

PAIGE L. FORBES

SSN: 000-00-0000

FINANCE OFFICE CLERK, GS-05 ANNOUNCEMENT #XYZ123

KSA #2: Ability to process a variety of medical and legal cases/records and documents.

Overview of my work experience: In the job described below, I have received a Certificate of Outstanding Performance every year and have been cited each year for performing all duties in an outstanding manner. I have been commended on numerous occasions for my expertise in preparing records and documents. Through my problem-solving and negotiating skills, I have in many instances resolved stubborn problems and difficult issues which could have resulted in serious liability problems involving theft, loss, etc.

In my current position as Supply Clerk, NF-2, I review, analyze, and prepare a wide variety of documentation and paperwork while assuring that paperwork is always within guidelines established by regulatory authorities and other authorities. While maintaining, updating, and utilizing a variety of data systems and using personal computers, I operate a GTA computer with WordPerfect software, Time Management Labor System software, Microsoft Office software to include Word, Excel, PowerPoint, and Access. I type all correspondence for Supply and Warehouse Section using the WordPerfect and Word software. One of my responsibilities is to maintain the internal supply budget on Excel software and prepare flyers for the MWR Auction on PowerPoint. Furthermore, I maintain and prepare all NAF time cards using the Time Management Labor System software. In addition, to maintain the annual budget for Supply & Warehouse and the Recycling Section, I use the internal software (NAF Financial Management Budget System). My knowledge of the computer and programs enables me to type all performance appraisals for all employees within the section, to type memoranda for the Chief, Technical Services Branch, to maintain and print all NAF time cards, to maintain annual budget for Supply and Warehouse and Recycling Section and Forward to Budget Office. I have operated a Zenith Data System computer with ADEPT and WordPerfect software to maintain the NAF property book, adding property when received, deleting property whenever it is turned in or missing.

Knowledge and Training related to this KSA:

- In 2003, I completed a Microsoft Office course at Galveston Technical Community College. This course enabled me to use Word, Excel, PowerPoint, and Access to type a variety of material and documents for the Supply and Warehouse Section.
- In 2001, I took 116 hours of IBM Operations at Western Texas Technical College. This gave me the knowledge, skills and ability to operate a computer.
- In 2000, I took a NAF Financial Management Budget System Course at Ft. Hood, TX. This course gave me the knowledge, skills and ability to maintain the NAF budget for Supply and Warehouse, and the Recycling Section.
- In 1999, I took 33 hours of word processing with Word at Galveston Technical Community College. This enabled me to type documents and material using Word.

Finance Office Clerk, GS-05 Announcement #XYZ123 KSA #2

Be specific.

FINANCE OFFICE CLERK

PAIGE L. FORBES

SSN: 000-00-0000

FINANCE OFFICE CLERK, GS-05 ANNOUNCEMENT #XYZ123

KSA #3: Ability to communicate orally.

Overview of my work experience: In the job described below, I have received a Certificate of Outstanding Performance every year and have been cited each year for performing all duties in an outstanding manner. I have been commended on numerous occasions for my outstanding oral communication skills as well as for excellent problem-solving, negotiating, and decision-making skills. Through my ability to communicate tactfully and graciously, to explain complex technical issues, and to train and motivate other employees, I have earned a reputation as an outstanding communicator in every aspect of my job.

In my current position as Supply Clerk, NF-2, I communicate with customers, vendors, and others in the process of performing my job. After I review, analyze, and prepare a wide variety of documentation and paperwork, I communicate orally with vendors, customers, and employees. I communicate orally with new or junior employees while training them to utilize a variety of data systems and using personal computers, I operate a GTA computer with WordPerfect software, Time Management Labor System software, Microsoft Office software to include Word, Excel, PowerPoint, and Access. One of my responsibilities is to maintain the internal supply budget on Excel software and prepare flyers for the MWR Auction on PowerPoint. Furthermore, I maintain and prepare all NAF time cards using the Time Management Labor System software. In addition, to maintain the annual budget for Supply & Warehouse and the Recycling Section, I use the internal software (NAF Financial Management Budget System). My knowledge of the computer and programs enables me to type all performance appraisals for all employees within the section, to type memoranda for the Chief, Technical Services Branch, to maintain and print all NAF time cards, to maintain annual budget for Supply and Warehouse and Recycling Section and Forward to Budget Office. I have operated a Zenith Data System computer with ADEPT and WordPerfect software to maintain the NAF property book, adding property when received, deleting property whenever it is turned in or missing.

> Notice how often the communication KSA comes up.

In my position as Personnel Clerk, I communicated orally with potential employees after receiving applications and briefed them about positions available. I communicated extensively through telephone conversations with Activity Managers to coordinate pickup of referrals and selection of new employees. I also telephoned applicants when they were accepted for the position.

Knowledge and Training related to this KSA:
- In 2003, I took a Microsoft Office course at Galveston Technical Community College. This course enabled me to use Word, Excel, PowerPoint, and Access to type a variety of material and documents for the Supply and Warehouse Section.
- In 2001, I took 116 hours of IBM Operations at Western Texas Technical College.
- In 2000, I took a NAF Financial Management Budget System Course at Ft. Hood, TX. This course gave me the knowledge, skills and ability to maintain the NAF budget for Supply and Warehouse, and the Recycling Section.

OFFICE CLERK

PAIGE L. FORBES
SSN: 000-00-0000
FINANCE OFFICE CLERK, GS-05 ANNOUNCEMENT #XYZ123

KSA #4: Ability to communicate in writing.

Overview of my work experience: In the job described below, I have received a Certificate of Outstanding Performance every year and have been cited each year for performing all duties in an outstanding manner. I have been commended on numerous occasions for my ability to communicate in writing in a concise, articulate, and effective manner. I have earned a reputation as an excellent writer.

In my current position as Supply Clerk, NF-2, I communicate extensively in writing in the process of reviewing, analyzing, and preparing a wide variety of documentation and paperwork while assuring that paperwork is always within guidelines established by regulatory authorities and other authorities. In creating documents for written communication and transmission, I maintain, update, and utilize a variety of data systems and using personal computers. I operate a GTA computer with WordPerfect software, Time Management Labor System software, Microsoft Office software to include Word, Excel, PowerPoint, and Access. I communicate in writing by typing all correspondence for Supply and Warehouse Section using the WordPerfect and Word software. One of my responsibilities is to maintain the internal supply budget on Excel software and prepare flyers for the MWR Auction on PowerPoint. Furthermore, I maintain and prepare all NAF time cards using the Time Management Labor System software. In addition, to maintain the annual budget for Supply & Warehouse and the Recycling Section, I use the internal software (NAF Financial Management Budget System). My knowledge of the computer and programs enables me to type all performance appraisals for all employees within the section, to type memoranda for the Chief, Technical Services Branch, to maintain and print all NAF time cards, to maintain annual budget for Supply and Warehouse and Recycling Section and Forward to Budget Office. I have operated a Zenith Data System computer with ADEPT and WordPerfect software to maintain the NAF property book, adding property when received, deleting property whoever it is turned in or missing.

Knowledge and Training related to this KSA:

- In 2003, I took a Microsoft Office course at Galveston Technical Community College. This course enabled me to use Word, Excel, PowerPoint, and Access to type a variety of material and documents for the Supply and Warehouse Section.
- In 2001, I took 116 hours of IBM Operations at Western Texas Technical College. This gave me the knowledge, skills and ability to operate a computer.
- In 2000, I took a NAF Financial Management Budget System Course at Ft. Hood, TX. This course gave me the knowledge, skills and ability to maintain the NAF budget for Supply and Warehouse, and the Recycling Section.
- In 1999, I took 33 hours of word processing with WordPerfect at Galveston Technical Community College. This enabled me to type documents and material using WordPerfect.

Finance Office Clerk, GS-05 Announcement #XYZ123 KSA #4

Sometimes the "oral" and "in writing" skills are joined in one KSA; sometimes they are separate as they are here.

PROJECT MANAGER

RICHARD ANDREWS

SSN: 000-00-0000

PROJECT MANAGER, GS-07 ANNOUNCEMENT #XYZ123

KSA #1: Knowledge of the functions and organizational structures of a major military headquarters.

In my current position at one of the largest U.S. military bases in the world, I have developed extensive knowledge of the functions and organizational structure of a major headquarters and have become increasingly knowledgeable of the hierarchy involved in order to accomplish the essential functions of my job within that structure.

Experience with the Special Operations Battle Lab Concept Directorate (SOBL-CD): Especially in my present job as secretary and personal assistant to the Director of Special Operations for the Department of Defense (2003-present), I have become very familiar with the functions and organizational structure of a major headquarters. I interact with individuals at all organizational levels of this major headquarters.

Interactions with officials throughout the organizational structure of SOBL-CD: Perform extensive liaison on a daily basis between the Directorate and officials of the U. S. Special Operations Command (USSOCOM), USASOC, TRADOC, the Combined Arms Centers (CACs), XVIII Airborne Corps, and the Advisory Group which consists of personnel from the North Atlantic Treaty Organization (NATO), National Reconnaissance Office (NRO), Office of Inspector General (DoDIG), and all branches of the Armed Forces including the National Guard. In addition, I coordinate daily with the chiefs of subordinate divisions and other personnel both within the Directorate and within the Department of Defense. Coordinate the Director's schedule to coincide with the Commanding General's and Assistant Commandant's calendars, when necessary.

Screen all incoming telephone calls and correspondence, directing requests for information to the appropriate individuals within the organization.

Knowledge of the structure and purpose of SOBL-CD: The Directorate is composed of several divisions, consisting of staff from civilian grades GS-03 through GS-12 and military personnel from MSG through COL. I maintain a solid working knowledge of the SOBL-CD mission in order to provide constructive feedback and recommendations to the director on administrative and clerical processes and procedures that could better accomplish the mission. The director is chairman of several special boards which involves preparing formal in-process reviews (IPRs), officers efficiency reports, decision and discussion papers, contracts, staff studies, and formal reports to higher headquarters. The SOBL-CD is responsible for future training operations, formulation, direction, and planning.

Education and Training related to this KSA:
Graduated with a B.S. degree in International Studies from the University of Maryland, College Park, MD, 2004.
Completed intensive 16-week training program related to Major Military Headquarters Operations, Washington, DC, 1999.

PROJECT MANAGER

RICHARD ANDREWS
SSN: 000-00-0000
PROJECT MANAGER, GS-07 ANNOUNCEMENT #XYZ123

KSA #2: Ability to communicate with high level civilian and governmental officials.

In my current position as secretary and personal assistant to the Director of Special Operations for the Department of Defense (2003-present), I demonstrate my ability to communicate effectively with high level civilian and military officials on a daily basis. I interact with civilian personnel as high as GS-12 and military personnel at all levels, arranging meetings and briefings between the Director and various high-ranking officers throughout the installation, including the Commanding General and the Assistant Commandant.

Within the Directorate, I have daily interaction with military and civilian personnel at all levels of rank. I also interact with the Director on a daily basis, making recommendations on administrative and clerical processes and procedures; and to suggest new policies or procedures to better accomplish the mission. While screening all incoming calls and correspondence, I determine the nature of the call and then direct it to the appropriate person within the organization.

From 1999-03, as Support Coordinator for the Branch Assistance Division of the Fort Polk Readiness Group, I worked under the general supervision of the Chief of Combat Arms and Combat Support Division. Planned and coordinated a number of program responsibilities, interacting with officials at all levels of civilian and military service on a daily basis.

Prepared and presented verbal briefings to Colonels from National Guard and Reserve Component units. Reviewed work load reports and procedures to ensure work load and manpower utilization were reported correctly, discussing discrepancies and recommended corrective action to the Team Chiefs. Communicated with officials within command channels and between other agencies, to conduct briefings and discuss recommendations to resolve problems and requests for assistance. Contacted the S-3 and DOIM when the computer terminal was down or not working properly, and scheduled a service call.

Earlier as Secretary for the Director of ADDS Test Division, I communicated with high level civilian and military officials while arranging official and social meetings and briefing, issuing telephone invitations and interacting with various officials to coordinate with the Director and resolve any scheduling conflicts.

Education and Training related to this KSA:
Graduated with a B.S. degree in International Studies from the University of Maryland, College Park, MD, 2004.
Completed intensive 16-week training program related to Major Military Headquarters Operations, Washington, DC, 1999.

Project Manager,
GS-07
Announcement #XYZ123
KSA #2

PROJECT MANAGER

RICHARD ANDREWS

SSN: 000-00-0000

PROJECT MANAGER, GS-07 ANNOUNCEMENT #XYZ123

KSA #3: Ability to communicate in writing.

In my present position as secretary and personal assistant to the Director of Special Operations for Department of Defense (2003-present), I use word processors and other computer software to prepare a variety of narrative and tabular material according to prepared formats, form letters, standard paragraphs, and mail lists. Provide writing assistance during the production and distribution of periodic performance evaluations, narratives for awards and medals, and memorandums. Proofread officer and enlisted efficiency reports and civilian performance appraisals for personnel under director's supervision. Provide support documents, ensuring that appropriate guidelines are followed and that efficiency reports and performance appraisals are completed on time.

Review documents prepared for signature of the director to include memorandum, nonmilitary letters, staff studies, etc., for conformance with regulatory guidance, grammar, format, and special policies of the directorate. Return these items to the originator for correction when not in conformance with known policies, or when correspondence regulations have not been followed. Compose personal, official, and other materials, assuring compliance with correspondence rules and regulations guidance and known viewpoints of director. Prepare a variety of narrative and tabular materials (e.g., correspondence, reports, and speeches), correcting errors in grammar, spelling, and punctuation. Refer to dictionaries, style manuals, and established typing/correspondence policies of the organization to ensure accuracy and precision of language as well as adherence to established formats.

In a previous position as Support Coordinator for the Branch Assistance Division of the Fort Polk Readiness Group (1999-03), independently prepared administrative correspondence and recurring special summary reports, ensuring that grammar, spelling, and punctuation were correct. Refer to dictionaries, style manuals, and established typing/correspondence policies of the organization to ensure accuracy and precision of language as well as adherence to established formats. Extracted pertinent information and consolidated manpower data, using this material to compose and prepare written reports to my supervisor for submission to higher headquarters.

Provided writing assistance during the composition and production of periodic performance evaluations, narratives for awards and medals, and memorandums. Proofread officer and enlisted efficiency reports and civilian performance appraisals for personnel under director's supervision. Provide support documents, ensuring that appropriate guidelines are followed and that efficiency reports and performance appraisals are completed on time.

Education and Training related to this KSA:
Graduated with a B.S. degree in International Studies from the University of Maryland, College Park, MD, 2004. Refined my written communication skills through preparing dozens of papers for various courses. Also prepared a senior-year paper on Historical Trends in Office Administration on which I received an "A."
Completed four-week training program sponsored by the Department of Defense in supply management, Washington, DC, 1999. Learned the "vocabulary of supply" and was trained to prepare specialized documents in the supply field including purchasing documents.

ABOUT THE EDITOR

Anne McKinney holds an MBA from the Harvard Business School and a BA in English from the University of North Carolina at Chapel Hill. A noted public speaker, writer, and teacher, she is the senior editor for PREP's business and career imprint, which bears her name. Early titles in the Anne McKinney Career Series (now called the Real-Resumes Series) published by PREP include: *Resumes and Cover Letters That Have Worked, Resumes and Cover Letters That Have Worked for Military Professionals, Government Job Applications and Federal Resumes, Cover Letters That Blow Doors Open,* and *Letters for Special Situations.* Her career titles and how-to resume-and-cover-letter books are based on the expertise she has acquired in 25 years of working with job hunters. Her valuable career insights have appeared in publications of the "Wall Street Journal" and other prominent newspapers and magazines.

PREP Publishing Order Form

You may purchase our titles from your favorite bookseller! Or send a check, money order or your credit card number for the total amount*, plus $4.00 postage and handling, to PREP, 1110 1/2 Hay Street, Fayetteville, NC 28305. You may also order our titles on our website at www.prep-pub.com and feel free to e-mail us at preppub@aol.com or call 910-483-6611 with your questions or concerns.

Name: _____

Address: _____

E-mail address: _____

Payment Type: ☐ Check/Money Order   ☐ Visa   ☐ MasterCard

Credit Card Number: _____ Expiration Date: _____

Put a check beside the items you are ordering:

☐ $16.95—REAL-RESUMES FOR RESTAURANT, FOOD SERVICE & HOTEL JOBS. Anne McKinney, Editor

☐ $16.95—REAL-RESUMES FOR MEDIA, NEWSPAPER, BROADCASTING & PUBLIC AFFAIRS JOBS. Anne McKinney, Editor

☐ $16.95—REAL-RESUMES FOR RETAILING, MODELING, FASHION & BEAUTY JOBS. Anne McKinney, Editor

☐ $16.95—REAL-RESUMES FOR HUMAN RESOURCES & PERSONNEL JOBS. Anne McKinney, Editor

☐ $16.95—REAL-RESUMES FOR MANUFACTURING JOBS. Anne McKinney, Editor

☐ $16.95—REAL-RESUMES FOR AVIATION & TRAVEL JOBS. Anne McKinney, Editor

☐ $16.95—REAL-RESUMES FOR POLICE, LAW ENFORCEMENT & SECURITY JOBS. Anne McKinney, Editor

☐ $16.95—REAL-RESUMES FOR SOCIAL WORK & COUNSELING JOBS. Anne McKinney, Editor

☐ $16.95—REAL-RESUMES FOR CONSTRUCTION JOBS. Anne McKinney, Editor

☐ $16.95—REAL-RESUMES FOR FINANCIAL JOBS. Anne McKinney, Editor

☐ $16.95—REAL-RESUMES FOR COMPUTER JOBS. Anne McKinney, Editor

☐ $16.95—REAL-RESUMES FOR MEDICAL JOBS. Anne McKinney, Editor

☐ $16.95—REAL-RESUMES FOR TEACHERS. Anne McKinney, Editor

☐ $16.95—REAL-RESUMES FOR CAREER CHANGERS. Anne McKinney, Editor

☐ $16.95—REAL-RESUMES FOR STUDENTS. Anne McKinney, Editor

☐ $16.95—REAL-RESUMES FOR SALES. Anne McKinney, Editor

☐ $16.95—REAL ESSAYS FOR COLLEGE AND GRAD SCHOOL. Anne McKinney, Editor

☐ $25.00—RESUMES AND COVER LETTERS THAT HAVE WORKED. McKinney. Editor

☐ $25.00—RESUMES AND COVER LETTERS THAT HAVE WORKED FOR MILITARY PROFESSIONALS. McKinney, Ed.

☐ $25.00—RESUMES AND COVER LETTERS FOR MANAGERS. McKinney, Editor

☐ $25.00—GOVERNMENT JOB APPLICATIONS AND FEDERAL RESUMES: Federal Resumes, KSAs, Forms 171 and 612, and Postal Applications. McKinney, Editor

☐ $25.00—COVER LETTERS THAT BLOW DOORS OPEN. McKinney, Editor

☐ $25.00—LETTERS FOR SPECIAL SITUATIONS. McKinney, Editor

☐ $16.95—REAL-RESUMES FOR NURSING JOBS. McKinney, Editor

☐ $16.95—REAL-RESUMES FOR AUTO INDUSTRY JOBS. McKinney, Editor

☐ $24.95—REAL KSAS--KNOWLEDGE, SKILLS & ABILITIES--FOR GOVERNMENT JOBS. McKinney, Editor

☐ $24.95—REAL RESUMIX AND OTHER RESUMES FOR FEDERAL GOVERNMENT JOBS. McKinney, Editor

☐ $24.95—REAL BUSINESS PLANS AND MARKETING TOOLS ... Samples to use in your business. McKinney, Ed.

☐ $16.95—REAL-RESUMES FOR ADMINISTRATIVE SUPPORT, OFFICE & SECRETARIAL JOBS. Anne McKinney, Editor

☐ $16.95—REAL-RESUMES FOR FIREFIGHTING JOBS. Anne McKinney, Editor

☐ $16.95—REAL-RESUMES FOR JOBS IN NONPROFIT ORGANIZATIONS. Anne McKinney, Editor

☐ $16.95—REAL-RESUMES FOR SPORTS INDUSTRY JOBS. Anne McKinney, Editor

☐ $16.95—REAL-RESUMES FOR LEGAL & PARALEGAL JOBS. Anne McKinney, Editor

_____ **TOTAL ORDERED**

_____ **(add $4.00 for shipping and handling)**

_____ **TOTAL INCLUDING SHIPPING** *PREP* offers volume discounts on large orders. Call us at (910) 483-6611 for more information.

THE MISSION OF PREP PUBLISHING IS TO PUBLISH
BOOKS AND OTHER PRODUCTS WHICH ENRICH
PEOPLE'S LIVES AND HELP THEM OPTIMIZE THE
HUMAN EXPERIENCE. OUR STRONGEST LINES ARE
OUR JUDEO-CHRISTIAN ETHICS SERIES AND OUR
REAL-RESUMES SERIES.

Would you like to explore the possibility of having PREP's writing
team create a resume for you similar to the ones in this book?

For a brief free consultation, call 910-483-6611
or send $4.00 to receive our Job Change Packet to
PREP, 1110 1/2 Hay Street, Fayetteville, NC 28305. Visit our
website to find valuable career resources: www.prep-pub.com!

QUESTIONS OR COMMENTS? E-MAIL US AT PREPPUB@AOL.COM